The FOOTBALL UNcyclopedia

Advance Praise for
The Football Uncyclopedia

"Adam Hoff is not the most ill-informed person I know."
– Michael Kun, *The Football Uncyclopedia*

"Michael Kun doesn't know much at all about football."
– Adam Hoff, *The Football Uncyclopedia*

"We will never work with these two idiots again."
– Publisher, Clerisy Press

A HIGHLY OPINIONATED, MYTH-BUSTING GUIDE
TO AMERICA'S MOST POPULAR GAME

The
FOOTBALL
UN*cyclopedia*

Michael Kun and Adam Hoff

CLERISY PRESS

Please memorize the following information:

Published by Clerisy Press
Printed in the United States of America
Distributed by Publishers Group West
First edition, first printing

For further information, contact the publisher at:

Clerisy Press
1700 Madison Road
Cincinnati, OH 45206
www.clerisypress.com

Library of Congress Cataloging-in-Publication Data:

Kun, Michael.
    The football uncyclopedia : a highly opinionated, myth-busting
        guide to America's most popular game / by Michael Kun and
        Adam Hoff. — 1st ed.
    p. cm.
    ISBN-13: 978-1-57860-311-4
    ISBN-10: 1-57860-311-0
    1. Football—Miscellanea—Encyclopedias. 2. Football—United
    States—Miscellanea—Encyclopedias. I. Hoff, Adam. II. Title.
    GV950.5.K86 2008
    796.332—dc22
                                        2008015722

Edited by Jack Heffron and Donna Poehner
Cover and interior designed by Stephen Sullivan
Production design by Annie Long

All photos courtesy of the following photographers with iStockphoto (page number follows credited photographer):

Simon Askham *5;* Kirsty Pargeter *13;* Kim Dailey *33;* Brian McClister *36;* Sean Locke *43;* Marisa Allegra Williams *46;* Matthew Coons *49;* iStockphoto *54;* Kriss Russell *96;* Eric Isselée *98;* iStockphoto *110;* Nicholos Sereno *118;* Bill Grove *121;* Jeff Chevrier *135;* Jazsef Szasz-Fabian *152;* Jacob Wackerhausen *156;* Brandon Laufenberg *193;* Sami Suni *207;* Andrew Manley *213;* Jorge Delgado *241;* Mikael Damkier *247;* Andrew Manley *252;* Nicky Blade *262.*

DEDICATION

★ ★ ★ ★ ★

To our wives
And all of your wives

response to

DEDICATION

★ ★ ★ ★ ★

You're dedicating a *football* book to us?
You really are a couple of morons.
—*The authors' wives*

Introduction

In the past several months, I have conducted an admittedly unscientific study relating to reading. That study demonstrates rather conclusively that no one—and I mean *no one*—reads the introduction to a book. Everyone—and I mean *everyone*—just flies right past the introduction and heads for the first entry.

At the same time, you should know that most publishers expect authors to write an introduction. It doesn't matter if it is complete gibberish, it just has to be there.

So, knowing that you're not going to read this, but also knowing that this must nevertheless be done in order to satisfy our publisher, I would now like to present the following chart as our introduction to this book:

Billy Kilmer	38%
The two-tight end formation	61%
The Baltimore Colts	B
The Indianapolis Colts	N/A
Referees	73.2%
Don Maynard	L
Red Grange	96%
Carl Eller	Tuesday

We hope you will agree with that analysis, knowing full well that you did not read a word of it. And we hope you will enjoy the book.[1]

---

[1] By the way, this book has footnotes in it. This is what a footnote looks like. It's up to you whether you want to read them. No skin off our noses if you don't. But half the cover price of the book is for the footnotes, so it might make sense to give them a look. After all, you paid for them.

We originally wrote it with ketchup on pages made out of ham.

And no one will ever question whether that statement is true.

Because no one will read this introduction.

Except maybe our publisher.

And that's a big *maybe*.

(MK)

Abdul-Jabbar, Karim: Karim Abdul-Jabbar Was *Not* Kareem Abdul-Jabbar's Son

There was once a running back named Sharmon Shah, who played for UCLA in the early 1990s. He was a two-time team MVP and the holder of numerous school records, yet relatively little attention was paid to this prolific runner.

Then in 1995, Shah converted to Islam and was given a new name.

That name? Karim Abdul-Jabbar.

Did I mention that he was a student at UCLA?

Oh, and that he wore the number 33?

For those readers who aren't fans of the NBA or college basketball, there happens to be a Hall of Fame center named Kareem Abdul-Jabbar, who just so happened to wear the number 33 and who just so happened to play his college ball at UCLA (although he was then known by his birth name of Lew Alcindor).

Naturally, the newly christened Karim Abdul-Jabbar started to get a lot more attention when he went back to campus for his senior year. People were intrigued by this fascinating coincidence. Many assumed that he wore 33 as a tribute to the former Lakers legend. (Not true. He wore it as a tribute to former Dallas running back Tony Dorsett.) Others assumed that Karim Abdul-Jabbar was Kareem Abdul-Jabbar's son.

Obviously, the people who thought this weren't terribly bright. Not only does such conjecture ignore the fact that both Karim and Kareem were given their names by their Imam, but it also assumes that Kareem forget how to spell his own name when he passed it on to his son.

So, no, Sharmon Shah-turned-Karim Abdul-Jabbar was not Kareem Abdul-Jabbar's son. And if there was any doubt about this fact whatsoever, it was put to rest when Kareem actually sued Karim over the use of his name.

That's right, he *sued*.

Even more amazing is the fact that Kareem won his lawsuit, forcing Karim to take the "Jabbar" off his jersey and forcing the Miami Dolphins, Karim's employer at the time, to pull all of the Abdul-Jabbar merchandise from the shelves.

Oh, by the way, Karim was obviously so distraught over losing the lawsuit against his non-idol, non-father Kareem that he changed his name to Abdul-Karim al-Jabbar.

All of this makes me think that if Kareem Abdul-Jabbar was Karim Abdul-Jabbar, er, sorry, Abdul-Karim al-Jabbar's father, he wouldn't have been a very good one.

Which, of course, he wasn't.

So, it's all good.

Although I remain troubled by Kareem suing Karim over his name. I may need to rethink my plan to change my name to Goar Vidal.

(AH)

AFL, The: The American Football League Did *Not* Use A Red, White, And Blue Ball

Several years ago, while sitting in an airport, I overheard a man discussing football with his young son. Specifically, he was talking about the American Football League, the renegade league of the 1960s that would eventually merge with the National Football League.

"The AFL," he explained, "had many great players like Joe Namath, Lance Alworth, and Len Dawson."

Correct.

"They generally had more wide-open offenses that changed the way the game was played."

Correct.

"And what made the league unusual was that they used a red, white, and blue ball."

Okay, the AFL didn't use a red, white, and blue ball. But you have to admit it would've been awfully cool if they had.

Uh, no.

The man was thinking of the American Basketball Association, not the American Football League.

The ABA was a *basketball* league.

The AFL was a *football* league.

It's awfully hard to confuse the two. I mean, they're two completely different sports. One involves tall men in shorts bouncing a round ball. The other does not.

In any event, not wanting to embarrass the man in front of his son, I didn't confront him. Someday, though, his son will learn the truth. Perhaps from this book. Perhaps he will give this book to his father for Father's Day and say, "You have embarrassed me for the last time, Dad. You have humiliated me in a book that will be read by millions!"

And the father will say, "Millions? How stupid are you?"

Then the mother will have to step in to stop the argument.

At least that's how I see this playing out.

(MK)

AFL, The Other: You Do *Not* Care About Arena Football

At this time, there is a professional football league called the Arena Football League.

They play football indoors on fields the size of a pool table, or at least it seems that way.

There are nets at the ends of the field, and there are boards around the field like you'd see in a hockey game.

When the Arena Football League was first created . . .

Oh, who really cares?

If you haven't already moved on to the next entry, you really should.

(MK)

Alworth, Lance: Lance Alworth Was *Not* Lance Rentzel

Lance Alworth was a wide receiver for the Chargers and Cowboys in the 1960s and 1970s.

Lance Rentzel was a wide receiver for the Vikings, Cowboys, and Rams in the 1960s and 1970s.

They were not the same person, although people frequently confused them because they shared the same first name and both had long blond hair.

Here's an easy way to remember them: Lance Alworth was one of the greatest receivers of all time.

Lance Rentzel was not.

See, it's easy.

(MK)

Answer, Trying to Figure Out The: You Do *Not* Know The Answer To This Trivia Question

Here's a football trivia question. Actually, it's more of a brain teaser.

There were two men who first played for the St. Louis Cardinals in 1973. Both wore number 21 for the Cardinals that year. In fact, both wore number 21 for the St. Louis Cardinals not only in 1973, but also in 1974, 1975, 1976, and 1977. Both had excellent rookie seasons such that one was named to the Pro Bowl, and the other was named Rookie of the Year. Both were exciting, speedy offensive players.

By the way, this is not a hypothetical. Everything you have just read is true.

How is this possible, you ask. How could two star players wear the same number for the Cardinals for the same five years?

If you lived in St. Louis in the 1970s, you might know the answer without having to give it a moment's thought. Otherwise, I'll bet you're scratching your head right now, at least figuratively.

Was it the same player, only he changed his name, like when Lew Alcindor became Kareem Abdul-Jabbar?[1]

No. They were two separate individuals.

Did the two guys alternate wearing the number 21?

No. They both wore 21 all the time.

Did all the Cardinals players wear some commemorative patch with the number 21 on it?

No. Although you get some points for being creative.

Did the Cardinals get some special permission from the league to have two players wear the same number?

No.

Did one of the players have to wear the other's jersey because his jersey was torn?

No. And what are the odds of one player's jersey being torn for *five straight years*? Don't you think the team would have repaired it?

---

[1] What are the odds of Kareem Abdul-Jabbar being mentioned in two of the first entries in a *football* book? Don't ask us. We just write this stuff.

Were they a father and son?

Huh?

So, how is this scenario possible, you ask. How could two star players wear the same number for the Cardinals for the same five years?

Give it some thought. Think about it for a day or two if you need to. If you still can't figure out the answer, take a look at *Question, Answer To The Trivia,* later in this book.

(MK)

Apples, Bad: All University Of Miami Football Players Do Not Have Bad Attitudes

As is probably obvious from the title, this is an entry based on the old expression "One bad apple can spoil the barrel." In this case, I've modified the cliché to read: "A few bad Hurricanes can spoil the reputation of an entire football program." A little wordier to be sure, but it gets the point across.

"The U" has had more than a few incidents over the years on the college gridiron, including a horrific fight against Florida International during the 2006 season. For the most part though, Miami's tarnished reputation has come about because of the behavior of its players once they graduate to the NFL.[2]

When one hears the words "University of Miami" in the context of the NFL, the mind tends to immediately gravitate toward negative thoughts.

Flamboyant and outspoken players.

Holdouts.

Cocaine and prostitutes.

Motorcycle accidents and notorious quotes comparing athletes to soldiers.

---

[2] I use the term "graduate" loosely, in the colloquial sense. Like many major universities, Miami sees many of its players leave school sans degrees. Such is the state of major collegiate athletics. But that's another book.

Murder charges.

Needless to say, "The U" doesn't always conjure up the most positive of sentiments.

The problem with that particular brand of word association is that it isn't fair to the dozens of former Miami players who went on to have great NFL careers without so much as a harsh word to the press or a brusque interaction with a clubhouse attendant. Players like Jim Kelly, Vinny Testaverde, Bernie Kosar, Dan Morgan, Reggie Wayne, Andre Johnson, Santana Moss, Bubba Franks, Bryant McKinnie, Cortez Kennedy, Russell Maryland, Ed Reed, D.J. Williams, and Jonathan Vilma create a legacy of outstanding performers possessing great character and work ethic.[3] Unfortunately, those aren't the names that one immediately associates with Miami. Rather than think of a classy great like Jim Kelly, the association is with the slightly bizarre Clinton Portis or the loudmouthed Warren Sapp. . . or worse.

Here are some of Miami's bad apples that are spoiling the barrel for their cohorts.

Michael Irvin. There is no denying that Michael Irvin was a great player, although his place in the Hall of Fame is questioned in the entry titled *Moore, Herman.* That is not what this entry is about. In fact, athletic greatness plays a huge part in the Miami reputation. It's not just, "those guys have an attitude and get in trouble." It's, "They are usually the best players but they have *serious* attitude problems and get in a *lot* of trouble." The fact that they are really good only accentuates the bad boy image. For that reason, Irvin is the ringleader. The flashy receiver set the NFL record for consecutive games with at least 100 yards receiving (11) on his way to a monster 111-catch, 1,603-yard 1995 campaign. For his career he caught 750 passes for nearly 12,000 yards.[4]

---

[3] Edgerrin James had a shot at making this list until he was quoted in an *FHM* magazine article as proudly proclaiming the University of Miami motto to be "Hit, stick, and bust [bad word for a male body part]. Then what? Talk [bad word for a bodily function]." I'm not even exactly sure what Edge meant here, but those comments got him moved into the "bad box."

[4] The yardage total was good for fourteenth all-time as of the final print deadline for this book.

However, stats and even Super Bowl rings (he had three) don't tell the whole Michael Irvin story. To do that you have to include the cocky demeanor on the field. The arrest for cocaine possession in 1991 and the subsequent five-game suspension by the NFL. The regular trips to the "White House."[5] Even fairly recently, as an ESPN analyst, Irvin was causing controversy and dodging in and out of legal trouble.[6]

Brian Blades. Blades reached a Pro Bowl and snagged 581 balls during his eleven-year career with Seattle, but he is perhaps better known for being briefly convicted of manslaughter in 1996. He was acquitted within seventy-two hours of the original decision, but the debacle was a highly publicized incident that only added to the growing Miami "legacy."

Ray Lewis. One of the best linebackers in the history of the game, Lewis often rubbed some people the wrong way with his propensity to celebrate excessively after even the most mundane of tackles. However, what really changed his image was a little thing called a murder charge. Lewis was arrested in January of 2000 for the murder of two people outside a nightclub. He wound up copping a plea and pleading guilty to obstruction of justice in exchange for his testimony against two friends. Lewis also eventually reached a settlement with the daughter of one of the victims, preempting a civil trial that was set to begin in June of 2004.[7]

Jeremy Shockey. The talented tight end reached four Pro Bowls in his first five seasons in New York, but stood out more for his outlandish attitude and extreme disrespect for authority.

---

[5] The "White House" was an establishment outside of Dallas that provided sexual services and other acts of debauchery to many Cowboys players. Without access to firsthand accounts, it is impossible to say exactly what transpired in this glorified brothel, but I'm guessing that whatever it was, it put the Minnesota Vikings' "Party Boat" of 2005 to shame.

[6] Most famously, he started a war between Terrell Owens and Donavon McNabb when he claimed that the 2005 Eagles (3–5 at the time) would be 8–0 with the aging Brett Favre as quarterback. He was also arrested for marijuana possession during the 2005 season.

[7] *The Baltimore Sun* reported that the settlement amount was in excess of one million dollars. Draw your own conclusions as to why Lewis would pay so much money.

His most infamous episode occurred when he called Bill Parcells a "homo" in a *Sports Illustrated* interview. He sometimes seems to milk his injuries to build his reputation for toughness. Additionally, he was shown partying in a luxury box with numerous empty drinks in front of him while his New York Giants teammates were slugging it out on the field during Super Bowl XLII and seemed to be sulking about the fact that his squad was doing better without him.

Kellen Winslow II. First, while at Miami, he became the poster child for irresponsible comments. During a game against the University of Tennessee, Winslow laid out a Volunteers receiver and then stood over him, taunting the injured player. After the game, he attempted to justify his actions by claiming (among other things) that "they're gunning for my legs," "we don't care about nobody but this U," and "I'm a soldier." Needless to say, he took a lot of heat for this incident, most specifically for calling himself a "soldier" when there were actual American soldiers fighting an actual war. Upon reaching the NFL, Winslow was once again in the eye of the storm (for all the wrong reasons) as he suffered career-threatening injuries while trying to learn how to ride a motorcycle, which was in blatant violation of his contract. When he finally got healthy and took the field for the 2006 season, he promptly blasted his coaching staff in press interviews.

Willis McGahee. McGahee's only real crime is thinking that he is much better than he really is. During a mediocre 2005 campaign, he made the unsubstantiated claim that he was the best running back in the NFL, despite record-breaking seasons in the making by the likes of Shaun Alexander, LaDainian Tomlinson, and Tiki Barber. After making those comments, McGahee went out and rushed for 50 yards in his next game, and only 639 yards and one touchdown in his final ten games. Football fans everywhere rolled their eyes and muttered, "Typical Miami player."

Najeh Davenport. In college, Davenport allegedly "went number two" in the closet of a female dorm room at Barry University. He eventually pleaded guilty and got the charges of burglary and "criminal mischief" dropped in exchange for community service. Additionally, Davenport was charged with domestic violence and endangering a child in a dispute with the mother of his five-year-old child in October of 2007. Classy guy.

Obviously, the players listed above run the gamut from "mouthy" (McGahee) to "indiscriminate pooper" (Davenport) and everything in between. However, when you consider that nearly 50 current NFL players graduated from Miami, that list doesn't seem so substantial. In reality, most players from The U are respected, they work hard, and they stay out of trouble, all while excelling on the field. Unfortunately, as the old saying goes, it only takes a few bad apples to spoil the barrel.

With that in mind, it is probably a good thing Miami never landed Adam "Pacman" Jones as a recruit.

(AH)

Appliances, Kitchen: William "The Refrigerator" Perry Was *Not* Actually A Refrigerator

Look, I'll be up front about this. I love a good nickname, so much so that I may actually root for a player just because I like his nickname. If the Titans had a wide receiver named Bob Jenkins, I couldn't care less. But if they had Bob "Red Top Hammer" Jenkins, he'd be one of my favorites. And I don't even know what "Red Top Hammer" could possibly mean.

Fortunately, pro football has had some great nicknames.

Red Grange was "the Galloping Ghost." I never saw him play, but I can say with 100 percent certainty that I would have rooted for someone nicknamed "the Galloping Ghost."

The same is true for Elroy "Crazy Legs" Hirsch.

Kitchen appliance or defensive lineman for the Bears?
The vegetable crisper should be a hint.

And Lou "the Toe" Groza.

Lance Alworth was "Bambi." If you ever watched him darting down the field after catching a pass for the Chargers, you understood why. That is, if you understood that "Bambi" was the name of a deer in a Disney movie, and that deer are fast and graceful.

The Cowboys' Ed Jones was never just "Ed Jones." No, he was "Too Tall Jones." And it was true. He was not just tall. He was too tall. You could always pick him out on the field.

Kenny Stabler was "the Snake." I don't know why, and I don't want to know why. The nickname just seemed to fit.

Joe Namath was "Broadway Joe."

Chiefs running back Christian Okoye was "the Nigerian Nightmare."

Dick Lane was "Night Train Lane."

The Steelers' Joe Green was "Mean Joe Greene."[8]

The Oilers' Billy Johnson was never just "Billy Johnson." No, he was Billy "White Shoes" Johnson, and shall always be Billy "White Shoes" Johnson. You see, he wore white shoes, and he danced in the end zone after scoring like the insides of his thighs were on fire.

Ted Hendricks was "the Mad Stork." If you saw him play, you knew why.

Thomas Henderson was "Hollywood Henderson."

Dolphins running back Eugene Morris was never, ever, "Eugene Morris." He was "Mercury Morris." I'll bet even his family didn't know his real first name was Eugene.

And then there was Walter "Sweetness" Payton and William "the Refrigerator" Perry, teammates on the 1986 Super Bowl champion Chicago Bears.

Payton, of course, was one of the greatest running backs the game has ever seen. And the nickname "Sweetness" aptly captured his style of play.

Perry was an enormous defensive lineman who was the approximate size and shape of a refrigerator. The fact that he liked to fill himself with food, and would eventually participate in organized eating contests, only made the nickname even more appropriate.

Now, there is a reason I saved Payton and Perry for last, and it has nothing to do with their nicknames. Like many football fans of a certain age, I tend to think of Payton and Perry together because of one of the worst coaching decisions in history. It wasn't a decision that affected the outcome of a game in any way. Instead, it was a decision that needlessly affected a great player's legacy.

---

[8] We have an entire section on Mr. Greene. See *Greene, Mean Joe*. Especially if you like the Steelers or Coca-Cola.

In Super Bowl XX, the Bears were ahead of the Patriots by the score of 37–3 in the second half. The game was already well out of hand. The Patriots' groundskeeper was playing quarterback, or might as well have been. With the ball on the Patriots' one-yard line, Bears coach Mike Ditka could have given Payton a chance to score a Super Bowl touchdown. Instead, playing to the fans, he inserted the enormous Perry in the backfield and called Perry's number. Perry plowed through the Patriots' defensive line, scored a touchdown, and celebrated in the end zone in a fashion that would have made Billy "White Shoes" Johnson more than a bit nervous.

It was a lot of fun to see the big man score a touchdown and celebrate. Everyone laughed and smiled. However, the record books will forever reflect that William "the Refrigerator" Perry scored a Super Bowl touchdown, but that Walter "Sweetness" Payton never did.

Payton was too much of a gentleman to ever complain about Ditka's slight.

But I'm not: Ditka screwed up. He should have given Payton a chance to score. And we all would have been just as delighted as we were when Perry scored.

(MK)

Asia, The Continent Of: It Is *Not* True That There Has Never Been An Asian To Play In The NFL

At the time we are writing this book, there has been a small amount of publicity about a wide receiver from Japan named Noriaki Kinoshita, who is trying out for the Atlanta Falcons. Repeatedly, the articles about Kinoshita have stated that he is trying to become the first Asian to play in the NFL. Repeatedly, the articles have been wrong, and a reporter should not have to think too long or too hard before realizing the inaccuracy of the statement that he would be the first Asian to play in the league. It's not as if you have to look in the history books to track down some obscure player who played on special teams in a single game back in 1974. No, all you have to do is think about one of the most prominent players on a recent Super Bowl champion team, who happens to still be playing at the time this book is being written and at the time the receiver from Japan is trying out for the Falcons.

All you have to do is think of Hines Ward, the wide receiver for the Pittsburgh Steelers.

Ward's mother is Korean.

And before you argue that he was adopted, stop. He wasn't.

And before you argue that you are not including Asian players who were born in the United States, think again. Hines Ward was born in Seoul, South Korea.

And before you argue that South Korea is not in Asia, let me suggest that you look at a globe or an atlas or a map. Look for the big area marked "Asia." Now look for the little area marked "Korea." See, there it is, right smack dab in Asia.

And before you argue that you do not know how to read a globe or an atlas or a map, stop embarrassing yourself.

Ward is not the only Asian to play in the NFL, either. There have been a few others, such as Dat Nguyen of the Cowboys, in case you were wondering.

So, if he ever ends up playing a down in the NFL, Kinoshita will not be able to say that he was the first Asian to do so.

He would be able to say that he was the first Kinoshita to do so.

Which is still quite an accomplishment for the Kinoshita family.

(MK)

Babes, The: Babe Parilli Was *Not* Babe Laufenberg

Babe Parilli was a quarterback for the Packers, Patriots, Browns, Raiders, and Jets in the 1950s and 1960s.

Babe Laufenberg was a quarterback for the Saints, Chargers, and Cowboys in the 1980s.

Babe Parilli's claim to fame was that he was a three-time Pro Bowl player who passed for more than 22,000 yards and threw 178 touchdowns.

Babe Laufenberg's claim to fame was that he was named Babe.

There is no reason to confuse these two people.

So don't.

(MK)

Backs, Running: Pro Bowl Running Backs Do *Not* Grow On Trees

During the incredibly long two weeks leading up to the 2006 Super Bowl, television and radio shows were bringing anybody and everybody onto the air in an effort to fill space and get a new angle. One of those guests was John Riggins, former Washington Redskins great, who commented that he had seen a shift in the way running backs were being valued by NFL teams. He noted that quarterbacks, always the highest paid players, were pulling away from ball carriers and that even wide receiver, cover corner, and offensive lineman were becoming more premium positions. Basically, he summarized the prevailing feeling in today's NFL: running backs are replaceable.

The timing of Riggins' comments was interesting because Shaun Alexander and Edgerrin James were both entering into free agency after being tagged as "franchise players" the previous season, and neither had been locked up by their current teams despite incredible individual seasons.[9] Their situations seemed to symbolize the wide-spread

---

[9] The dreaded "franchise player" tag is a tool that every NFL team possesses in an ongoing effort to stay under the salary cap. The short version of the rule is that each team can designate one player as its franchise player, which allows them to pay that player a set rate for the next season. Most NFL players find the designation frustrating and unfair, as it delays the opportunity to enter into a long-term contract with either their current team or a new organization. I can't say I disagree with them.

belief in pro football that a good running back can be found anytime, anywhere. That they indeed "grow on trees."

Obviously, such sentiment isn't completely without merit. It seems that every year a hidden gem is unearthed in the form of a Willie Parker or Chris Warren or whoever the Broncos play at tailback that season. It is also true that running backs seem to be at greater risk of injury than most players. Throw in the fact that running backs tend to suffer the most noticeable drop in performance after turning thirty, and you start to see why the position lacks certainty. For all of those reasons, NFL teams are right to be cautious about signing just any random running back to a huge, long-term deal. There is only one thing: we aren't talking about just "any random running back."

The biggest misconception about running backs is that there are a lot of great ones playing at any given time. This is an important point because if that were true, then teams would be justified in cutting loose superstars at the position. However, that is simply not the case. In almost any season in NFL history, there has always been a clear upper echelon of NFL running backs. Players who were superior at that time, and proven to be superior in hindsight as well.

In the early 1960s, Jim Brown and Jim Taylor were the best running backs in the game.[10] In the late 1960s it was Gale Sayers and, to a lesser extent, Cleveland's Leroy Kelly.[11] The 1970s saw an explosion of incredible running backs, led by O.J. Simpson, Larry Csonka, and Franco Harris. They were joined later in the decade by elite running backs such as Walter Payton, Earl Campbell, and Tony Dorsett, all three of whom remained dominant into the 1980s, a decade that also featured the likes of Marcus Allen, Roger Craig, Eric Dickerson, and even Joe Morris, Herschel Walker, and George Rodgers.

The 1990s were dominated by Thurman Thomas and Ricky Watters early; by Jerome Bettis and Terrell Davis in the middle; by

---

[10] Brown needs no explanation, but Taylor is overlooked because he peaked a few years too early, before the popularity of the game exploded. In his prime, Taylor was one of the most dominant players in football for the Green Bay Packers.

[11] See the entries *Piccolo, Brian* and *Kelly, Leroy.*

Marshall Faulk, Curtis Martin, and Eddie George late; and by Emmitt Smith and Barry Sanders throughout.

All of which leads us to the current decade, where the likes of Corey Dillon, LaDainian Tomlinson, Shaun Alexander, Edgerrin James, Tiki Barber, Priest Holmes, and Larry Johnson all have made their significant marks.

Pundits and experts would have you believe that this last group of backs was expendable all along. The Colts parted ways with James after losing in the 2006 playoffs, preferring to throw their money at wide receiver Reggie Wayne. The Seattle Seahawks rode Alexander's record 28 touchdowns to the 2006 Super Bowl and didn't sign him until the last possible minute. Did they have access to a time machine? How could they have known that his production would drop off so dramatically?

The prevailing theory is that the secondary option is good enough at running back, so there is no need to pay the established star. However, can you look back through history and find that to be the case? Was Alex Webster really going to fill in for Jim Brown? Essex Johnson for Franco Harris? Mike Pruitt for Walter Payton? No. Yet that is what NFL teams are banking on when they let a proven star go, with hopes of filling the hole by plugging in a cheaper replacement.

Coaches and front offices have seen Denver cycle through running backs with great success. They watched the unstoppable Larry Johnson take over for Priest Holmes in Kansas City without missing a beat and noted the way Rudi Johnson filled in nicely for Corey Dillon in Cincinnati. It has all added up to the belief that they can have the same success by scaling back. The problem is that they are ignoring the flipside. Dallas spent years searching for a consistent running game after Emmitt Smith. Same with Detroit after Barry Sanders. It took the 49ers almost a decade to plug the hole left by Ricky Watters. The Patriots had four different leading rushers in the four years after losing Curtis Martin. The list of inadequate replacements goes on and on, and it reads a lot longer than the success stories.

History bears out a different and more compelling reason to change horses: age. A friend of mine compares running backs to tires. You want to get good ones and treat them well, but when they are done, don't hesitate to get new ones. That is why the Colts replaced Edgerrin James with rookie Joseph Addai in 2006 and why guys like Jamal Lewis, Thomas Jones, Ahman Green, and Corey Dillon were all on the move in the winter of 2007. It isn't that teams believe their stars are expendable. They just believe they are old, tired, and worn out. Like a set of tires.

(AH)

Bay, Green: A City Need *Not* Be Large To Be A Great NFL Town

This entry could have been filed under the title "Angeles, Los" as well, which pretty much gives away where I'm going with this.

Question: How can the city of Green Bay, Wisconsin, located in Brown County, population 190,000, sustain one of the proudest franchises in all of American sports, while the city of Los Angeles, California, located in Los Angeles County, population 9.5 million, can't even keep an NFL team in town? How does that make any sense at all?

There is obviously a reason for this. There has to be.

The first explanation typically proffered for the "Green Bay Experience" is that the tradition and history of the franchise fosters a special connection between the fans and the team. The Packers have won three Super Bowls (including the first two). They've been around since 1921. They have a legacy of great football names like Hutson and Lombardi and Starr and Favre. The Packers play their home games on the famous frozen tundra of Lambeau Field.[12] There is a ton of tradition here.

The only problem with using tradition as the reason that Green Bay is a better football town than a place like Los Angeles, is that L.A.

---

[12] See the entry titled *Tundra, Frozen.*

has plenty of its own NFL tradition. Obviously, Los Angeles is best known for some of the dominant eras of USC football on the college level. The "Student Body Left" years of O.J. Simpson, Anthony Davis, Ricky Bell, Charles White, and Marcus Allen were legendary, and the recent run led by Pete Carroll, Matt Leinart, and Reggie Bush was arguably one of the greatest teams in college football history. Besides, L.A. is not without its fair share of NFL lore as well.

The Rams played in Los Angeles from 1946 until 1994 (including the seasons they played in Anaheim, California). That is nearly fifty years of football history. While in L.A., the Rams reached four NFL Championship games, where they went 1–3. Once the Super Bowl era began, they became a fixture in the NFC playoffs, reaching post-season play every year from 1973 to1980 and playing in five NFC title games.[13] The franchise has featured such players as Norm Van Brocklin, "Crazy Legs" Hirsch, Deacon Jones, Dick "Night Train" Lane, Roman Gabriel, Merlin Olsen, Jackie Slater, and Eric Dickerson. There is a ton of history here.[14]

Another common theory on why people love the Packers is that they are often competing for titles. To contrast that, many would point to the Rams' poor play in the years leading up to the move as an excuse for waning fan interest.[15] However, in the twenty-four years between winning Super Bowl II and the first year of the Brett Favre era, the Packers enjoyed only *five* seasons above .500. Five! Yet the luster was never lost, the fans kept packing the stadium, and the Packers remained the absolute pride of Green Bay. So even if you subscribe

---

[13] Part of the reason the Rams aren't remembered as being more of a force during that decade is that they won only once in those five conference championship bouts. Consider them the predecessors to the Philadelphia Eagles of 2001–2004.

[14] Obviously, the Raiders also had a stint in L.A., but they are largely remembered as the Oakland Raiders, considering that is where they started as a franchise and where they play today. However, while the Raiders' stay in Los Angeles was brief (13 years), they went 118–81 during that span, reached the playoffs in seven of those seasons, and won Super Bowl XVIII. I hate to reduce that sort of success to a footnote, but when the discussion revolves around history and tradition and fan connection, you really can't hold Los Angeles accountable for failing to hold on to a "borrowed" franchise.

[15] The Rams suffered six consecutive losing seasons before moving to St. Louis, where they had four more campaigns under .500 before breaking through and winning the Super Bowl in the 1999 season.

to the faulty logic that fans will only support great teams, success (or lack of success) isn't the reason L.A. can't support a football team.

A third reason offered for Green Bay's popularity is that Packers' games have become more than just a game, that they are an "event." The stories of people waiting for season tickets, the legend of the town shutting down during Packers games, the commercials depicting these scenarios. . . it all adds up to a certain mystique and hype that tends to continue on in perpetuity. Packers games will always be insanely popular because everyone knows that they are supposed to be insanely popular. It's very circular logic, but indisputable all the same. However, this also doesn't really separate Green Bay from Los Angeles, because L.A. is the one city on the planet that loves an event. This is the land of "see and be seen."

Lakers games have always sold out, even when the team was briefly terrible and Kobe Bryant was hoisting up forty shots a night. Why? Because everyone wants to be spotted at a Lakers game. They want to tell their friends they went to the Lakers game the night before. Leave the parking pass on the dashboard. Wine and dine clients in a corporate suite. Lakers games are a big event in the City of Angels. Given that the Lakers play forty-one home games each season, not including any playoff contests, wouldn't you think that a mere eight NFL games would be a bigger draw? We've already pointed out that the Rams and Raiders were both good NFL franchises, so the handful of Sundays each year when the NFL was in town definitely qualified as an "event." So that's not it.

That leaves one major comparison between Green Bay, Wisconsin, and Los Angeles, California: the weather. If you were charting a destination for a vacation in late October, which place would you pick? How about early December? How about ever? The simple fact is that when the sun shines every day, your options for entertainment multiply in a hurry. Golfing, hiking, picnics, surfing, beach volleyball, jogging, skateboarding, bike rides, kite flying, lawn bowling, outdoor basketball, softball, playing catch, barbequing, pool parties, outdoor shopping, driving along the coast with the top down, tennis, sunbathing, neighborhood strolls, washing your car, teaching your dog to fetch, eating ice cream on a bench, and swimming are all activities you can participate in when it is seventy-five degrees with a blue sky overhead. Very few, if any, of those activities are available to people living in Green Bay, Wisconsin in November, December, or January.

Ultimately, that is the answer, and it is a very simple one. A city does not need to be large to be a great NFL town. It just needs to be cold.

(AH)

Bowl, Bud: Bud Light Did *Not* Have A Clutch Quarterback

As readers of this book know very well, far too many people now watch the Super Bowl not for the game itself, pitting what is ostensibly the best team from the AFC against the best from the NFC, but for the commercials shown during the game. Advertisers spend a small fortune to buy advertising time during the game, and they frequently create new commercials just for the event, often involving highly paid celebrities, or special effects, or both. The thinking in a nutshell is, "We're spending a million dollars for a minute of advertising time, so we might as well do something special and memorable with it."

Knowing that advertisers want to create something special and memorable to justify their ridiculously large investments, Super Bowl party attendees frequently talk and eat and drink during the game itself, but demand silence when the commercials come on. Because nothing demands our attention so much as the new Doritos ad.

Will they have an attractive woman doing the splits while eating a Dorito this year?

Maybe they'll have a giant Dorito that crushes a city!

Then, in the newspapers the next day, not only is there an analysis of the game, but there is also an analysis of the Super Bowl commercials, identifying the "winners" and the "losers."

Does it make sense?

Of course not.

We should be going to the restroom, or loading up on food, or getting another drink during the commercials, not sitting in rapt attention.

Surely, this says something about our society. And, surely, it isn't something good.

When did this phenomenon start exactly?

It's hard to say. Maybe it was in 1984 when Apple spent a fortune creating a futuristic advertisement that seemed to mimic George Orwell's *1984*, with a solitary figure destroying the enormous screen projecting the face of a Big Brother-like figure as he monitored a roomful of people working. That is the first Super Bowl commercial I remember people discussing the next day.

Regardless of when the phenomenon started, the Bud Bowl certainly didn't help matters.

What is the Bud Bowl, you ask.

Well, back in 1989, the makers of Budweiser beer decided it would be a good idea to use their very expensive commercial time to stage a football game. Between bottles of beer.

Yes, you read that correctly.

Bottles of beer playing football.

One team was comprised of bottles of Budweiser. The other was comprised of bottles of Bud Light.

The commercials would show the two teams of beer bottles moving around on something that resembled a football field. They had little helmets on the tops of the bottles so you would not confuse the two teams. They kept score just as you would in a normal football game played between teams of human beings. Eventually, the game would end, and one team would be crowned the Bud Bowl champion.

Hooray!

Here are the final results of the Bud Bowls:

Bud Bowl I	Budweiser 27, Bud Light 24
Bud Bowl II	Budweiser 36, Bud Light 34
Bud Bowl III	Bud Light 23, Budweiser 21
Bud Bowl IV	Budweiser 27, Bud Light 24
Bud Bowl V	Budweiser 35, Bud Light 31
Bud Bowl VI	Bud Light 20, Budweiser 14
Bud Bowl VII	Budweiser 26, Bud Light 24
Bud Bowl VIII	Budweiser 27, Bud Light 24

That's right: this promotion was so popular that they played eight—or, technically, VIII—Bud Bowls.

And Budweiser won six of the eight—or, technically, VI of the VIII—games.

As you can see, all of the contests were very close—the types of games that teams with clutch quarterbacks tend to win.

Which is an awfully strong indictment of the Bud Light quarterback, don't you think?

In any event, the really sad thing is that some people used to bet on the outcome of the Bud Bowls.

Really.

They bet actual, hard-earned money that could be used to buy life's necessities.

They bet that money on a commercial. A commercial showing a football game. Between teams of beer bottles. I am embarrassed to have to point this out, but because beer bottles cannot actually play football or even, well, move, the commercials were filmed in advance using stop-motion photography. Meaning that the outcomes of the games were determined and filmed well in advance, and yet people still bet real, honest-to-God money on these games.

Imagine sitting in front of the television set praying that a bottle of beer doesn't get tackled by another bottle of beer.

Imagine perspiration dripping from your brow as the play clock is running down and a bottle of beer is scooting down the sideline.

Imagine the devastation when that bottle of beer gets tackled just inches from the goal line.

Imagine having to explain to your wife that you can't pay the mortgage because you bet on Bud Light to win Bud Bowl VII.

Imagine having to explain to her that if they'd just kicked a field goal, you'd be rolling in cash.

It would probably just be easier to lie and say you spent the money on a hooker.

A very expensive hooker.

(MK)

Bowl, Bud: It Is *Not* Difficult To Find Statistics For The Bud Bowls

A decade ago, it would have taken forever to track down the scores for all of the Bud Bowls.

Now, with this thing they call a computer, I was able to find them in a matter of seconds.

I don't know about you, but I'm beginning to think this computer thing may be more than a fad.

Perhaps time will prove me wrong.

(MK)

Bowl, Pro: You Do *Not* Care About The Pro Bowl

In the 1992 Pro Bowl, which the AFC won 41–13, the AFC took the lead by . . .

You already moved on to the next entry, didn't you?

Heck, I would, too.

I'd rather read about the Bud Bowl than read about the Pro Bowl.

I'd rather read the bottom of a Kleenex box than read about the Pro Bowl.[16]

Isn't it about time they just cancelled that stupid game?

And they can cancel the Hall of Fame game, too, while they're at it.

(MK)

Bowl, Pro: The NFL All-Star Game Should *Not* Be At The End Of The Season

Mike is right; nobody cares about the Pro Bowl. But they should! And they would, with one simple change.

Every year the best players in professional football compete in an annual All-Star game. The game is played in beautiful Hawaii, "where the air is so dewy sweet that you don't even have to lick the stamps."[17] The participants get to fraternize with rivals and friends alike, walk around wearing leis[18], represent their teams and conferences, and put their skills on display for all the world to see.

Oh, wait. Never mind. Nobody actually watches the Pro Bowl.

Think about the big three American sports: baseball, basketball, and football. Two of them feature All-Star games in the middle of the season; one tacks on its star-studded exhibition at the end. Is it a coincidence that both the baseball and basketball All-Star games are far more exciting and relevant?

Consider the sheer controversy that surrounds roster choices. The selection of the Major League Baseball All-Star teams is perhaps the most arduous and difficult process this side of peace talks with North Korea. Fans pick the starters, then players pick some reserves, then coaches pick a few pitchers and reserves, then the fans round

---

[16] By the way, did you know that the bottom of a Kleenex box provides an 800-number to call if you have any questions about using the product? What questions could someone possibly have? "Do I put the Kleenex up to my nose before I blow, or after?"

[17] I am quoting Newman of *Seinfeld*.

[18] And no doubt beating the "you just got leid" joke into the ground.

things out—all while conforming to representation rules,[19] injury concerns, and politics. Every year there is a storm of controversy swirling around the All-Star game. Who is going to be the starting pitcher? Will the manager try to screw over a divisional rival by pitching their ace on short rest? Who will the fans vote in to replace the injured Ken Griffey, Jr.? What deserving American League shortstop will Derek Jeter beat out this year? And so on. Throw in the fact that the winning league gets home-field advantage in the World Series, the Home Run Derby, and everything else, and you are looking at a *major* event.

The NBA version of All-Star weekend (creatively titled "All-Star Weekend") doesn't have quite the mystique of the Midsummer Classic, but it, too, features controversial picks, fan voting, limiting rules,[20] and sideshows like the Dunk Contest and the Three-Point Shootout. At the very least, it flares up as a major story midway through the NBA season and it always serves as a spotlight in which All-Star players can get their due recognition. For instance, despite the fact that Orlando was abominable in 2003–2004, Tracy McGrady still got a chance to be acknowledged for his fine play and be part of something positive for a few days. In other words, players in the NBA and in Major League Baseball actually get a chance to enjoy their All-Star appearances. People actually notice that they *are* All-Stars.

The Pro Bowl offers none of this. There is no debate over roster choices, because by the time the playoffs start, nobody cares about stuff like that. The players get very little recognition because the exhibition itself gets so little coverage. There are no festivities, nothing on the line, no ambience. At least a dozen players beg out with suspicious injuries. This is a real shame.

Not only are football players and fans just as deserving of a quality exhibition game as their basketball and baseball counterparts, there is also potential for a higher quality game in the NFL. Think about it. The NBA All-Star game has long been guilty of being a layup line

---

[19] Every team in baseball must be represented with at least one All-Star. Why? God only knows.
[20] Like when the requirement that two centers be selected for each team led to Jamal Magloire making the Eastern Conference All-Star team in 2004. Who is Jamal Magloire, you ask. Thank you for making my point.

disguised as a basketball game. *Nobody* plays any defense. The reason for this is obvious: there are very few, if any, NBA All-Stars who get their paychecks for being defensive stoppers. They all score points, so if Vince Carter gives up a wide-open lane to the basket to Steve Nash, it is no problem at all, as he will just get it back on the other end with a crowd-pleasing dunk. In the Pro Bowl, the level of play is actually pretty good (this remains a secret because, as noted above, people don't actually watch the Pro Bowl), mainly because *half* the players in the game—and on the field at any given time—are defensive players. Obviously, they are going to give pretty close to a maximum effort on defense, because they don't want to look like idiots. Reputations and paychecks are on the line. For that simple reason, you inherently have a better brand of ball than you do in the NBA All-Star game.

The NFL also has the potential for a more exciting game than that offered by Major League Baseball. This is primarily because it is easier to manipulate a football game to ensure a certain level of excitement. You can tweak the rules to increase passing and scoring, both teams can air it out and put crazy formations on the field, and so on. However, baseball is limited completely by chance. If the pitchers are throwing strikes with good stuff, it might not matter how explosive the hitters are, the game could be headed for a 4–2 snoozer. Baseball—even exhibition baseball—always has the possibility of tremendous drama, but it is very unpredictable. Football can assure a more consistently exciting game.

If football is American's most popular sport and more conducive to an exciting and competitive All-Star game, why is the Pro Bowl an afterthought? Why would the league throw away millions and millions of dollars? Obviously, there are scheduling issues and injury concerns, but those are present in any sport. The NFL could eliminate the current staggered bye-week system, and give everyone the same bye in the middle of the season. The Pro Bowl could be played on a Thursday night (since there is little need for extensive preparation), and the players could be back with their respective teams with over a full week to rest and prepare for the next game. It seems so simple.

One thing is for sure. The Pro Bowl is the best sporting event that no one is watching, and the NFL's All-Star players are not getting their due. The games are exciting, the setting unique and surreal, and the players the very best at what they do. It seems natural that the NFL would want to find a way to package this and present it for all the world to see. The first weekend of November, on the heels of the World Series, seems like the perfect time. How about it, Commish?

(AH)

Bowl, Pro: Adam Is *Not* Right

Okay, having just read Adam's last section, I must say I disagree. The problem with the Pro Bowl isn't with *when* it is played, but rather *how* it is played.

Football is simply too complex a game for a group of men from different teams to be able to put together a coordinated, high-quality effort after only a few days together.

In a baseball All-Star game, the manager can pretty much sit back and watch because the players know what to do. There are no "plays." There are no complex "defenses."

Basketball and hockey All-Star games can be played with only a few "plays" and—as has been shown—no "defense" whatsoever.

But football?

To play it properly, an offense needs a complex playbook, and a defense needs an equally complex set of defensive schemes. Dumbing it down for the Pro Bowl by only having a few plays makes for a different, less exciting game.

So just cancel it.

Please.

(MK)

Browns, Cleveland: The Current NFL Team In Cleveland Should *Not* Share The Former Name Of The Team That Used To Be Known As The Cleveland Browns But Is Now Known As The Baltimore Ravens

Long title, huh? There is a reason for that. I wanted to try to confuse you as much as the NFL has confused me over the years. During the 2006 NFL Playoffs, the Indianapolis Colts traveled to Baltimore to play the Ravens in an AFC Divisional game. This meant that the Colts were heading back to their former home where they were the Baltimore Colts from 1953 to 1983.

Obviously, that storyline was not terribly confusing. Intriguing, certainly, but not confusing. In sports, teams often go back to their former homes to compete. The New Orleans Hornets travel to Charlotte to play the Bobcats. The Los Angeles Lakers had an intense Western Conference Finals series with the Minnesota Timberwolves in 2003. The Dodgers and Giants annually go back to New York to play the Mets. This is not an entirely uncommon experience.

What makes the Colts-Ravens clash so odd is that there is history on both sides of the equation. In all of the examples cited above, the team that moved is replaced by an expansion team. However, in the case of the Ravens, they are actually the old Cleveland Browns, masquerading as a team from Baltimore that wears purple uniforms. Did you forget about that? If so, it is probably because there actually is an expansion team called the Cleveland Browns. Which means there is an old Cleveland Browns and a new Cleveland Browns. How incredibly stupid is that?

The rationale for granting Cleveland a new expansion team and naming them the Browns was supposed to be a nod to tradition and history. Some kind of "The NFL is better off if we have a team called the Cleveland Browns involved" argument. Maybe that was a nice thought, but it really makes no sense at all. After all, where do their stats belong? If you go to some Web sites and look over the history of the "Cleveland Browns," it starts in 1950 and keeps on going to the present, with a gap from 1996 to 1998. Others show the Browns as starting in 1999, while all those other years are tacked on to the Baltimore Ravens' history.

In addition to all this confusion, the Browns Debacle has created a perverse situation where football fans remember the Mayflower Incident[21] with great clarity, while completely forgetting the way owner Art Modell hijacked the Browns from Cleveland. Because Indianapolis kept the same name and uniform, people still remember Jim Irsay's treachery over twenty years later. However, when Modell moved the team from Cleveland and was forced to change everything from the mascot to the uniforms to the team name, he helped brainwash everyone in the NFL. This process was completed by the league itself when they created the new Cleveland Browns.

Now, unless you really think hard about it, you forget that any of this Browns-Ravens-Browns stuff even happened. And if you think too hard about it, you start to get confused, and then you get a headache.

I hate headaches. Thanks a lot, NFL.

(AH)

Buccaneers, Tampa Bay: The Buccaneers Do *Not* Play In Tampa Bay

For years, it bothered me that people referred to the Buccaneers simply as "Tampa." It just didn't sound right. After all, when the Jets come into town to play the 49ers, nobody says that "New" is on the road facing "San." They also don't chop it up to say "York" goes against "Frisco." Well, maybe they say Frisco, but not very often.

The point is that it seemed lazy. The name of the team is the Tampa Bay Buccaneers, so why shorten it to just Tampa? It used to drive me crazy.

---

[21] This refers to March 29, 1984, when Colts owner Jim Irsay packed the team up into Mayflower Transit trucks and moved everything in the dead of a snowy night from Baltimore to Indianapolis. Mike, my co-author, will proudly tell you that he was living in Baltimore when it happened. As if that somehow makes him special.

No, the Bucs do not play their games under the Sunshine Skyway Bridge ... although it would be pretty awesome if they did.

Eventually, I got over my little problem with the liberal use of Tampa, but I remained curious about the phenomenon. For starters, taking the lazy route to refer to the Bucs as Tampa is technically accurate. The Bucs play their games at Raymond James Stadium, which is located on the east side of the city of Tampa, out near the Tampa International Airport. In fact, using only "Tampa" is so logical that one wonders where the "Bay" came from in the first place.

The reason is actually fairly obvious: using Tampa Bay as the geographic identifier opened the door for more fans. The Minnesota Vikings, Carolina Panthers, New England Patriots, and Arizona Cardinals are all examples of NFL teams using states or broad regions to appeal to a larger fan base.[22] Tampa Bay is a large body of water that cuts a huge chunk out of the Florida coastline and happens to double as the nickname of a region that spans three counties and

---

[22] In baseball, the Los Angeles Angels of Anaheim are an example of a team that has covered this strategic ground in its entirety. They began as the Los Angeles Angels, moved to Anaheim and went with the California Angels, switched back to using Anaheim, and now have decided to use two city names at the same time. You can read about this in great detail in *The Baseball Uncyclopedia*.

includes the cities of Tampa, St. Petersburg, and Clearwater. Talk about expanding your fan base.

The strategy was obviously a good one, as the Bucs have consistently packed the house despite the fact that they were embarrassingly bad for many decades and even now continue to display a ridiculous pirate ship behind one end zone.[23]

Now whenever an announcer mentions that "Tampa" is running the ball well or an analyst says that "Tampa" looks playoff bound, I let it slide. After all, they do play in Tampa. However, it raises an entirely different issue: the fact that the Buccaneers don't actually play in Tampa *Bay*.

If they did, they would be underwater.

(AH)

Bush, Reggie: Reggie Bush Did *Not* Have The Greatest Postseason Performance By A Rookie Running Back

In January of 2007, Reggie Bush burst onto the national scene with a huge rookie performance in the playoffs. In two games—a win over Philadelphia and a loss to Chicago—Bush racked up 225 total yards and two scores. Both touchdowns were dramatic in fashion and featured the classic Reggie Bush flip into the end zone.

People immediately started gushing that he had turned in the greatest performance by a rookie running back in the history of the NFL Playoffs.

This is not true.

Reggie Bush is an exciting player. He might wind up being one of the most dominant and valuable players in league history. Or he might wind up being a huge bust.[24] Either way, Reggie Bush did not have the greatest postseason by a rookie back in the history of the league.

---

[23] The same strategy has not proved to be as successful in baseball, as the Tampa Bay Devil Rays consistently draw some of the most embarrassing attendance totals in the major leagues. Of course, they play their games indoors in a building with all the charm of a bowling alley.

[24] At the time of this book's printing, the verdict is very much still out.

A quick look through the record books proves this.

Tony Dorsett, the seventh all-time leader in rushing yards, ran for four touchdowns during the playoffs while leading the 1977 Cowboys to a Super Bowl title.

Fred Taylor hung 162 yards and a score on New England in his playoff debut for the 1998 Jaguars and tacked on another 86 rushing yards in a loss to the Broncos.

Jamal Lewis ran for 338 yards and four scores while leading the Ravens to the 2000 title.

And Timmy Smith of the Redskins ran for 204 yards and a pair of touchdowns in Super Bowl XXII.

Granted, the list doesn't get much longer than that. Curt Warner, Earl Campbell, and Marcus Allen all notched similar rookie performances, but there aren't a whole lot of players that were *better* than Bush was for the Saints in his first postseason.

Still, there were at least four. Which proves my point.

Barely.

(AH)

Busts, Drug: Playing Professional Football Does *Not* Kill The Dream Of Becoming A Drug Kingpin

One of the most bizarre sports stories in recent memory occurred in 2001 when Nate Newton, six-time Pro Bowl offensive lineman for the Dallas Cowboys, was arrested for toting around 213 pounds of marijuana in the back of his van.

Newton was pulled over for a moving violation, acted suspicious and nervous, and the next thing he knew, the Louisiana State Troopers were busting him. Newton was stashed in the St. Martin Parish Jail and charged with possession of marijuana with intent to distribute.

None of this in and of itself is all that interesting. People get locked up for hauling around drugs all the time. What is interesting is that Newton was an individual so good at football that he was able

The next best thing to a pair of shoulder pads and a ten-million-dollar signing bonus.

to succeed at the highest level the game had to offer. Why would someone like that still dabble in drug peddling? Perhaps the craziest part of all is that Newton isn't even that rare of a commodity. In fact, there have been plenty of current and former NFL players who have been busted for being part of the drug trade. Here are some of the recent would-be George Jungs:

> **Timmy Smith.** You might remember Smith as the rookie running back who somehow managed to set the Super Bowl record with 204 rushing yards in Washington's 42–10 victory over the Broncos in Super Bowl XXII. You might remember this because it was mentioned in the preceding entry of this very book.[25] This was pretty much Smith's only memorable moment as a professional football player, and it obviously came at the expense of Denver. However, the city got its revenge when Smith was busted there in 2005 for trying to sell cocaine to an

---

[25] For those of you keeping score at home, Timmy Smith has now been mentioned in two entries of this book. Same as Kareem Abdul-Jabbar. Jerry Rice? No mentions.

undercover police officer. He was sentenced to over two years in a federal prison system for conspiring to distribute cocaine.

Barry Word. The NFL's Comeback Player of the Year in 1990, Word actually got his pro drug-dealing career off the ground before his pro football career. After graduating from the University of Virginia and being drafted in the third round of the 1985 draft by the Saints, Word was indicted and convicted for attempting to distribute cocaine. Thanks to his willingness to cooperate with the authorities, Word only received five months in prison and was then able to go on to sign a three-year contract with the Saints.[26]

Bam Morris. It's shame that a guy with the name of "Bam" is remembered for anything but slamming into linebackers. (Unless "anything" includes orbiting the moon, curing a disease, or rescuing cats from trees—those are all worthy accomplishments. But you get the idea.) Unfortunately, that is the case with Bam Morris, who won the Doak Walker Award as college football's best running back in 1993 and rushed for 73 yards in a Super Bowl game, yet went down in the annals of football for his federal drug trafficking indictment that resulted in a lengthy stint in the Leavenworth federal penitentiary.

Jamal Lewis. Perhaps the most infamous member of the Nate Newton Club, Lewis was the target of a federal sting operation that began before he even left the University of Tennessee and that culminated in him being charged with the attempt to distribute cocaine. This got Lewis four months in prison, two months in a halfway house, five hundred hours of community service, and a two-game suspension. It also seemed to change Lewis for several years, as he went into prison one of the NFL's most dynamic running backs and came out as a lumbering

---

[26] It is a little odd that Word won the Comeback Player of the Year award. His career was delayed because he was a drug dealer, which meant that by the time he showed up to play with the Saints he was stuck behind Rueben Mayes and Dalton Hilliard on the depth chart. So then he sat out for the entire 1989 season before being picked up by the Chiefs and then rushing for 1,015 yards in 1990. I suppose he technically "came back" from something, but this all seems a little perverse to me.

stiff.[27] It took three years for Lewis to rediscover even a shred of his former ability, when he rebounded with the Cleveland Browns in 2007 and averaged 86.9 yards per game and 4.4 yards per carry on the ground.

Lawrence Taylor. Actually, Taylor was not a drug dealer. The huge amount of cocaine he possessed in the 1980s might have had you confused, but know that it was all for personal use. Just wanted to clear that up.[28]

Adam "Pacman" Jones. The presumption that Jones might be a drug dealer is actually the least of his troubles. Pacman has put on display a cornucopia of troublemaking skills since coming into the NFL. In 2005, he was arrested on charges of assault and felony vandalism after a nightclub incident. He was also busted for probation violations that year. In 2006, Jones was arrested for an incident of disorderly conduct (again at a nightclub) as well as a misdemeanor assault when he spit on a female from Tennessee State at (drum roll, please). . . a nightclub! And during the 2007 NBA All-Star Weekend, Jones got into all kinds of trouble for "making it rain" at a strip club, an incident that led to a total fiasco.[29] Supposedly Jones became enraged that one of the dancers started grabbing up money without his permission, so he smashed her head on the stage. When a security guard intervened, Jones allegedly bit that guy in the leg. Then in the chaos that followed, someone started firing shots into the crowd, hitting three people. Immediately following this disaster, Jones was linked to known drug dealer Darryl Moore and eventually slapped with an unprecedented one-year suspension by the NFL. So, the drug-dealing is more of a "feather in his cap" situation than anything else.

---

[27] Before prison, Lewis averaged 99.1 yards rushing per game and 4.7 yards per carry from 2000 to 2003. In the three years after his time in the clink he managed just 70.1 yards per game and 3.7 per carry.

[28] Taylor himself said that "my place was like a crack house."

[29] Making it rain: throwing money up into the air around the stage. In this case, eighty-one thousand dollars in a trash bag.

Todd Marinovich. The former USC golden boy never amounted to much as an NFL player, but he has certainly had a colorful career in the world of drugs. Some of his most notorious moments include being arrested in a public bathroom in Newport Beach and fleeing from the police on a bicycle; getting busted for skateboarding in a prohibited area and being found to have methamphetamines in his pockets; and a heroin possession charge that got him booted out of the Arena Football League. However, he lands on this list for his 1997 arrest and three months in prison as a result of growing marijuana. He's been busy, that's for sure.

Sherman Williams. Michael Irvin got the headlines for his cocaine use and Nate Newton is the headliner of this entry, but it was backup running back Sherman Williams who was the real drug kingpin of the Dallas Cowboys during the late 1990s. Williams was busted in 2000 for being the leader of a drug ring that supplied over one thousand pounds of marijuana to the Mobile, Alabama, area.

Williams has already served six years in prison and isn't set to be released until 2014, but all the reports indicate that he's pretty pleased with his situation. He was quoted as saying, "I'm cool with that. It's no problem. Do I look like a guy that's doing hard time?" He also chalked up his lengthy prison stint as nothing but a business risk. "Whenever you're a businessman, there's always a risk. The most successful businessmen in the world are going to be high risk takers. The bigger the risk, the bigger the reward. Me, I just was a risk taker."

Get Donald Trump on the phone, I think we have the next Celebrity Apprentice.

(AH)

Cap, Salary: You Do *Not* Understand The Salary Cap

The NFL has a players' salary cap in place meant to control costs and ensure some minimal amount of parity—two perhaps equally important goals for the league.

In short, the thinking is that if all teams spend approximately the same amount of money on talent, they should be able to field teams that are comparable, which will create more competitive games each week and put more teams in contention for the playoffs, which in turn will create more fan interest, which in turn will create more revenue, which in turn will create more profits for the league and its owners, which in turn will lead to an increase in the salary cap, which in turn will give me a headache.

In any event, the salary cap is not as simple as requiring that each team spend no more than X number of dollars per year on player contracts. Instead, it is so convoluted that many teams retain "cap-ologists" whose sole task is to help the team manage the salary cap, taking into account signing bonuses, rookie contracts, performance bonuses, retirements and renegotiations. Some things are prorated, some things aren't. Some things count toward the salary cap, some things don't.

At the end of the day, I am confident that I do not really understand how the cap works, and you probably don't either.

Now, I suppose that some of you will say, "Why the heck are you writing about it if you aren't going to explain it to us?"

Well, hang on a second there, sport. I'm not writing about the salary cap. I'm writing about how we don't understand the salary cap.

And if you're asking that question, then I believe I've made my point.

And if you're not asking that question because you understand the cap, then you don't need anyone to explain it to you.

(MK)

Cardboard, Pieces Of: Football Fans Do *Not* Care About Collecting Football Cards

Baseball fans keep their old baseball cards in firm plastic sleeves to protect them from bending, fading, or otherwise being defaced. Baseball fans keep track of the value of their old baseball cards by perusing magazines devoted entirely to the hobby of baseball-card collecting.

Baseball fans believe that a Fergie Jenkins rookie card in "mint" condition is worth one hundred dollars more than a Fergie Jenkins rookie card in "good" condition.

Baseball fans go to baseball card conventions where they buy and sell old baseball cards.

Baseball fans believe that a Honus Wagner card is actually worth 1.5 million dollars, assuming it is in "mint" condition.

Baseball fans take out insurance on their baseball-card collections.

Baseball fans store their baseball-card collections in safe deposit boxes or in sturdy containers to preserve them.

Baseball fans include their baseball-card collections in their wills.

Football fans understand that a small piece of cardboard with a photograph of an athlete on it has no intrinsic value whatsoever.

Football fans do not care about saving those pieces of cardboard.

Football fans could not care less if one of those pieces of cardboard is bent or damaged.

Football fans keep their old cards in shoeboxes in the attic, if they keep them at all.

Football fans would never even consider going to a football-card convention to buy and sell old pieces of cardboard.

Football fans could not give two craps about collecting football cards.

I offer this as Exhibit A for why football fans are smarter than baseball fans.

Exhibit B, by the way: baseball fans will fly all the way to Florida to attend a spring training game, while football fans understand that exhibition games are a waste of time and money.

Exhibit C? Football fans cook their own food in the parking lot before the game instead of paying a fortune for a hot dog at the concession stand.

(MK)

Cheerleader, That Hot: The Cheerleader Who Smiled At You Does *Not* Want To Date You

You had a great seat for that big game your favorite team was playing.

It was a fantastic game, the game that put your favorite team in the playoffs, or kept them in contention, or kept them from prolonging a losing streak, or something along those lines.

In the fourth quarter, as your team was mounting its improbable comeback, you were on your feet cheering them on because that is what you do.

And on the sidelines, right in front of you, the team's cheerleaders were jumping and dancing and pumping their arms.

"Let's go, team!" they were shouting. "Let's go!"

And for one instant, it seemed you made eye contact with one of the cheerleaders. The blonde one.

And she looked right at you as she shouted, "Let's go, team!"

And you looked right back as you screamed, "Let's go, team!"

And she smiled and shook her pom-poms before turning away.

Let me tell you something about that cheerleader.

She is probably a lovely person.

And she is not interested in dating you.

That moment that you believe you shared with her? It's her job. She has hundreds of moments like that during every game. She smiles and shouts and looks into the stands, and occasionally, often accidentally, she makes eye contact with a generic male figure in the stands who is wearing the same colors as the team for which she cheers. And when she happens to make eye contact, she smiles because that's her job. It says it right on the job description. "Essential functions of job: leap, cheer, smile."

That moment that you will remember the rest of your life? She was forgetting it as it was happening.

Dream on, buddy. Dream on.

Do not tell your friends that you "shared a moment" with that cheerleader.

Do not tell your friends that you are going to track her down to see if she wants to go on a date.

Do not spend your time at work fantasizing about the date you are going to go on with that cheerleader, or about how she is going to become your girlfriend and come to the office Christmas party.

Do not spend your time at work trying to imagine what she looks like in her underwear, or naked.

Do not go to your favorite team's Web site to see if you can find her name.

Do not call the front office to see if they can tell you her name.

Do not send flowers to her in care of your favorite team.

Do not send a note to her in care of your favorite team, particularly a note referring to "the moment you shared."

Do not send her a note asking her to meet you somewhere for a drink.

Do not send her your photograph to jog her memory about "the moment you shared."

Just leave her alone, and get on with your life.

Trust me.

There's a reason courts issue restraining orders.

(MK)

Cities, Cold Weather: The Super Bowl Should *Not* Be Played In Any City Other Than Miami Or San Diego

In February 2006, Super Bowl XL was played at Ford Field in Detroit, Michigan. The night before the game, it snowed. To keep an entire crowd from being morbidly depressed and frozen in place, they put the roof on for the big showdown. However, while the teams, spectators, and Rolling Stones wax figures were cozy and comfortable for the actual game, the week leading up to the biggest event in American sports was spent with people huddling inside their parkas, piling into People Movers, and doing pretty much anything they could to stay indoors.[30] Is this how the Super Bowl should be enjoyed?

Now, I am not the first to advance the "warm weather only" theory regarding the Super Bowl host city. *Washington Post* columnist Michael Wilbon has espoused this particular idea many times on the popular ESPN show *Pardon the Interruption*. However, Wilbon isn't writing this book, so it is up to me to carry the flag. Besides, it makes too much sense to play the game in Miami or San Diego. These are fun cities with good stadiums and great climates.[31] There is no need to subject people to harsh northern winters. It is simple common sense.

There is another reason that cites like Detroit should be avoided come Super Bowl season, and it goes beyond suntans and boardwalks and anything else directly related to the "experience" of at-

---

[30] The Rolling Stones were a controversial decision to headline the halftime show, considering that the game was being played in Detroit. You know, Motown. Hard to believe they passed on Stevie Wonder (who performed during the pregame) and other famous artists from the legendary record label.

[31] Although I should acknowledge that the 2007 Super Bowl was played in near monsoon conditions in Miami. So, even the best locations aren't foolproof.

tending a Super Bowl. This is the "real" reason and it has to do with the simple fact that the Super Bowl is supposed to be a game held at a neutral location.

Obviously, no matter how good the intentions are, this concept of neutrality can be lost given the fact that Super Bowl sites double as home stadiums for NFL teams during the season. If the Dolphins win the AFC and the title bout is being held in Miami, it is going to be tough to eliminate a home-field advantage. Same with the Chargers and San Diego. Short of building a state-of-the-art facility in Bermuda, there is always going to be the chance that a home-field advantage occurs.

The real problem comes when the game is played in a place like Detroit. Not only could the Lions have reached the Super Bowl and held a huge crowd advantage, but six other NFL teams are within a five-hour drive from the Motor City.[32] Had Buffalo, Cincinnati, Cleveland, Indianapolis, Chicago, or Pittsburgh reached the Super Bowl, they would have been playing a few hundred miles from their hometown crowd.[33] Stop me if you know where I am going with this. That's right, one of those six teams, the Pittsburgh Steelers, the same squad that had to win three games on the road in the AFC playoffs, got to play what amounted to a home game in the supposedly neutral Super Bowl.

Obviously, there were many other factors that played a role in the Steelers winning Super Bowl XL by the score of 21–10 over the Seattle Seahawks.[34] However, there is no doubt that the crowd was one of those factors. If you saw and remember the game, you know what I am talking about.

A sea of black and yellow.

"Terrible Towels" waved by four of every five set of hands.

---

[32] Obviously, reading "Not only could the Lions have reached the Super Bowl" in the context of the 2005–2006 season is hilarious. However, the NFL couldn't be sure that the Lions would be terrible when they awarded the game to Detroit.

[33] As it turned out, four of those six teams—Chicago, Cincinnati, Indianapolis, and Pittsburgh—were playoff teams.

[34] Among others: poor red zone play, dropped passes, and horrible clock management by the Seahawks, and officiating that could most charitably be described as "questionable."

Deafening roars of approval for the Steelers.

By all accounts, this was a home game for Pittsburgh. More importantly, it was a road game for the Seahawks, a team that went 13–3 during the regular season, landed the top seed in the NFC, breezed to the Super Bowl, and then was "rewarded" with a trip to Detroit to face a crowd that was the definition of partisan.

To Seattle's credit, they didn't complain about the crowd factor. Nor should they have stooped to that level. After all, tickets were available to both teams, and Steelers fans certainly did nothing wrong by getting excited for a Super Bowl and going to the game. It is the NFL that should seek to ensure this sort of thing doesn't happen.

The league needs to be more proactive in preventing a possible home-field advantage. As mentioned above, even the NFL's best efforts may wind up being thwarted. However, simple math indicates that it would be better to play the game in Miami or San Diego than it would be to host it in a place that is as centrally located as Detroit.

In addition to the seven teams (including the Lions) that are within a five-hour drive of Detroit, there are another five teams less than ten hours away. Fans from St. Louis, Philadelphia, Green Bay, Minneapolis, and Nashville could make the trip with a solid day of driving. Even fans from New York face no more than an eleven-hour

The only reason the Super Bowl should be held here is if. . . well, actually, there is no good reason.

drive. It makes no sense to host a game in a city with that kind of access. Teams from Seattle and Miami and San Diego would have no hope of balancing out a crowd from a nearby city.

Contrast the plethora of proximate major cities to a place like Detroit with the ideal options of Miami and San Diego. Beyond the obvious fact that the Dolphins and Chargers play in those cities, the potential for a "home game" occurring in the two prime "warm weather" locals is dramatically lower. Phoenix, at a little over five hours away, is the only city that could be considered even remotely close to San Diego. Both Bay Area fan bases would face a trip over eight hours in length. Anything else is either a really, really long day of travel, an overnighter, or a flight. In all, four teams are close enough to San Diego to realistically be cause for concern—two in each league.

As for Miami, the Buccaneers and Jaguars are obviously close (four hours away), but other than that, only Atlanta, at nine hours way, is anywhere nearby. That puts Miami at four total teams that could turn a Super Bowl into a home game—one AFC team and two NFC squads.

Miami and San Diego combined don't offer the risk of hosting the game in a place like Detroit. By putting the Super Bowl in a central location, the NFL was inviting the possibility that one team would have a significant advantage in terms of bringing fans to the host city. In fact, based purely on the fact that fourteen fan bases (including the New York teams) were a day's drive away from Detroit, the risk was almost 50 percent. Compare that with hosting the game in San Diego or Miami (12 percent), and it seems insane to play the Super Bowl somewhere like Detroit.

Factor in the more obvious and rehashed reasons dealing with weather, entertainment, and quality of life, and it becomes a no-brainer. Keep the NFL's title game in San Diego and Miami. The event is supposed to be fun and memorable, and the game itself is supposed to be decided on a neutral field. Miami and San Diego. Repeat after me, NFL: Miami and San Diego.

(AH)

Coaches, Conservative: Structural Engineers Are *Not* The Most Risk-Averse Professionals On The Planet

During the 2006 NFL Playoffs, the Philadelphia Eagles were trailing the New Orleans Saints late in the fourth quarter when they faced a fourth-and-ten near midfield. With just a few minutes left on the clock and the Saints' ground game already at over 200 rushing yards, Eagles' head coach Andy Reid made the obvious call to go for the first down. After all, just one first down by New Orleans would end the game.

With the home crowd of New Orleans nearly tearing the roof off the Superdome, quarterback Jeff Garcia dropped back and found receiver Hank Baskett for an improbable completion and what appeared to be a first down. Unfortunately for Philly, a false start was called on the play and they were forced to do it all over again, this time facing fourth-and-fifteen. Obviously, it is tough to complete an improbable pass once, let alone twice, and the added yardage only increased the difficulty. That said, this is the same franchise that once beat the Packers in the playoffs on a miraculous fourth-and-twenty-six completion from Donavon McNabb to Freddie Mitchell. Surely they would line up and go for it again. Right?

Wrong. For reasons that will probably never be made clear, Reid sent out the punter and booted the ball away with just 1:56 left on the clock. A few snaps and a Deuce McAllister first down later, and the Saints were kneeling the ball and running out the clock. Based on the time and score situation in the game, it was an egregious decision to punt the ball away.

However, just because it was a bad call by Reid doesn't mean it was surprising. In fact, we've come to expect nothing less from NFL coaches. Based on the decisions they make during games, NFL head coaches appear to be the most risk-averse professionals in the world—ahead of even structural engineers or corporate attorneys or chief information officers. It is unbelievable. They kick field goals

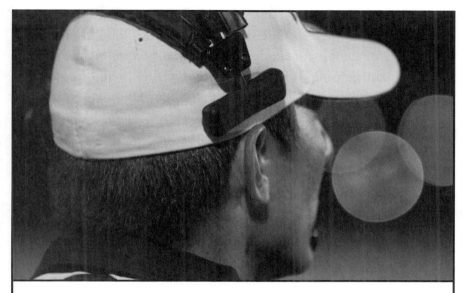

There is a good chance this man is ordering a punt on fourth-and-one at this very moment.

even when all common sense indicates that they can punch it in from the goal line. They order punts when they need just a few yards for a first down, and when they are in the opponent's territory, and when the odds dictate that they will only gain a net of about 15 yards of field position. They are like robots with headsets, automatically choosing the safe route in every situation.

The crazy thing about this is that the safe route isn't always the most practical decision. In fact, it often is not. Most people who are risk-averse take that trait and use it to build rational frameworks for all their decisions. They study the odds and master cost/benefit analysis, and generally turn every decision into an exercise of calculated odds and percentages. With that in mind, you would think that if anything, NFL coaches would be extremely rational and dependent on the cold, hard numbers. Many baseball managers are this way, going to a left-handed pitcher to face a left-handed batter based purely on the stats, even if the pitcher seems inferior to the guy at the plate.

NFL coaches don't do this. If they did, they would never punt on fourth-and-three from the opponents' 35-yard line. Because they would know that the odds of picking up the first down are in their favor (the average NFL play nets about 5 yards), while the odds of actually landing a punt inside the ten are not. They would balance the information and realize that going for it was the *only* decision to make. No, most NFL coaches do not engage in that type of analysis. They just feel their sphincters tighten, worry about what the armchair quarterbacks will say the next morning, and kick the ball away. In actuality, this is more blame avoidance than risk avoidance.

This kind of lunacy ignores everything valuable about statistical analysis and rational thought (two keys of risk avoidance), and instead embraces only the most rudimentary element of risk management, which is to be as conservative as possible, at all times.

This kind of behavior drives fans crazy and leads to losses that shouldn't happen and ultimately (when too many of those losses add up) gets the coach fired.[35] Of course, for all that, NFL coaches do get the title of most risk-averse professional in the world. So there's that.

(AH)

Control, Birth: Travis Henry Did *Not* Pay Attention During His High School Sex Education Class

At the time we are writing this book, the starting halfback for the Denver Broncos is Travis Henry.

Henry, who starred at the University of Tennessee, is a gifted player who has bounced around the league a bit, having previously played for the Bills and Titans before joining the Broncos.

---

[35] There is obviously quite a bit of irony involved here. Coaches order ridiculous punts and make overly cautious decisions to avoid blame. They don't want to stand out as the reason for a loss. However, because they are going against the most favorable odds, they are actually increasing their chances of losing the game. And when they do this over and over and over, the losses pile up and they get blamed, and the result they have been trying to avoid on a play-by-play basis winds up happening on a much larger scale. In effect, embracing risk and potential blame would make coaches more effective and, therefore, more impervious to blame in the long run.

I could give you a few of his statistics—more than 1,200 yards rushing in three seasons to date, for example—but there is one statistic that is so astounding that it will forever be the first thing I think of whenever I hear Henry's name mentioned.

According to several sources, Henry, who is only twenty-eight years old at this time, is the father of nine children.

By nine different women.

In four different states.

Wow.

I just reread those last few sentences, and, again, all I can say is, "Wow."

Nine children.

By nine women.

In four states.

Now, I have no interest in using this space to offer my opinions about promiscuity, responsibility, commitment, or birth control. I'll save that for *The Promiscuity, Responsibility, Commitment, and Birth Control Uncyclopedia.*

And I have no interest in taking up your time talking about morality. I'm a lawyer. What the hell do I know about morality?

No, I just want to focus on Henry's remarkable achievement in the field of producing children.

Having nine children by the age of twenty-eight isn't the easiest thing in the world to do. You'd have to start early, stay healthy, and be very active sexually. Very, very active. You'd also have to be very, very lucky. Or unlucky, depending on your perspective.

Having the nine children with nine different women only increases the degree of difficulty. If he'd had nine children by three different women, well, that just seems easier somehow, doesn't it?

Then add the fact that the women are in four different states.

Wow.

I'm not saying that what Henry has accomplished in this particular field has not been accomplished by others. Perhaps it has been. What I'm saying is, simply, "Wow."

I have one child.

By one woman.

In one state.

And I can barely handle that.

Nine children, by nine women, in four states?

Wow.

If he is playing any role at all in the lives of these children—and, again, I am not going to editorialize—I can't imagine how Henry even has the energy to get up in the morning, let alone try to wriggle his way through a defensive line every Sunday.

There is more.

As sports fans, we like to project statistics based upon a small sample. We like to determine what a player is "on pace for," even when we know that there is no way in the world that anyone would keep up the early pace he has set. For instance, if someone rushes for 200 yards in the first game of the season, we all like to say that he's "on pace for" 3,200 yards for the year. (Two hundred yards multiplied by 16 games equals 3,200 yards.) If someone catches seven passes in the first quarter, we like to say that he's "on pace for" 28 receptions in the game. (Seven receptions times four quarters equals 28 receptions.) You know what I mean.

Well, assuming that Henry began his sexual activity at age eighteen, he's only been active for ten years.

Assuming he remains active for another thirty years, he's "on pace for" thirty-six children.

By thirty-six different women.

In sixteen different states.

Wow.

Really, that's all I can say.

Wow.

Somewhere in Henry's hometown of Frostproof, Florida, there's a high-school sex education teacher saying the exact same thing.

Or, more likely, a former high-school sex education teacher, as I imagine she got fired the moment the school board discovered how little Henry had learned in her class.

(MK)

Control, Birth: I Did *Not* Pay Close Enough Attention To The News

The Travis Henry story is right up my alley. Seriously. Breaking down the "Serial Fathers" who populate the sports world has long been a favorite pastime of mine, right up there with golf, traveling, and long walks on the beach. In fact, I've often wished we were writing *The Basketball Uncyclopedia* just so I could hammer out an entry on some of the most infamous "Serial Fathers" of all time, such as Calvin Murphy, Larry Johnson (the "Grandmamma" version, not the Chiefs running back), and Shawn Kemp. But, alas, football is a more popular sport and isn't being ruined by shoe contracts, plummeting television ratings, and refs on the take. So, *The Football Uncyclopedia* it is.

Then, the Travis Henry story broke.

The story I'd been waiting for.

And Mike beat me to it. Which is something I might never get over.

All I can say is, you're going to pay for this, Mike.

(AH)

Cunningham, Randall: Great NFL Quarterbacks Do *Not* Belong In The Marble Business

Before I dive into this, let me admit something up front: I *loved* Randall Cunningham. Forgive me if I remember his career more fondly than most or if I anoint him as "great" while withholding that same term from every single quarterback that ever played for the Raiders. Not only do I think this is an accurate assessment of Cunningham as a player, but also I simply can't help myself. I'm a Randall fanatic.

I remember the way he redefined the quarterback position and thrived in an era when black quarterbacks were still an anomaly in the NFL. I recall with great fondness (even though I was just ten years old) the 1988 campaign when he threw for 3,808 yards and ran for 624 more while finishing second in the Associated Press Player of the Year voting, while winning the Bert Bell version of the MVP. Also the 942 yards rushing and NFL Offensive Player of the Year award in 1990, complete with another Bert Bell MVP award. The 95-yard touchdown against Buffalo in 1990 (when he ducked under Bruce Smith and heaved the ball 65 yards in the air). The incredible 91-yard punt into the wind against the Giants in 1989. And on and on.

However, what I remember most about Cunningham is the second half of his career; when he was done wrong by the NFL, left the game to run his own business, and then came back to dominate the league once again.

We've all heard the famous quote that there are no second acts in American lives, and we also all know by now that this statement

We can't prove it, but this might be the work of Randall Cunningham— just before he returned to the NFL and won the MVP award.

is nowhere near the truth. It was especially untrue for Randall Cunningham.

In 1993, after starting the season as the NFL's Offensive Player of the Month for September, Cunningham broke his left fibula and missed the final 12 games. The year 1994 was a successful statistical campaign, but he never seemed quite right under center. By 1995, Cunningham was benched by the Eagles and forced to play out his contract as a backup. Despite this downward spiral, it seemed obvious that he had plenty left in the tank. Yet not one single NFL team signed him for the 1996 season. You can imagine how distraught I was at the time, having known no other NFL than one featuring my guy Randall Cunningham.

To Randall's credit (that's right, we're on a first-name basis now), he didn't just sit around moping during that 1996 campaign. He did a little work for TNT and moved back to Las Vegas where he stated his own business, Custom Marble and Granite Accessories. Cunningham spent his days hauling around heavy stones and making custom countertops for remodeled and new homes. By all accounts he was a skilled craftsman, a fine businessman, and a tireless worker. As the owner of a marble business, Cunningham did himself proud.

Of course, whether he was a complete hack or a modern-day Michelangelo is beside the point. The man had no business cutting stone when he should have been dicing up NFL defenses. Fortunately, after running into Minnesota coach Dennis Green, Cunningham returned to the NFL in 1997 as the Vikings' backup quarterback.[36] He didn't get a ton of action that first season back in the game, but he did throw for 331 yards in a second-round playoff loss to the San Francisco 49ers.

Cunningham started the 1998 season on the bench, but did so with a "at least I'm not cutting metamorphic rocks with a circular saw" smile on his face. He wasn't on the bench long as he took over for Brad Johnson (broken leg) in week two and promptly led the Vikings into Green Bay the next week, where Minnesota snapped the

---

[36] Ironically, Randall was backing up Brad Johnson, who would later become the headliner among old NFL backups and even go on to become the backup on the Vikings a full decade later.

Packers' twenty-nine-game home winning streak behind 442 yards and 4 touchdowns from Cunningham.

Randall never looked back during that incredible 1998 campaign. He threw for 3,704 yards and 34 touchdowns in just over fourteen games, leading the Vikings to a 15–1 record and an appearance in the NFC Championship Game.[37] That game resulted in a disappointing end for Cunningham and the Vikings, as Gary Anderson missed his first kick of the *entire season* in the waning minutes of the contest—a kick that could have extended a 27–20 lead over Atlanta and put the game out of reach.[38] Nevertheless, Cunningham still pulled down his third MVP award and helmed a Minnesota offense that set the NFL record for total points in a season with 556.

Needless to say, it was the second act to top all second acts and all the proof I will ever need that great quarterbacks should be playing football, not running a marble business.[39]

(AH)

Curse, Madden: Jinxes Are *Not* Something To Take Lightly

The *Sports Illustrated* Cover Jinx is well known among most sports fans.

The Madden Curse has surpassed it in terms of brutal power.

Simply put, if you appear on the cover of a *Madden* football game, you will be severely injured.

Until the release of *Madden 2000,* EA Sports had featured John Madden himself on the cover of their signature football game. Put-

---

[37] If you are NFL kicking legend Gary Anderson, and you are reading this book, now would be a good time to turn away.

[38] Perhaps the worst thing about the kick was the fact that Anderson was the first kicker in NFL history to go an entire regular season without a miss and, up to that point, was 39 for 39 on field goals and 67 for 67 on extra points. Now *that* sucks.

[39] If you count the marble business, Cunningham is now on his fourth act as he went back to UNLV to get his degree, became an ordained minister, founded a church, and opened a recording studio.

ting aside the question of whether a photo of John Madden should ever be allowed on the cover of anything, it was not until that year that they pictured a player, Barry Sanders, on the cover.

Sanders promptly retired.

The 2001 version featured Eddie George on the cover. George eventually bobbled a key pass in the playoffs that was intercepted for a touchdown by Ray Lewis. He followed that up with the first serious injury of his career the next season and was never the same again.

The 2003 game featured Marshall Faulk, who then suffered an injury and had the worst season of his career. He has not run for 1,000 yards in a season since, and at the moment I write this entry, he is providing commentary for the NFL Network.

For the 2004 version, Michael Vick landed on the cover and then managed to break his leg in a preseason game the *day after* the game was released. A few years later, Vick was embroiled in the infamous dogfighting scandal.

Donovan McNabb suffered the disintegration of the Eagle's playoff run, a series of injuries capped off by a groin tear, and a highly publicized dispute with Terrell Owens. . . all after gracing the 2006 cover.

Coming off an MVP and record-breaking 2006 season, Shaun Alexander landed on the cover of *Madden,* and then broke his foot and had the worst season of his career.

Vince Young was the toast of the football world after his "he just wins" rookie campaign of 2006, but after his appearance on the *Madden* cover, he spent the 2007 season flinging interceptions and struggling with quadriceps injuries.

You may say it's a coincidence.

Fine.

But you'd still be wise to turn down any offer to appear on the next *Madden* cover.

(AH)

Davis, Terrell: Terrell Davis Could *Not* Be Stopped In The Playoffs

Most football fans—especially those who live in the Rocky Mountain region of the United States—know that former Denver Broncos running back Terrell Davis was the halfback on two championship teams. Most of those same fans know that his career was cut short by injury. And that he helped John Elway to finally win a championship. And that he was a perfect fit for Mike Shanahan's famous zone-blocking running scheme. The one thing they probably don't know? Just how good he was.

In the conversation of great running backs who had careers that ended too early, the central figures are Barry Sanders and Jim Brown—two NFL legends who hung up the cleats at the top of their games. Terrell Davis doesn't get the same mention, which is a shame.

There are a variety of statistics and stories that would provide support for any pro-Terrell Davis argument. His 2,008-yard, 21-touchdown season of 1998 would probably be a good place to start.[40] Going from a little-known, sixth-round draft pick to NFL MVP isn't too shabby either.

However, there probably isn't a single stat that tells the story of Terrell Davis' brief dominance better than his postseason performances.

As a second-year player in 1996, Davis made his playoff debut with 91 rushing yards, 24 receiving yards, and a touchdown in a surprise 30–27 loss to Jacksonville. Never again would he log less than 100 rushing yards in a playoff game. Seven times over the next two seasons Davis suited up for postseason football. Seven times he ran for more than 100 yards, while helping the Broncos to a pair of Super Bowl titles. He rushed for more than 150 yards four times and scored multiple touchdowns four times as well.

---

[40] Unfortunately, Davis logged 392 carries to get those yards. Aaron Schatz, author of *Pro Football Prospectus*, has written about the "Curse of 370," which details all of the horrible things that happen to running backs the year after they log more than 370 rushing attempts. Sure enough, Davis's career was forever altered the very next year when he tore both his anterior cruciate ligament and medial collateral ligament while trying to make a tackle following an interception.

All told, in eight career playoff games, Davis racked up 1,140 yards and 12 touchdowns. He averaged 5.6 yards per carry against the stiffest possible competition, and he won a Super Bowl MVP award.

It will be a long time before a running back has that kind of career in the postseason, and an even longer time before this author forgets how good Terrell Davis was.

I hope you won't forget either.

In fact, maybe you should make a point of rereading this entry every couple of months. Just a suggestion.

(AH)

Dempsey, Tom: Missing Half Your Foot Does *Not* Give You An Advantage Kicking A Football

Like many of you, I have heard more than my share of idiotic statements in my lifetime.

Statements like, "There is no proof that cigarette smoking causes cancer."

And, "George W. Bush defeated Al Gore in the 2000 Presidential election."

And, "*Brokeback Mountain* was a great movie."[41]

What's the stupidest comment I've ever heard? It's hard to say. But way, way, way up on the list has to be this one: "Tom Dempsey had an advantage as a place kicker because he was missing half of his foot."

What?!?!?!

As you may know, Tom Dempsey was a kicker in the late 1960s and early 1970s. If you are a younger reader, you may not know that Dempsey was born with half a right foot and no right hand. Nevertheless, he was a good athlete, and wearing a special shoe with a flat toe, he was a very good place kicker. How good? Good enough to sign with the New Orleans Saints in 1969.

---

[41] Smoking does cause cancer. Gore really did defeat Bush, despite what the Supreme Court had to say. And *Brokeback Mountain* was as overrated as Ryan Leaf. Although, we would like to suggest that you read the entries titled *Leaf, Ryan*.

In 1970, Dempsey would become famous. His picture would appear in virtually every newspaper and on virtually every news program in the country. It was then that, trailing the Lions 17–16 with only seconds remaining in the game, the Saints lined up for a field goal attempt. And not just any field goal attempt. No, they were attempting the longest field goal in NFL history, the holder kneeling down 63 long yards from the goal post. You could see the Lions players shrug as they walked up to the line to defend the kick, knowing that no one had any chance of making such a kick. The ball would fall ten yards short, they must have been thinking, and then we can go home. But then the ball was snapped, Dempsey took a few quick steps forward and connected. Incredibly, the ball floated, and just kept floating and floating, until it finally squeaked past the goal post. Immediately, Dempsey was mobbed by his stunned teammates, who probably had shared the same thoughts as the Lions had about Dempsey's chances. Now, they jumped on Dempsey like he had money coming out of his jersey. He had just kicked the longest field goal in NFL history, a 63-yarder to help the Saints turn a 17–16 defeat into a 19–17 victory. It would be twenty-eight years before Jason Elam of the Denver Broncos would equal the mark by kicking a 63-yarder himself. No one has ever kicked one farther.

Dempsey was an inspiration to many, and rightly so. Kicking a record-breaking field goal made him interesting. Doing it with half a foot made him heroic. But from time to time you would hear people whisper that Dempsey's accomplishment wasn't really that special. You would hear them whisper that Dempsey actually had an unfair advantage as a kicker. You see, the argument would go, because he had only half a foot, he could wear that special, flat-toe shoe that would allow him to smack the ball like a polo mallet.

That anyone would try to minimize Dempsey's accomplishment is both ridiculous and insulting. He had a disability. And he overcame that disability. Making the argument that he had an advantage even more ridiculous and insulting is that fact that many kickers both before and after Dempsey used flat-toe shoes. While most kickers today use the "soccer" style of kicking, that style did not become popular until the mid-1970s. Before then, most place kickers used a straight-ahead style. And they wore shoes with flat toes. None of those other kickers who used flat-toe shoes kicked a 63-yard field goal, did they?

Nope.

Just Dempsey.

So, wherever you are Mr. Dempsey, I hope you had a nice, long celebration after kicking your record-breaking field goal.

I just hope it didn't involve having a smoke because, despite what you may have heard, smoking, in fact, does cause cancer. Really. It does. Just ask President Al Gore.

(MK)

Detmers, The: You Do *Not* Know The Difference Between Ty And Koy Detmer

Ty and Koy Detmer both played quarterback in college and in the NFL.

Ty won the Heisman Trophy in 1990 when he was the quarterback at Brigham Young University.

Koy did not win the Heisman Trophy at any time while quarterbacking at Colorado.

They both played for the Eagles at one time, and they both had relatively unremarkable pro careers.

Ty was mostly a backup for the Packers, Eagles, 49ers, Browns, and Lions.

Koy was a backup for the Eagles.

I am sure they are both fine people. Fine sons, fine husbands, fine teammates, etc.

But, for the life, of me I cannot remember which one is which. I remember that Ty won the Heisman, but beyond that they both had such nondescript careers that it is impossible to remember who is who.

And I'll bet the guys who played with them on the Eagles can't remember which Detmer they played with either.

Seriously, let's call up Donovan McNabb right now and ask him which Detmer was his backup in 1999.

Ten bucks says he gets it wrong.

(MK)

Detmer, Ty: Throwing Seven Interceptions Does *Not* Automatically Result In A Loss

Unlike Mike, I can tell Ty and Koy Detmer apart. It is because of a single game. In a 2001 contest, longtime backup quarterback Ty Detmer got the call as the starter for the Browns. He promptly went out and threw a whopping 7 interceptions in that single game.

Pretty amazing, right? After all, he had to make that many bad throws. The defenders had to catch them all. His coaching staff had to leave him in the game after the third, fourth, fifth, and sixth interceptions. This was a real "perfect storm" situation.

But there is something even more amazing about this feat, and that is that Detmer's Cleveland Browns somehow won the game, 24–14.

How is that possible?

Wait for it. . .

You got it. He was playing the Detroit Lions.

(AH)

Dilfer, Trent: You Do *Not* Need A Good Quarterback To Win A Super Bowl

Brilliant quarterbacks are synonymous with Super Bowl victories. Starr, Namath, Bradshaw, Montana, Elway, Brady, Manning: each with that all-important ring.

Then there are many of the quarterbacks on the losing side of the equation, guys who couldn't get it done, with names like O'Donnell, Grossman, Humphries, Chandler, Morton, and Eason.

Because the quarterback is such an important position on the field, and so many great ones have led teams to titles while less-than-great quarterbacks did not, many make the assumption that QB greatness is a necessary ingredient for winning a Super Bowl.

This is not the case.

There are more than a few examples of teams winning the Super Bowl with quarterbacks who were merely average. In fact, the Redskins won two Super Bowls behind Doug Williams and Mark Rypien, neither of whom will ever be appearing on any all-time lists. Jim McMahon was never a transcendent quarterback. Brad Johnson was, um, average. Yet all of these players were able to get the job done.

You could argue that all of those guys turned it up a notch during the Super Bowl season or that the talent surrounding them elevated their games. However, there is one Super Bowl-winning quarterback who was mediocre through and through: Trent Dilfer of the Baltimore Ravens.

The Ravens won the Super Bowl in 2000 behind a fantastic defense and a bruising ground game, and all they asked of Dilfer was that he not screw it up. This is a guy who ran an inept Tampa Bay team in the years preceding his one season in Baltimore and then served as a backup in Seattle immediately afterward. In fact, think about that: he only played *one season* for the Ravens. And in that season, he wasn't even their leading passer (that was Tony Banks). He threw 12 touchdowns and 11 interceptions in 2000. In the four postseason games that year, he threw for just 590 yards and completed only 35 out of 78 passes. He simply wasn't very good. Yet the Ravens got 336 yards and 4 touchdowns from rookie running back Jamal Lewis, allowed only 23 points in the four games, and managed to take home a Super Bowl title.

No offense to Trent Dilfer, but I think this proves you can win a Super Bowl without a good quarterback. So take hope, everyone.

(AH)

Dryer, Fred: All Football Players Are *Not* Bad Actors

Putting aside the fact that they each offer entertainment to their patrons, there are some fundamental differences between the arts and sports worlds that likely need not be articulated here, but that I will articulate nonetheless.

Generally speaking, the arts—paintings, sculptures, books, movies, music, etc.—are meant to speak about the human condition.

And sports—football, baseball, basketball, etc.—are supposed to be about winning, pure and simple.

The arts are open to interpretation. What one person finds valuable, the next person may think is garbage. (The work of Jackson Pollack comes to mind.)

In sports, there is no interpretation of the final product. You know by the scoreboard which team won and which team lost.

Now, if you think back to your high school graduating class, you can readily picture the persons who were involved in the arts: the budding actors, writers, painters, and so on, most of whom wore black clothes and often could be seen hugging and crying in the cafeteria. And you can just as readily picture the athletes: the football players, the baseball players, the wrestlers, and so on, most of whom wore T-shirts and jeans and could be seen making out with cheerleaders outside the gym.

You would never, ever, confuse someone in the arts group with someone in the sports group. Okay, maybe the star quarterback was in a skit at the senior talent show but that doesn't count, and you know it.

For the most part, as adults, the groups remain separate.

You would never see a world-renowned poet play for the Cowboys.

You would never see a famous painter in a Steelers uniform.

You would never see an accomplished novelist returning a kickoff for the Dolphins.

Why?

Because they were not trained to do that. And they know better than to try to do something they have not been trained to do.

That being the case, why the heck do professional football players keep trying to do things they have not been trained to do?

Specifically, why do they keep trying to act when they have little or no training?

Exhibit A: Alex Karras on the television show *Webster*. Painful.[42]

Exhibit B: The pre-murderous O.J. Simpson in *The Towering Inferno* and the *Naked Gun* movies. More painful.[43]

Exhibit C: Joe Kapp grunting his way through *The Longest Yard*. Ouch.

Exhibit D: Joe Namath struggling to play "Joe Namath" in an episode of *The Brady Bunch*. Perhaps he should have researched the role.

Exhibit E: Brian Bosworth in whatever the hell that movie was where he rode a motorcycle and solved crimes. Holy crap.

If you witnessed any of these performances, you likely reached the inescapable conclusion that football players simply can't act.

Of course, we probably shouldn't expect them to be able to act in the first place, just as we shouldn't expect an accountant or a veterinarian or a cashier to be able to act. Nevertheless, someone hired and paid them to act, so we notice when they try and fail.

That said, there are a couple of notable exceptions to this rule: football players who actually were fairly decent actors. And that is something that you cannot say about athletes in any other sport.

---

[42] If you have never seen *Webster*, it was essentially the same show as *Different Strokes*. A white family adopted a black child and hilarity ensued, as they say. Only *Webster* had Alex Karras. And Alex Karras had cue cards. It always looked like he was reading his lines for the first time.

[43] A little trivia. Did you know that the producers had considered O.J. for the part of the terminator in *Terminator*, but decided not to cast him because they didn't think audiences would believe him as a killer?

I defy you to name a single baseball player who was even a mediocre actor. Reggie Jackson's futile effort to play himself on *The Love Boat* still haunts my dreams.

How about a basketball player? Did you see Julius Erving in *The Fish That Saved Pittsburgh*? Or Shaquille O'Neal in that movie where he played some kind of enormous genie?

Hockey players? Let's be serious.

Golfers? Come on.

But there actually were a few football players who had legitimate acting careers. Two come immediately to mind.

First, there was former L.A. Rams defensive lineman Merlin Olsen, who received very good reviews for his performances in *Little House on the Prairie* and *Father Murphy*. Neither of which I actually saw. I swear. However, I did see his commercials for FTD Florists, which almost made me want to order some flowers for someone I cared about.

Then there was former L.A. Rams defensive lineman Fred Dryer, who was actually very good in his own detective show, *Hunter*. He and a short, curly-haired woman ran around and solved crimes and flirted. (A little bit of television trivia: Dryer was actually one of the finalists for the role of Sam Malone in the television show *Cheers*, where Ted Danson and a short, curly-haired woman ran around and poured drinks and flirted.)

Unfortunately, there hasn't really been a decent football player/actor since Olson and Dryer.

Probably because there aren't any L.A. Rams defensive lineman anymore.

Since there aren't any L.A. Rams anymore.

I honestly can't tell if this is an argument for bringing football back to Los Angeles, or against it. But if they ever put another football team in L.A., there's a chance we might just see another decent acting performance by a football player. Until then, we can await the next Brian Bosworth movie.

(MK)

Elway, John: The Browns Would *Not* Be Looking For Their First Super Bowl Championship If John Elway Had Just Signed With The Colts

Football fans do not always have the best of memories. Which is not necessarily a bad thing.

Baseball fans memorize and analyze every little detail of the sport, and often forget to actually enjoy themselves in the process.

Football fans enjoy themselves, even if they occasionally don't recall the details precisely right.

Take John Elway, for instance.

Many football fans, including fans of the Denver Broncos (the team for which Elway starred from 1983 to 1998), believe that Elway was drafted by the Broncos.

There's nothing wrong with believing that, if you want.

It's wrong, but it doesn't make you a bad person if that's what you believe.

In fact, Elway was drafted by the Baltimore Colts with the first pick of the 1983 draft.

If you don't recall ever seeing Elway in a Colts uniform, there's a good reason. He never wore a Colts uniform, unless he and his wife liked to play "dress up" behind closed bedroom doors.

For reasons I have never quite understood, as I have always loved Baltimore, Elway was adamant that he would not play football in that city. It didn't matter what the team offered him, it just wasn't going to happen.

How adamant was Elway?

So adamant that he signed a minor-league-baseball contract with the New York Yankees and claimed, with a bit of a smile, that he would devote himself to a career in baseball instead of football. Well, eventually the Colts realized that he was serious, at least about not wanting to play in Baltimore, so they traded him to the Broncos.

The rest is history. The Broncos went on to become one of the finest teams in the league, with Elway leading them to two Super

Bowl victories, setting a number of NFL passing records along the way. And the Colts packed their bags and moved in the dark of the night to Indianapolis. For fans who believe this to be an exaggeration, it is not. They literally left in the night, sneaking out of town in Mayflower moving vans. I lived in Baltimore at the time. It was quite a scandal, and the city still has not gotten over losing its beloved Colts, even after the Browns packed their bags and moved to Baltimore, becoming the Ravens. (I have yet to understand why Baltimoreans felt it was so heinous for Indianapolis to steal their football team, but utterly appropriate for Baltimore to steal Cleveland's team. Where I come from, this is called "hypocrisy.")

History could have been different. Very, very different.

Now, I fully recognize that there are consequences to every action, and that history would change, sometimes dramatically, if we were to go back in time and change any one detail. It's called the "butterfly effect." Go back in time and kill a single butterfly, and all of history changes, with one event changing another, and so on and so on.[44]

If Mr. and Mrs. Hitler had never met, their son never would have been born, the Holocaust and World War II would have been avoided, and the world would be a very different place today.

If Abraham Lincoln had decided not to go to the theatre, he might have stuck around to be elected president for another term or two, effectively changing every presidential race thereafter and, in turn, leaving us with a very different country today.[45]

On a much, much smaller scale, how different would the world of football have been if Elway had actually signed with the Colts?

Pretty darned different. Particularly for fans of the Cleveland Browns.

What does this have to do with the Cleveland Browns, you ask. A lot.

---

[44] The "butterfly effect" has been the subject of a number of science fiction books and movies. There was even a terrible Ashton Kutcher movie about this called *The Butterfly Effect*. Unfortunately, no one has been able to go back in time and stop production of that movie.

[45] Before anyone writes to us to say that presidents are limited to two terms, the term limits were not implemented until after Lincoln's presidency, after FDR was elected to four terms.

Just bear with me here.

Had Elway signed with the Colts, a pretty fair argument could be made that the Colts never would have left Baltimore. Instead, with his hotshot new quarterback in the fold, owner Robert Irsay may well have had the leverage to negotiate the concessions he wanted to keep his team in Baltimore. With Elway on his squad, the Colts, not the Broncos, might have become one of the top teams in the AFC in the 1990s, perhaps even winning a championship or two along the way. There would not have been a team in Indianapolis (at least for a while), and when the NFL eventually decided to expand, they might have bypassed Indianapolis altogether and put a team in Los Angeles instead. Without Elway, the Broncos may well have struggled for some time. And the Colts likely would not have been in a position to draft Peyton Manning with the first pick in the 1998 draft. No, assuming that the Colts and the Broncos histories during the Elway era would have swapped—an unfair assumption, but one worth making for this analysis—the Broncos may have been the team with the first pick in the 1998 draft, and Manning may well have become their quarterback.

What does this have to do with the Browns, you ask again.

I'm getting there, I promise.

If the Colts had not moved from Baltimore to Indianapolis, the Browns would not have moved to Baltimore. Simply, there would have been no possibility of moving to Baltimore because there already would have been a team there. Perhaps the Browns still would have moved to some other city, but perhaps they would not have moved at all. Perhaps they would have stayed in Cleveland. And instead of the Baltimore Ravens winning the Super Bowl in 2001, the very same players would have been wearing Cleveland Brown uniforms when they hoisted the championship trophy over their heads.

So, if Browns fans did not already hate Elway enough for the torture he inflicted upon them during his career, they now have this, too: had Elway not refused to sign with the Colts, the Browns might have stayed in Cleveland and won a Super Bowl!

Imagine that, Browns fans.

Then try to forget it as swiftly as you can.

(MK)

Exception, The Marshall Faulk: Teams Should *Not* Trade For Star Running Backs

In the entry titled *Backs, Running* I mentioned that a friend of mine once compared NFL running backs to a set of tires. Get them cheap, use them up, and then trade them in for a new set. That entry discussed the fallacy that all elite running backs are replaceable, but accepted the notion that you do want to change horses when tailbacks start closing in on that dreaded age of thirty.

It would stand to reason that the opposite is also true. That while trading for an older running back is risky business, acquiring a younger stud rusher might be worth the price. It might surprise you to learn that it almost never makes sense to trade for a star running back, whether the guy is young or old. The reason: the cost is too high.

Second-tier backs can often be had for a song. In the 2007 off-season, the Ravens and Jets both patched holes at tailback by trading very little in exchange for solid runners in Willis McGahee and Thomas Jones. However, snagging a star running back requires paying a far steeper price.

In 1987, the Indianapolis Colts had to do quite a lot of work to pry twenty-seven- year-old Eric Dickerson away from the Rams. First, they sent the rights to unsigned first-round pick Cornelius Bennett to the Buffalo Bills in exchange for running back Greg Bell, a 1988 first-round pick, and a first- and second-round pick in 1989. The Colts turned around and traded Bell, those three picks, and their own 1988 first-round and second-round picks, and a 1989 second-round pick in order to get Dickerson. To summarize, they gave up three first-round picks and three second-round picks, which is a whole heck of a lot.

In 1989, the Minnesota Vikings traded five players and a whopping six draft picks (including the picks that produced Emmitt Smith,

Russell Maryland, and Darren Woodson, three players who played in a combined fourteen Pro Bowls and won one combined *Dancing With the Stars* competition) to the Dallas Cowboys in order to acquire a twenty-seven-year-old Herschel Walker. While Walker was an incredibly accomplished back and a freak of nature, I think it is safe to say the Vikings didn't get their money's worth.[46] Walker ran for just 2,264 yards in three seasons with Minnesota.

A decade later, Mike Ditka and the New Orleans Saints traded *all* of their 1999 picks as well as two early picks in 2000 to move up to the number-five spot in the 1999 draft in order to take Ricky Williams. After that didn't work out very well, the Saints traded him to the Dolphins in 2002, a move that cost Miami two first-round picks of their own.

Clinton Portis is an example of the danger of trading for even the youngest star running back. Portis had consecutive 1,500-yard seasons for Denver in 2002 and 2003 and then was acquired by the Washington Redskins. He's been terrific (when healthy) in the nation's capital, but it doesn't appear any level of production will be enough to offset the loss of one of the NFL's best cornerbacks, Champ Bailey, which was the ransom charged by Denver in exchange for Portis' services.

These are just a handful of examples in which the cost of a prime-time running back was steep and, ultimately, not worth it.

However, as with any rule, there is always an exception. In this case, that exception is Marshall Faulk. Taking advantage of Faulk's potential hold-out situation in Indianapolis, the St. Louis Rams moved in with a fairly paltry offer of a second- and fifth-round pick in exchange for a guy coming off a season in which he led the NFL with 2,297 yards from scrimmage. While the Colts would move on behind Edgerrin James, there is no doubt that the Rams pulled off one of the great trades in NFL history.

In his first year with the Rams, 1999, Faulk became the headliner

---

[46] I can still remember the *Sports Illustrated* article about Walker's training regimen, which included doing over one thousand crunches and fifteen hundred push-ups every day, many of them with his wife sitting on his back.

of St. Louis' "Greatest Show on Turf" offense. He broke Barry Sanders' record for yards from scrimmage with 2,429 and joined Roger Craig as only the second player in NFL history to tally over 1,000 yards rushing *and* receiving. He also scored 12 touchdowns, won the NFL's offensive player of the year award, and led the Rams to a Super Bowl title. I'd say that is worth a second- and fifth-round draft pick.

The next year Faulk scored 26 touchdowns (the NFL record at the time) and won the NFL MVP Award. In 2001 he won his third straight offensive-player-of-the-year award and led St. Louis to a 14–2 record. Over that three-year period, he racked up an unbelievable 6,765 yards of total offense.

So, while NFL teams normally should avoid paying through the nose to acquire a big-time running back, there is always an exception. The Marshall Faulk Exception.

(AH)

Fans, Raiders: Raiders Fans Are *Not* Like Other Fans

The Oakland Raiders, formerly the Los Angeles Raiders, formerly the Oakland Raiders, are well known for their rowdy, crazed fans.

Let's see how good you are at spotting a Raiders fan.

You are standing alone in a room. Three men walk into the room.

You are told that one is a Raiders fan, one is a Giants fan, and one is a Rams fan.

All three men are the same height.

They are all the same weight.

They have similar builds, hair color, and eye color.

They are all about the same age.

They are all wearing identical clothing that does not indicate in any way where they are from or which team they root for.

Now, without asking them any questions at all, which one is the Raiders fan?

Easy.

He's the one who's beating the crap out of you.

(MK)

Fartpiss, Penisnose: Dick Butkus Did *Not* Have The Worst Name Of Any Pro Football Player

Dick Butkus was one of the NFL's great linebackers. Some would argue that he was the greatest linebacker ever, and you would have a hard time proving them wrong. When you watched a Bears game, Dick Butkus was the player to whom your eyes were drawn. He may not have been involved in every tackle, but it sure seemed that way. And it sure looked like receivers and running backs flinched whenever they were near him. And, in football, flinching is not a good thing.

Dick Butkus was one tough SOB.

I have always contended that one of the reasons he was so tough was that he had to be tough. He had to be tough because he was saddled with a name that probably resulted in more than a few schoolyard taunts . . . until Dick pounded the stuffing out of whoever was stupid enough to taunt him. Then the taunting probably stopped.

I had hoped not to have to do this, but it appears I will need to as many readers and younger fans may not be familiar with Dick Butkus or the pronunciation of his last name. His last name is pronounced "butt-kiss."

So, his first name is a euphemism for male genitalia. His last name is a description of the act of placing one's lips upon another's buttocks.

Dick. Butt. Kiss.

Get it?

I know more than a bit about being taunted about your name. My last name is Kun. It is pronounced as if you replaced the *t* with an *n* in the word cute. However, all too frequently, kids would add a *t* to the end of my last name to spell (actually, to misspell) a crass euphemism for female genitalia. How crass is that word? If you ever want your girlfriend or wife to leave you, call her that name. If you ever want to get fired from a job, call someone that name.

Unfortunately, unlike Mr. Butkus, I did not develop into a large and muscular athlete who could frighten people so that they would cease making fun of his name. Nope, I had to use my wit instead and make fun of anyone who taunted me. Which, of course, resulted in more taunting.

In any event, I have digressed.

For more than three decades, Dick Butkus had the worst name of any professional football player. Frankly, it wasn't even close.

Then, in 2005, the Houston Texans signed a free-agent safety from Alcorn State named Penisnose Fartpiss. Penisnose Fartpiss played in fourteen games for the Texans that year, starting eight of them. He had 2 interceptions, including picking off a Peyton Manning pass and returning it for a touchdown in the Texans' upset win over the Colts. But, in my mind, his most glorious moment was when he first stepped on the field and became the player with the worst name in football history.

(MK)

Fartpiss, Penisnose: We Do *Not* Know Anything About The Houston Texans

If, after reading that last entry, you ran to the computer to find out more about Houston Texans' safety Penisnose Fartpiss, please do not be embarrassed. I would have done the exact same thing.

You see, none of us knows anything about the Houston Texans. It's one of the problems with expansion. Years ago, when there were a handful of teams, football fans knew everyone on every team. Seriously, we knew everyone, or it seemed that way. But now, with more teams than you can count, it's hard enough just to remember who the teams are and which division they are in, let alone their players.

Oh, sure, you could probably name the starting quarterbacks for most teams. But the safety? For the Texans? No way.

So, as Penisnose Fartpiss is nothing but a figment of our imaginations, Dick Butkus still holds the title for the worst name in football history.

Sorry, Dick.

Please don't hurt me.

(MK)

Flags, Penalty: Penalty Flags Have *Not* Always Been Yellow

Penalty flags have not always been yellow.

They used to be white.

The NFL changed the color in 1965.

If you'd like to read more about this, you should seek help.

(MK)

Flutie, Doug: The Dropkick Is *Not* Dead

As you well know, there are several ways to score points in a football game.

Score a touchdown, and you get 6 points.

Kick the ball through the uprights after a touchdown, and you get a point.

Pass or run the ball into the end zone following a touchdown, and you get 2 points.

A safety will get you 2 points.

And kicking a field goal is worth 3 points.

Now, we've all seen how a field goal is kicked. We've seen it hundreds of times. The holder kneels on one knee 7 yards behind the line of scrimmage; the kicker takes a few steps farther back; the ball is snapped to the holder; the holder spins the ball so the laces are facing the goal post and places the ball vertically on the ground; the kicker steps forward and swings his foot; the ball flies through the air; and, if it actually sails through the goal posts, the other members of the team will pretend for a moment to actually care about the kicker's existence. They may even pat him on the head.

But there is actually another way to pick up 3 points for your team. The dropkick.

What exactly is a dropkick, you ask.

Well, it looks an awful lot like a punt. You hold the ball. You drop the ball. You kick the ball. But, unlike a punt where you strike the ball before it hits the ground, with a dropkick you strike the ball right after, or as, it hits the ground. If the ball flies through the goal posts, congratulations—you get 3 points. (You only get 1 point if you use a dropkick for an extra point after a touchdown.)

Now, the dropkick was a very popular means of racking up points in the early days of the game. Players would try it from virtually anywhere on the field. What might look like a running play could suddenly, and surprisingly, turn into 3 points as the ball carrier would stop short and kick the ball through the uprights. The reason it was so popular was fairly basic: the balls used at the time were rounder than they are now and, as a result, could be expected to bounce somewhat predictably. Drop one of today's footballs right on its nose, and you have no idea where it might wind up. There's a good chance it will dart off to one side when you try to kick it.

Because of those changes to the shape of the ball, the dropkick died a quiet death in the 1930s—although it was used in a game in 1941—and it has rarely even been referred to in recent years.

But the dropkick has remained in the rule book, and, technically, anyone could still use it at any time. They just chose not to.

Then, after more than sixty years without anyone so much as seeing a dropkick in an NFL game, along came Doug Flutie. Flutie had first gained national recognition as a college quarterback at Boston College, tossing an improbable 48-yard touchdown pass to Gerald Phelan to defeat the Miami Hurricanes in the last seconds of their 1984 contest, before being awarded the Heisman Trophy. Thought to be too small to play pro ball, he quarterbacked the USFL's New Jersey Generals. Then, after failed stints with the Bears and Patriots, starred in the CFL before returning to the NFL to the Bills, where he became one of the league's top quarterbacks. It was a circuitous route, that's for sure, but he had proved what many had doubted—that such a short man could succeed as an NFL quarterback. He finished his career as a backup for the Chargers and the Patriots. It was as a backup for the Patriots that he made history.

In his last professional game on January 1, 2006, against the Dolphins, Flutie came off the bench following a touchdown. He lined up for what appeared to be a 2-point conversion. Fans rightly assumed that he was being given a chance to score one last time before his retirement. Either he would make one of his mad dashes toward the end zone, or flip the ball to one of the four receivers who were on the field. But Flutie lined up far deeper than normal, 12 yards behind the line of scrimmage to be precise, and no one had any idea what the heck he was up to. The ball was snapped to him, and instead of running or trying to find a receiver in the end zone, he dropped the ball to the ground and kicked it through the uprights to score an extra point for his team. It was his last play in the NFL. And one that certainly had the fans talking. To say that fans were surprised would be an understatement. A good percentage of fans likely had no idea what they had just witnessed. And those who understood likely had large smiles on their faces.

It was a fitting play for such a unique player to make as he left the game of football.

(MK)

Football, Electronic: Pong Was *Not* The Worst Game Ever Invented

If you grew up in the United States in the 1960s or 1970s, you were subjected to a lot of bad, silly, or poorly designed games and toys, all of which look even worse when compared to the games and toys that are available to kids these days.

Today, kids play with their Playstations. We had Pong.

What was Pong, you ask.

Basically, it was a game you played on your television set. Each player had a line.

A line?

Yes.

And you moved the line up and down using a dial.

Up and down? How about sideways?

Sorry, but you could only move up and down.

And you hit a small ball back and forth until someone missed it. Every time the ball hit one of the lines, it would make a sound like "boop." When the other player missed the ball, it made a sound like "beep-boop," and you got a point.

That's it?

Yup.

How did you know who won or lost?

Well, whichever player got bored first was the loser.

Pong is just one example of how the toys and games we grew up with, well, sucked.[47] While kids today play with somewhat realistic action figures with moveable parts and exciting gadgets, we had G.I. Joe. He had a scar.

A scar?

Yippee!

---

[47] Pong should not be confused with another game that was known as Gnip Gnop. Gnip Gnop was a board game that allowed us to simulate the thrills of playing ping pong. In fact, Gnip Gnop was *ping pong* spelled backwards, which made it even more exciting! What was the obsession with creating games to simulate ping pong? Heck if I know. I mean, it's friggin' ping pong. Did we really need to simulate it at all? Couldn't we just play ping pong when we wanted?

And while kids today have a variety of incredibly high-tech football computer games like *Madden NFL Football,* which allow the players to call plays and have graphics so crisp they almost appear to be actual film, we had electronic football.

What was electronic football, you ask.

Hmm, how to explain electronic football? Well, it was a green metal board with a football field painted on it and plastic goal posts at each end. There were two teams of tiny plastic football players with magnetic bases, and a small piece of felt meant to represent a football. You and your friend would each line up your players on the field, then push a button.

What happened when you pushed the button?

Well, it would produce a noise like a bomber plane passing over your house, and all twenty-two players would shake as if they were being electrocuted simultaneously. Just like in real football! At some point, you and your friend would just decide arbitrarily that the play was over, then line up the twenty-two players again, press the button and watch the players shake again. Normally, you would do this five or six times before you and your friend just threw up your arms and said, "This is ridiculous. Want to go look at the *Playboys* my dad has hidden in the garage?"[48]

Sadly, I fully expect that we will receive more letters complaining about this description of electronic football than about any other section of this book. Why is that? Well, it seems that some people loved electronic football. I mean, really loved it. As in, "I'm going to spend my entire vacation playing electronic football." As in, "I'm staying home Friday night to play electronic football. Alone." As in, "If I could find a woman who I loved as much as electronic football, I would marry her." There are actually leagues where grown men face off against each other in electronic football competitions. With money being awarded to the champion. Seriously. I couldn't make that up if I tried.

---

[48] Note: My father did not keep *Playboys* in the garage. They were in the basement. Under the workbench. In a box marked "Tax Records." What does this have to do with football? Well, some *Playboy* issues mentioned the word "football." Or "foot." Or "ball." Usually "ball."

I'm not criticizing those people.

Really.

If I could find a Pong tournament, I'd be there in a heartbeat.

Seriously, I ruled in Pong.

And I was pretty awesome in Hungry Hungry Hippo, too, if you don't mind me bragging.

(MK)

Footnotes, Reading The: You Are *Not* Reading All Of The Footnotes

You're not reading all of the footnotes, are you?[49]

That's fine. We told you at the beginning of the book that it was up to you whether to read them.

But you missed something really interesting a couple pages back.

Trust me.

(MK)

Game, It's Only One: Winning A Super Bowl MVP Award Does *Not* Guarantee A Great Career

The Super Bowl is the single biggest game in American athletic competition. It is the culminating event of the nation's most popular sport, a winner-take-all showdown decided in sixty minutes of action, and the single greatest excuse for corporations everywhere to blow their advertising budgets.

By that logic, you might guess that the player most responsible for winning The Big Game would almost always be a superstar. After all, presumably two of the NFL's finest teams are competing, which certainly means that anyone getting playing time is already exceptional to begin with. Furthermore, to actually play a large enough

---

[49] For instance, you're not reading this, are you? Too bad, because we were about to say how handsome and smart you are. Yes, you. We were even going to mention you by name.

role in the contest to tip the balance in his team's favor, that player would have to be of the highest caliber. It wouldn't be a stretch to guess that winning a Super Bowl MVP serves as a sort of earmark of greatness; an honor reserved for only the game's elite.

For much of the Super Bowl's history, this hypothesis would have proven true. A glance at the list of MVP winners from 1967 to 1986 reveals the names Bart Starr, Joe Namath, Len Dawson, Roger Staubach, Larry Csonka, Franco Harris, Lynn Swann, Fred Biletnikoff, Terry Bradshaw, Joe Montana, John Riggins, and Marcus Allen. Hall of Famers, all of them. In fact, the first twenty (or should I say, XX) Super Bowls saw a future Hall of Fame player win the MVP a whopping sixteen times.[50] Three of the other four MVP's were standout players, with fifteen Pro Bowl appearances between them.[51] Only one of the first twenty Super Bowls saw the Most Valuable Player award go to a player that could be described as "average."[52]

The last twenty-one Super Bowls tell a different story. Whereas the first twenty Big Games featured sixteen Hall of Famers, four Pro Bowl players, and one mediocre quarterback,[53] the next batch offered far more variety. In the second crop of MVPs, we see only five Hall of Fame winners (Joe Montana again, Steve Young, Jerry Rice, Troy Aikmen, and John Elway), twelve Pro Bowl-caliber recipients,[54] and four players who have never even reached a single Pro Bowl.

---

[50] It should be noted that Super Bowl XII featured co-MVPs from the Dallas Cowboys. Harvey Martin, a fierce defensive end in the third of four straight Pro Bowl seasons was not a Hall of Fame player, but his teammate Randy White has a plaque in Canton, Ohio. This is also a good time to point out that Randy White possessed one of the great nicknames of all time: "The Manster," so given because he was said to be half man, half monster. This is the sort of nickname we need in today's NFL—a subject that will be covered in great detail later in the book.

[51] Super Bowl V MVP Chuck Howley was named to the Pro Bowl six times as a linebacker for the Dallas Cowboys. In Super Bowl VII the award went to Miami defensive back Jake Scott, who was in the third of five straight Pro Bowl seasons. Super Bowl XX winner Richard Dent was a four-time Pro Bowl defensive end for the Chicago Bears.

[52] In fact, Super Bowl XV MVP and Oakland Raiders quarterback Jim Plunkett was less than average. Research reveals that he only completed 51 percent of his passes during the 1980 regular season, while throwing a mere 18 touchdowns against 16 interceptions. Hardly the stuff of legends. This was probably the second-best season of his career. Yet Plunkett is somehow remembered as a very good quarterback.

[53] Remember the co-winners in Super Bowl XII. The twenty-one total MVPs you are tallying is not because I'm bad at math. Although that is true.

[54] Phil Simms, Ottis Anderson, Mark Rypien, Emmitt Smith, Desmond Howard, Terrell Davis, Kurt Warner, Ray Lewis, Hines Ward, Peyton Manning, and Tom Brady (twice).

Obviously, breaking it down into such simple terms isn't entirely fair to the more recent winners. All of the MVPs from the first twenty Super Bowls have had ample opportunity to become eligible for Hall of Fame voting and to be measured fairly over time. Many of the last twenty-one winners have yet to reach the ballot, while many more are still active in the league. Certainly a player like Emmitt Smith will gain entry into Canton when his time comes. Tom Brady and Peyton Manning look like locks. However, even if we wave those five players on through, and throw in Ray Lewis and Terrell Davis (no certainty, due to his career being cut short by injury) for good measure, that only brings the count to eleven Hall of Fame-caliber recipients (Brady counts twice)—less than two-thirds of the total that garnered the hardware through the first half of Super Bowl history. Clearly, the game's über elite no longer dominates the award.

However, it is doubtful that anyone thinks an MVP *must* be a Hall of Famer. While it makes sense to see guys like Elway and Montana holding trophies aloft, it is also understandable when a terrific quarterback like Phil Simms or a pass-rushing defensive end like Richard Dent carries the day on the game's biggest stage. One expects to see a multitude of "great-but-not-quite-a-Hall-of-Famer" type players fill up the rest of the list. This is where things really go off the rails. As was pointed out above and detailed in the footnotes (as Mike always says, read the footnotes!), there was only one "average" MVP during the first twenty years the Super Bowl was played. In the last twenty-one, we have had *at least* four. Doug Williams, Larry Brown, Dexter Jackson, and Deion Branch are all players who have failed to reach even a single Pro Bowl.[55]

However, there have been more than four "merely average" Super Bowl MVP winners from this time period. Desmond Howard and Ottis Anderson were both technically Pro Bowl players at some point during their careers; however, a closer look reveals that they

---

[55] One would imagine that Branch is the only member of that group with any chance to change this fact. Doug Williams would have to stage the most improbable comeback in the history of sports, given that he is fifty-five years old. Larry Brown is also out of the league, and Dexter Jackson is a journeyman safety who intercepts about one pass a year.

were not in Pro Bowl form the year they won the MVP. Howard was a dynamic kick-return specialist for the Packers, but he wouldn't go to his one-and-only Pro Bowl until three years later. Anderson was ten years removed from his last Pro Bowl appearance and was a 3.5-yards-per-carry rusher for the 1990–1991 Giants. It seems appropriate to add these two players to the "average" side of the ledger rather than to count them as Pro Bowl-caliber winners.

All told, the breakdown of winners from 1986 to 2007 indicates that the MVP award has gone to a Hall of Fame-level star eleven times, a Pro Bowl-caliber athlete four times, and an average player six times, including four times in the last twelve years. Obviously, things have changed dramatically. Why is this? One reason might be the increased specialization that dominates the game. The brand of football played in today's NFL often forces a team to rely on schemes rather than individual players. Ray Lewis was symbolic of a great Ravens defense in Super Bowl XXXV; Dexter Jackson took advantage of Tampa Bay's great defensive pressure in Super Bowl XXXVII to nab 2 interceptions; and Desmond Howard showed the importance of special teams and got some hardware for his efforts.

A more likely cause of the shift is that the media members voting on the award have evolved. They are more sophisticated in their understanding of the game. Rather than just assume that the quarterback led the way or that the running back should win the award because he had a lot of yards, they actually look to see who had the biggest impact on the outcome of the game. Certainly technology plays a role, as easy access to stats and highlights have aided in this process. However, not only are voting members more sophisticated, they are also eager to break from convention. Steve Nash won the 2005 MVP award in the NBA because voters were eager to display some "outside the box" thinking. The very same thing may apply here.

Whatever the reason, one thing is for sure: winning the MVP of the Super Bowl no longer means a whole lot in the grand scheme of things. It used to mean that you were a great player 95 percent of the time and that there was an 80 percent chance you were going to wind up in the Hall of Fame someday. Now those odds look more like 68 percent and 53 percent, respectively, and going down fast. I guess the lesson is this: if you win the award for being the Most Valuable Player of the Super Bowl, enjoy your moment in the sun. Unlike in the good old days, it may not last.

You still get to go to Disneyland though. (Don't you?)

(AH)

Game, The "Heidi": You Did *Not* See One Of The Greatest Comebacks Of All Time

Ever change channels while watching a game, only to find out later that you had missed a great comeback?

I'll bet you have, and I'll bet you were kicking yourself the next morning.

Well, back in 1968, millions of fans missed one of the greatest comebacks of all time—and not because they switched channels.

In November 1968, NBC was broadcasting an AFL game between the defending champion Oakland Raiders and the upstart New York Jets. The Jets were leading 32–29 with a little more than a minute left, and then the clock struck midnight. Or, more accurately, the clock struck 7:00 p.m.

Why is that time important?

That was the time when NBC was scheduled to show the movie *Heidi*, the story of a Swiss girl who does things in Switzerland. She may have had a dog.

So, what did NBC do?

They stopped the broadcast of the Raiders-Jets game with sixty-five seconds remaining so they could begin the movie on time.

Why would they do such a thing?

Did they not like the Raiders or the Jets?

Did they not care about the game?

Did they not care about the fans who were watching the game?

No.

No.

And no.

The answer, my friends, is that NBC was *contractually obligated* to start the movie at 7:00 p.m. That's right, they had a contract with the company that was sponsoring the movie to start the movie at 7:00 p.m.

Now, I know what you're thinking. You're thinking, *It's not like the sponsor was going to sue if they started the movie a couple minutes late.*

Oh, really? You don't know many lawyers, do you?

That's precisely the type of miniscule, technical issue that lawyers love to file suits over, clogging our courts with trivial little lawsuits. Don't believe me? Go down to any courthouse in any large city any day of the week, and just move from courtroom to courtroom and observe the silly little issues that lawyers file suits over. It will make you sick to your stomach.

So, was NBC right to honor their contract and start the movie at 7:00 p.m., just as they had agreed to do?

Absolutely.

Should they have agreed to that in the first place?

Well, that's a different question, isn't it? What they should have done, and what the networks have done since, is make sure that their various contracts allow for the completion of broadcasts of events like football games.

Now, why was this even an issue?

Who cares if NBC started to show *Heidi* when there were only sixty-five seconds left in the game?

Jets fans, Raiders fans, and anyone else who loves a great comeback cared.

In those final sixty-five seconds, the Raiders scored not 1, but 2 touchdowns. More accurately, they scored those 2 touchdowns in a span of *nine seconds*. First, Daryle Lamonica led a quick drive culminating in a touchdown pass to Charlie Smith. Then, Raiders special teamer Preston Ridlehuber recovered a fumble on the ensuing kickoff and took it into the end zone. Final score: Raiders 43, Jets 32.

Great game.

Shame no one saw it.

(MK)

Gates, Antonio: NFL Teams Should *Not* Employ Tight Ends Who Have Never Played Basketball

For years, Tony Gonzalez of the Kansas City Chiefs was the best receiving tight end in the NFL. No other player at his position combined the athleticism, soft hands, feel for the game, and ability to use his body that Gonzalez regularly exhibited in becoming the dominant element of the Kansas City passing game. He was Trent Green's favorite target in the red zone and in the middle of the field. On first down and third down. For short routes or deep posts. Gonzalez was awesome and unique in nearly every way.

As many people know, Gonzalez was also a fairly productive college basketball player at the University of California. He didn't dominate by any means, but he could rebound, score in the post, and set a mean pick. There is no doubt that the skills that got him on the court in the first place—and then were honed during those years of Pac-10 basketball—were a big reason he was so good as a tight end. It's just that nobody really put two and two together.

The funny thing is that while Gonzalez was the guy you heard about in the context of two-sport athletes at the position, he was actually joined in the NFL by Marcus Pollard, whose sport of choice at Bradley University was of the hard-court variety.[56] The two of them were extremely adept receivers who were putting their basketball skills on display every Sunday. Still, while it made for a nice anec-

---

[56] Although choice might have had little to do with it, as Bradley did not even have a football team.

dote, nobody seemed prepared to actually attribute their success in any way to their basketball pasts.

Then, along came Antonio Gates. Gates was a star football and basketball player at Detroit's Central High School and wanted to play both sports at Michigan State. However, MSU football coach Nick Saban told Gates he had to commit to football. This set Antonio off on a wild basketball journey that began at Eastern Michigan, took him to multiple junior colleges, and then finished with a magical run to the NCAA Tournament's Elite Eight with Kent State. The NBA didn't come calling though, so Gates lined up workouts with NFL teams. San Diego was first on the list, and they wasted no time in snatching him up.

Now Gates uses his quick feet and great hands—which he developed on the basketball court—to dominate NFL defenses. In the process of redefining the position, Gates hauled in 316 passes and scored 41 touchdowns in three seasons between 2004 and 2007. No wonder eight of the top ten tight-end prospects in the 2007 NFL Draft had significant basketball backgrounds.

The trend started with Gonzalez and Pollard, was popularized by Gates, and now goes well beyond those three guys. Nearly all of the best tight ends in the NFL as of 2007 had some hoops in their backgrounds.

The sixth pick in the 2006 Draft by the 49ers, Vernon Davis, played for basketball powerhouse Dunbar High School in Washington, D.C.

Kellen Winslow II has an uncle, David Winslow, who played pro hoops in Australia.

Jeremy Shockey played ball at Oklahoma's Ada High School.

Todd Heap played for the Arizona State basketball team during his freshman year.

Jason Witten averaged 15 points and 12 rebounds a night for Elizabethton High School in Tennessee.

Greg Olsen, 2007 first-round draft pick averaged 16 and 8 at Wayne Hills High School in New Jersey.

At this point, an NFL GM is pretty much crazy if he takes a tight end who didn't play basketball.

(AH)

Greene, Mean Joe: Mean Joe Greene Was *Not* Mean And His Name Is *Not* Joe

In the 1970s, the Pittsburgh Steelers featured one of the most fearsome defensive lines in football. Known as the "Steel Curtain," they were led ostensibly by a man named Charles Edward Greene. (Not incidentally, the other members of the "Steel Curtain" were L.C. Greenwood, Dwight White, and Ernie Holmes.) If you mention the name "Charles Edward Greene" to even the most dedicated of football fans, they are likely to respond, "Who?"

Very few people, other than perhaps his family and his accountant, are likely to know Charles Edward Greene as "Charles Edward Greene."

Instead, they know him by his nickname. Or, should I say, his nicknames, plural.

Big Chuck Greene?

No.

Fast Eddie Greene?

No.

Choo-Choo Chuckie Greene?

Nope.

Charlie "The Machine" Greene?

No.

Steady Eddie Greene?

No.

Lean Ed Greene?

No.

Choo-Choo Chuckie Greene?

Didn't we try that one already?

In fact, for some reason, Charles Edward Greene was known as "Joe" Greene, although, to my knowledge, "Joe" is not normally a nickname for "Charles" or "Edward." It is normally a nickname for "Joseph." Which is not one of Joe Greene's given names.

And Joe Greene was not really known as "Joe Greene," at least not when he was in the NFL. No, he was known as "Mean Joe Greene."

Aha, now you know who I'm talking about.

Yes, Mean Joe Greene, cornerstone of the Steelers defense, who helped the team to four Super Bowl championships in the 1970s. And, perhaps just as memorable, the same Mean Joe Greene who tossed a young boy his game jersey after the boy shared his Coke with him in a television commercial that was so popular it actually spawned a TV movie. Seriously. The movie was called *The Steeler and the Pittsburgh Kid*, and it starred no less than Mean Joe Greene himself and Henry Thomas, the boy who played Elliott in *E.T.: The Extra-Terrestrial*.

As the commercial and the movie taught us all, Mean Joe Greene really wasn't mean at all. He was just a big softy who liked carbonated beverages.

(MK)

Hand, Talk To The: Heisman Trophy Winners Are *Not* All Earmarked For Mediocre Pro Careers

We proclaim this book to be about busting pro football myths (among many, many, many other things), and there is no bigger myth than the supposed curse of the Heisman Trophy. More than the dreaded *Sports Illustrated* Jinx or the new and powerful Madden Curse, the myth that the Heisman Trophy winner cannot have success in the pros has become a pervasive force in the world of football.[57]

How else can you explain the fact that people were still talking about the Heisman Curse during the 2005 season, as stud pro prospect and 2004 winner Matt Leinart was handing off to eventual

---

[57] You can read more about the Madden Curse in the entry titled (perhaps not surprisingly), *Curse, Madden.*

2005 winner Reggie Bush at USC, all while 2002 winner Carson Palmer was tearing through NFL defenses?[58]

Some might say that there has been a shift and that the award has only recently been awarded to legitimate pro prospects, but that too would be inaccurate. A quick glance over the list of past winners reveals names like Roger Staubach, O.J. Simpson, Tony Dorsett, Earl Campbell, Herschel Walker, Marcus Allen, Tim Brown, Barry Sanders, Eddie George, and Charles Woodson. Not a bad group of NFL players. So what gives?

First, it is important to drill down on what this myth is all about. If it was a simple "hex," I might be able to live with that. After all, 1982 and 1984 winners Walker and Doug Flutie lost potential years in the NFL while playing in the USFL and Canadian Football League, respectively. Bo Jackson, the 1985 winner, suffered a freak hip injury that ended his career. Sanders retired suddenly and without warning. Charlie Ward chose to play basketball. Ricky Williams: well, we all know about Ricky "the Holistic Healer." So if the claim is merely that an inordinate number of weird things happen to Heisman winners, then maybe I could get behind this supposed curse.

However, that isn't what people are saying when they throw jabs at the famous statue. The real implication is that winning the Heisman Trophy means that you are going to suck. Not that you will wig out and retire or that you will fracture your hip or any of that. That you will suck.

As mentioned above, it is obvious that winning the Heisman Trophy means no such thing. In addition to the stars listed above, there have been plenty of solid NFL players with Heisman pedigrees. Guys like Billy Simms (three Pro Bowls), Charles White (led the league in rushing in 1987), George Rogers (led the NFL in touchdowns in 1986), Vinny Testaverde (sixth all-time in passing yards), and Desmond Howard (Super Bowl MVP) have all carved out a meaningful place in the game. No matter how you define the term "suck" in

---

[58] Of course, Palmer pretty much got his knee ripped in half during the 2006 Playoffs, so maybe we can't rule this curse thing out entirely.

reference to a player's ability at the NFL level, there is no way to say that all, or even most, Heisman Trophy winners go on to suck in the NFL. Yet the myth persists.

There seem to be two reasons why the connotation of NFL mediocrity has attached itself to the hardware like a thin layer of dust. The first is the unrealistic expectations placed on the winners to succeed. The second is the dramatic and complete nature in which a select group of Heisman recipients have flopped at the next level.

Unrealistic expectations are not unique to college football players who win the award for being the best at their sport. Number one picks in the NBA draft, tennis wunderkinds, top minor-league-baseball prospects, leading money winners on the PGA tour—they are all expected to take it to the next level. There is a reason that Kwame Brown is one of the most constantly and harshly criticized players in the NBA. He was drafted before *any other player in the world*. Of course there are expectations. Football is no different. The player who wins the Heisman Trophy award is supposed to be better than all the other young men who put on pads that season. By extension, people expect that player to keep playing better than everyone else on the field.

This kind of thinking is entirely unfair and horribly misguided. For starters, winning the award as college football's top player has nothing to do with NFL prospects. A guy doesn't go to Manhattan and accept a big hunk of metal for being the first pick in the draft. This has nothing to do with potential and everything to do with performance during the college season, against college players.

However, even beyond the contextual issues that tend to warp expectations, there is still the stark reality that those with the brightest futures will often fail. A look at some of the number-one picks in the NFL draft reveals the names of great players. John Elway, Bruce Smith, Troy Aikman, Peyton Manning, and Carson Palmer are a few names that stand out from the past twenty-five years. However, there are just as many busts on that same list. Guys like Aundray Bruce, Steve Emtman, Dan Wilkinson, Ki-Jana Carter, and Tim Couch just never put it all together. Whether it was injuries, attitude problems, or simply a lack of the necessary talent, these players could not live up to the hype. But do you hear about a "Curse of the Number-One Draft Pick"? Of course not.

Certainly the unrealistic expectations are a big part of the problem. However, the blame also falls on a handful of players for bombing so unceremoniously that they've given the trophy a bad name. Here is the progression of NFL futility that put the luster of the Heisman Trophy award in serious jeopardy. The cast of characters that conjured up talk of curses.

Andre Ware, 1989. The Houston Cougars quarterback put up insane numbers when he set NCAA records for yards (4,699) and touchdowns (46) during his award-winning junior season. However, he went on to fail miserably in both the NFL and the Canadian League. That, combined with the equally incredible numbers put up by his successor, David Klinger, led many to believe that Ware was simply a product of a great passing system.

Gino Torretta, 1992. Ty Detmer, the 1990 winner, was left off this list, but it goes without saying that we had a few rough quarterback transitions from college to the pros. At least Detmer was able to cobble together a career as an NFL backup quarterback.[59] Torretta had no such luck. He played in two games in his NFL "career" after being a seventh-round pick by the Vikings in the 1993 NFL Draft. Even worse than Torretta's lack of success was the fact that he won the award in controversial fashion over a star running back from San Diego State. That running back's name? Marshall Faulk. You could say that the Gino Torretta Experience was not a good one for the Heisman.

Rashaan Salaam, 1994. The former Colorado Buffalo ran for over 2,000 yards during his junior season, but was one of the biggest busts in recent NFL history. He got off to a decent start by clearing 1,000 yards and scoring 10 touchdowns in his rookie season for the Bears, but it was all downhill after

[59] Unless you are a member of the Detmer family, you might enjoy the entry titled *Detmer, Ty.*

that. He fumbled an incredible 14 times during his three years (31 games total) with Chicago; broke his leg in 1997; and then admitted that he played his entire career in the Windy City while high on weed. There is a silver lining in all of this though: he is the fourth-leading rusher in XFL history.[60]

Danny Wuerffel, 1996. Another "system quarterback," the former Florida Gator threw for 12 touchdowns and 22 interceptions during his NFL career. Adding insult to injury was the fact that he couldn't even get on the field while playing for former college coach Steve Spurrier in Washington. If ever there was a year to give the Heisman to an offensive lineman, it was 1996. Ohio State's Orlando Pace finished fourth and went on to be just as dominant in the NFL as he was in the Big Ten.

Eric Crouch, 2001. This one doesn't take a whole lot of analysis. Anytime a Heisman Trophy-winning quarterback goes into training camp as a wide receiver and then retires before ever playing a game, well, that is a bad sign. I think it is safe to say that Willis McGahee might have been a better choice here.

Jason White, 2003. The sentiment against the Heisman Trophy probably spiked to an all-time high during White's reign. With Crouch out of the league, and Carson Palmer riding pine at the time in Cincinnati, fans really became disillusioned when White won the award in 2003. The Sooners' field general was the classic case of a guy who could amass great numbers playing on a stacked college team, while obviously lacking the physical tools to succeed in the NFL. Sure enough, White has failed to make an NFL roster. Meanwhile, the runner-up in 2003, Larry Fitzgerald, has quickly become one of the top wide receivers in the NFL. This is why a transcendent receiver should always beat out a statistically impressive quarterback. The former comes along once in a decade, and the latter happens pretty much every season.

---

[60] Salaam ran for 528 yards for the Memphis Maniax of the XFL, which might be my favorite stat in this entire book.

Thanks to the performances of Ware, Torretta, Salaam, Wuerffel, Crouch, and White, the Heisman Trophy lost its luster. Fans and members of the media seemed capable of living with a mediocre career like that of 1983 winner Mike Rozier or a career cut short like Bo Jackson's. They were even doing okay with Charlie Ward choosing the Knicks over the pigskin. However, when the flurry of Heisman flops hit the scene, they simply had to react. Out came the columns questioning whether the award was in fact an honor, the jokes, the degradation of the Heisman race itself. It was only a matter of time before the whole thing morphed into the latest and greatest "sports hex."

Now the fate of the Heisman Trophy, as well as the fate of common sense, is in the hands of Matt Leinart and Reggie Bush. Only the recent USC winners can restore order. To the former Trojans, I offer this: Go in the footsteps of the 2004 Boston Red Sox and 2005 Chicago White Sox. Reverse the curse.

(AH)

Heads, Bobble: Football Fans Do *Not* Collect Bobblehead Dolls Of Their Favorite Players

See the sections titled *Porcelain, Collecting* and *Cardboard, Pieces Of.*

Replace "porcelain" with "bobblehead dolls."

Then go have an ice-cold beer to celebrate having read another entry of this book. You deserve it.

(MK)

Iron, Nine: Golf Is *Not* A Good Hobby For NFL Players

These days, it seems that every professional athlete worth his salt plays golf. The sport was already popular among retired athletes and select stars before Tiger Woods came along, revolutionized the game, and made golf infinitely more appealing to pretty much every male on the planet, particularly those under the age of forty.

That meant that NBA stars and Cy Young pitchers and stud NFL receivers no longer had to wait until retirement to pick up the flat sticks and start wearing checkered pants and soft spikes. The future was now!

Except that squeezing in a round at a nice private club still might not make for a great idea *while* the season is going on.

You are probably thinking, "Why not? What could happen?" Well, for starters, you could be struck by a golf ball. Tiger planted an approach shot right into a woman's head during the 2007 British Open, and while that was a spectator taking the worst of it, other players have been known to get domed by errant shots. (Why do you think "Fore!" is the most commonly heard phrase on the golf course?)

And that is just being hit by the ball. There are also horror stories of thrown clubs winding up lodged in necks, golf carts running over feet, and people falling into water hazards and being attacked by crocs.[61]

Many star athletes might read all of that and scoff, believing themselves too graceful and lucky and star-kissed to ever join such a list of freak accidents. Tales of doom and gloom might not be enough to push their favorite hobby back until the offseason.

Well, then they might want to take Derrick Mason into consideration. Mason, a wide receiver named to the Pro Bowl four years in a row, from 2001 to 2004, nearly saw that string of successes come to an end when he suffered a broken hand during the 2003 offseason.

Want to know what crazy activity Mason was participating in? You can probably guess that he was golfing. But surely he must have done something stupid, right? Something that other stud athletes could easily avoid during a leisurely day of eighteen holes.

Nope. Derrick Mason broke his hand *while teeing off*. All he did

---

[61] I'm pretty sure that last one only happened in the Adam Sandler movie *Happy Gilmore*.

was hit the ball. Some fluke combination of grip, swing speed, and angle of contact caused an awkward tee shot and. . . snap.

Mason quickly healed and was ready to go for the 2003 season (a Pro Bowl season, as mentioned above), but had he been squeezing in that round of golf on a rare in-season off day, and his Pro Bowl campaign might have been over.

And if that had happened, Mason might have been forced to actually use the excuse that he joked about with reporters—that he slipped while rescuing his dog—because I'm guessing that NFL teams wouldn't take too kindly to the truth.

Which is why NFL players should never play golf during the season. That sport is just too dangerous for football players.

(AH)

Coaches, get your players away from this vehicle right away!

Irrelevant, Mr.: The Last Player Selected In The NFL Draft Is *Not* A Bad Player

For several decades now, the last player selected in the NFL draft has been referred to jokingly as "Mr. Irrelevant." He is also given an award called the Lowsman Trophy.

That, you see, is supposed to be funny because the Heisman Trophy is awarded annually to the best college player in the country. And Heisman is pronounced "highs-man." So "lows-man" would be the opposite of "highs-man."

Get it? Highs-man? Lows-man?

Okay, let's acknowledge that it really isn't that clever.

And, worse, the implication of the award is wrong.

While the Heisman Trophy is awarded, ostensibly, to the best college player in the country, the Lowsman Trophy is not awarded to the worst college player in the country. The worst college player in the country is the fifth-string defensive back for Podunk State University, who didn't get off the bench all season and wears a uniform his sister knitted for him because Podunk's athletic program's budget ran out of money. The award does not go to that guy. Instead, it goes to the last pick in the draft, who is about the 260th best college player in the country (or, at least, the 260th best player eligible for the draft, as it does not include most underclassmen).

That's who "Mr. Irrelevant" is.

He's not the worst college player in the country.

Not even close.

No, he's one of the best.

Good enough to be drafted by an NFL team, which is more than you can say for thousands upon thousands of college football players each year.

Now, I understand that the "Mr. Irrelevant" tag is intended in good fun. And I'm all for good fun. But the next time you or one of your buddies wants to joke about how bad a player is because he was the last player drafted, remember this: you weren't drafted at all.

And the guy you're making jokes about? Guaranteed he could beat the stuffing out of you or your buddy if he wanted to. And he might want to if he heard you were mocking him.

So watch yourself.

(MK)

Itself, The Football: Footballs Are *Not* Made Of Pigskin

Yes, everyone refers to footballs as "pigskins."

And, yes, footballs originally were made of pigs' bladders.

And, yes, it's pretty disgusting to be tossing around a pig's bladder.

But, no, footballs are no longer made of pig's bladders.

They've been made of leather for years.

I don't know about you, but I don't see a football when I look at this cute little guy. No, I see a ham sandwich.

And leather is the skinned hide of an animal.

And tossing around the skinned hide of an animal is disgusting, too, if you really think about it.

So, just don't think about it, okay?

(MK)

Jersey, Falcons: Oakland Raiders Jerseys Are *Not* King Of The Junior High Bad Boy Fashion World Anymore

My junior-high years were pretty good to me, all things considered. Based on every depiction of that period of life that I'd ever seen in a sitcom or film, I came away relatively unscathed. Most of the credit for that small victory goes to luck and the various rules my parents enacted that kept me out of trouble. That said, I like to think that part of my success came courtesy of an innate ability to spot trouble in the form of Oakland Raiders paraphernalia.

My junior-high years dawned during the era of the Starter jacket. You remember these gems, right? They came in two predominant styles: the traditional snap-button jacket in some sort of shimmering satin material, and the puffy polyester-nylon parka. And let's not forget the giant team logos on the back (stitched in, no less) or the trademark Starter patch sewn onto the sleeve. The jackets were overpriced, but they were the epitome of cool.

I had two Starter jackets. The first was a Kansas City Royals jacket that I received for free because I was a batboy for the local American Legion team, the Vancouver Royals. The second was a mammoth Atlanta Braves parka that my parents caved in and bought for me as my winter coat for eighth grade. I loved that jacket. It was all navy with red piping around the sleeves and a massive *A* stitched in cursive on the back. That thing was awesome, and, to be honest, I still throw it on for the occasional snowball fight.[62]

Not all of the kids at Pacific Junior High had classy Atlanta Braves jackets, however. A large percentage of the Starter jacket crowd instead wore the sleek silver and black of the Oakland Raiders. And just as the Starter jacket generally worked like a bat signal for being hip and cool, so, too, did the Raiders version of the jacket act as a flag for boorish behavior. All the tough kids wore Raiders jackets. All the kids your parents warned you to avoid and who got detention and smoked cigarettes behind the portables and drove their older brothers' cars without a license.

In other words, all the kids who dominated the junior-high-school social scene.

I was drawn to this misbehaving pack of Raiders-jacket-wearing

---

[62] My younger brother, Drew, had an Anaheim Mighty Ducks Starter jacket. He's embarrassed by this fact, which is why I'm including it.

deviants like the proverbial fly to honey, but I was equally terrified of them. It is unclear which way I ultimately would have decided, but when a group of them stole my clothes during track practice and then threatened to beat me to a pulp when they were caught, it made the decision quite a bit easier.

The best news is that from that point forward, the Raiders jacket acted as a lighthouse beacon. For troubled girls who liked bad boys, it was a light pointing the way. For me, it was more like a giant beam illuminating a jagged rock that my boat was about to crash into. Either way, there was real value in being able to wear the clothing of one professional sports team and send those kind of signals.[63]

Why the Raiders?

There are probably a lot of reasons, but the biggest seem to be:

• The black and silver colors. Bad guys wear black, right?

• The "colorful" history of the Raiders franchise, complete with a maverick owner in Al Davis, wild partiers playing quarter- back, and the terrifying fans in McAfee Coliseum known as The Black Hole.

• The adoption of Raiders gear as the uniform of choice by the rap group N.W.A.

Once Ice Cube started voicing his disdain for the Los Angeles Police Department while wearing a Raiders Starter jacket in videos popularized by MTV, the choice was clear to any kid who wanted to send a message and who didn't have parents who read Newsweek and knew what that message was.

Thus, a longstanding junior-high tradition was born. And while it has been years since I've spent any significant time in a junior high school, my suspicion is that Raiders gear was still going strong as

---

[63] I would be remiss if I didn't note that the Raiders jacket was often paired with a black, fitted Chicago White Sox hat. The "Sox" hat would be doctored with a touch of black magic marker and effortlessly turned into a "Sex" hat. These were just as popular as Raiders jackets, but worn by a larger cross section of the junior-high population (such as class clowns), so they didn't serve as accurately as a signal. Chicago Bulls jackets are another example of a popular item that was worn by the bad-boy crowd, but also by a wide swath of the junior-high population, making it an unreliable marker.

recently as a few years ago.

Now? Not so much.

You see, the Oakland Raiders jersey is quickly being replaced by the choice of a new generation: the Atlanta Falcons. As always, there are a variety of reasons for this fashion evolution.

The first is that the Raiders have become more of a running joke than a fierce antiestablishment symbol. The return of Art Shell as head coach in 2006 was the ultimate low point, and when Randy Moss was traded to the Patriots in the offseason, all hope of retaining street cred slipped out of the Oakland locker room along with that number 18 jersey.

Coincidentally, just as the sinister Raider Nation was imploding, the Atlanta Falcons kept emerging as a bad-boy powerhouse. First, they popped up in the social consciousness with the "Dirty Bird" team that reached the 1998 Super Bowl and eventually made its way into a Ludacris song. Then, they drafted Michael Vick in 2001 and crept ever closer to cultural relevance. The rise to bad-boy power was pretty much complete when they made the switch to black uniforms in 2003 (because, again, bad guys wear black), and if there was ever any doubt, it was erased when Michael Vick was sent to a federal penitentiary in 2007 for being the mastermind of a dogfighting operation. I mean, nothing seals up street cred among fourteen-year-old boys like an infamous plea bargain.

The torch has been passed. Junior highs are now populated with black Atlanta Falcons hooded sweatshirts, red number 7 Vick jerseys, and fitted Falcons hats.

Sorry, Oakland, your day in the sun is over. The most ruthless, misguided, and jaded of the adolescent community now fly the black and red flag of the Falcons. They now rule the cafeteria.

(AH)

Jewels, Family: NFL Players Are *Not* Required To Wear Cups

If you read the NFL rulebook backward and forward, you may notice what seems to be an omission.

NFL players are required to wear helmets to protect their heads.

Yet there is not a word in the entire rulebook requiring NFL players to protect, well, how do we say this politely? Let's just say that there is nothing requiring the protection of a player's reproductive organs.

It's actually kind of funny if you think about it. The NFL has to remind players to put on a helmet, as if a player might actually choose to take the field without one, but at the same time the league recognizes that there is no need whatsoever to remind players to wear a cup. No, wearing a cup is a given.

Tells you which body part NFL players believe is more important to them, doesn't it?

(MK)

Jewels, More Family: We Do *Not* Know What Happened To That Guard In *The Longest Yard*

The Longest Yard was a fantastic movie that I will watch over and over again until the day I die.

The Longest Yard is one of the worst movies ever made, and I race to change the channel whenever it pops up.

Completely inconsistent statements?

Not at all.

I love *The Longest Yard*—the 1974 movie starring Burt Reynolds as a former star quarterback thrown into prison and forced to coach a team of prisoners in a game against the prison guards.

And I hate *The Longest Yard*—the 2005 remake starring Adam Sandler as a former star quarterback thrown into prison and forced to coach a team of prisoners in a game against the prison guards.

Yes, you read that correctly.

Adam Sandler. Star quarterback.

Never in the history of film has an actor been so sorely miscast as an athlete. And I'm including Gus, the mule who kicked field goals in the movie *Gus*. I'm also including Anthony Michael Hall as the high-school quarterback recruited by all the top college programs in *Johnny Be Good*. At least Anthony Michael Hall, the dweeby actor who starred in *The Breakfast Club,* had grown considerably and had packed on some muscle, enough that you could imagine that he might actually play sports beyond the intramural level—but not enough that you could imagine him dating, then dumping, Uma Thurman, which his character does in the movie.

Anthony Michael Hall dumping Uma Thurman?

Yeah, right.

In any event, I have digressed.

Back to Adam Sandler, star quarterback.

While I am sure that Sandler is a fine person and that he sincerely loved the original version of *The Longest Yard*, that does not mean that the movie should have been remade or that Sandler should have been cast in the role of the star quarterback. If he'd loved *The Godfather*, they wouldn't have remade the movie with him as Don Corleone, would they? What if he'd loved *Ice Castles*? Or *Steel Magnolias*?

One of the main reasons the original *The Longest Yard* was so entertaining was that Burt Reynolds, playing star quarterback Paul Crewe, actually looked like a star quarterback. He looked like a football player because he was a football player—he'd played halfback at Florida State, after all. And he had that swagger and charisma and self-confidence that successful quarterbacks have. He looked like a leader.

Now, I have seen the original version of *The Longest Yard* at least twenty times.

I am always sad when Caretaker dies. I still can't believe that fink rigged the light bulb so it would explode. (Sorry if I spoiled that scene for you. I probably should have warned you first).

I am always thrilled by the slow motion, last-second touchdown run.

I always get a chill when I hear the fans chanting "Mean Machine! Mean Machine!" which is the name of the prisoners' team. (It's also the name of the guards' team, by the way. The prisoners stole the guards' jerseys that had "Mean Machine" sewn on them.)

I am always afraid the guard is going to shoot Burt Reynolds in the back after the game as Reynolds walks toward the stands, with the warden yelling "Shoot him! Shoot him!" Of course, Reynolds is not trying to escape. He's merely retrieving the game ball.

But there is one scene that has always puzzled me, and fans of the movie will not need much description to remember the scene.

During the big game, one of the prison guards is continually putting pressure on Reynolds whenever he drops back to pass. His offensive line just can't stop the guy. So, in the huddle, Reynolds advises his teammates to let the guard come through untouched on the next play. When he does, Reynolds rears back and throws the ball directly into the guard's groin. The guard falls to the ground, and everyone has a good laugh. After several moments writhing on the field, the woozy guard stumbles to his feet and lines up just in time for the next down. Again, Reynolds steps back and drills the ball right into the guard's groin, sending him to the ground once again.

Eventually, medics come onto the field to check on the guard's condition. He is on his back, absolutely motionless. They wave smelling salts under his nose, and he does not even twitch. Eventually, they cart him off the field and the game goes on.

Now, here is my question: did the guard die?

He was motionless, and everyone refused to perform mouth-to-mouth on him.

No one I have ever spoken with knows if the guard died during that scene—nor, oddly, do they seem to care. And none of the players on the field seemed to care, either.

If you know what happened, send me a note in care of our publisher, okay?

Thanks.

(MK)

Jones, Bert: Bert Jones Was *Not* The Next Johnny Unitas

When he was drafted by the Baltimore Colts in 1973, quarterback Bert Jones was touted as the next Johnny Unitas.

He wasn't.

Which doesn't make him a bad person.

It just means that the expectations were too high.

Although Jones had a fine career—more than 18,000 career passing yards and 124 touchdown passes—it wasn't the career that Colts fans were expecting. Colts fans were expecting more. They were expecting championships. They were expecting last-minute comebacks. They were expecting another Unitas precisely because they were told that Jones would be the next Unitas.

That's an awful lot of pressure to put on someone, saying that he would become as great as one of the all-time greats. See *Unitas, Johnny*.

If someone had said that Jones might be the next Gary Cuozzo, then we would all look back with great fondness at Jones' stellar career, rather than looking at it with more than a hint of disappointment.

Life's all about expectations, isn't it?

And if you don't know who Gary Cuozzo is, then I've just made my point.

(MK)

Kaufman, Napoleon: Napoleon Kaufman Should *Not* Have Been A Backup

This might seem random, but I just wanted to point out that former Oakland Raiders running back Napoleon Kaufman was much, much better than anyone—namely his coaches—ever realized. The lightning-fast back averaged a whopping 4.9 yards per carry in 91 career games, was a first-round draft pick, and once piled up 227 yards on the ground against the Broncos. So why couldn't he nail down a regular gig as a starting running back?

Good question.

Kaufman wasn't a big man—five feet nine inches and 185 pounds—but that didn't stop similar players like Warrick Dunn from becoming legitimate NFL running backs. Not only that, but in his two years as the full-time Oakland tailback, the former Washington Huskies great threw up 2,215 yards.

Despite that, for reasons that will never be entirely clear, the Raiders put Kaufman into a timeshare with Tyrone Wheatley. Jon Gruden—then the coach of the Raiders—is a smart man, but why he gave Wheatley (3.9 yards per carry) 242 totes to Kaufman's (5.2 yards per carry) 138 is beyond me. Of course, that isn't as perplexing as the fact that he did it again in 2000, handing off to Wheatley (4.5 yards per carry) 232 times, while giving Kaufman (5.4 yards per carry) the ball just 93 times.[64]

Perhaps that is why Kaufman decided to take off the shoulder pads and become an ordained minister instead of a football player.

All I know is that it isn't every day you see a guy average 5.4 yards per carry and then retire from the game. It seems entirely possible that nobody has ever quit after amassing that high of a number. Jim Brown retired after posting a 5.3 in 1965, but I can't find anything higher than that.

Napoleon Kaufman, you were robbed.

(AH)

---

[64] I will grudgingly admit that the Raiders went 12–4 that year and reached the AFC Championship game. So, maybe Gruden wasn't entirely crazy.

Kelly, Leroy: Leroy Kelly Was *Not* Jim Brown

Jim Brown was an incredible running back. So incredible in fact that whoever tried to replace him in the Cleveland Browns backfield was sure to fail to fill Brown's legendary shoes. And Leroy Kelly did fail to fill those shoes, which is only to say that he wasn't Jim Brown. It is not to say that he wasn't very good, because he was. In fact, Kelly was a fantastic player. He led the NFL in touchdowns each season from 1966 to1968. And you know what? He's the *only* guy to lead the league in scores for three straight seasons since Brown himself did it from 1957 to 1959. Furthermore, Kelly finished with 74 trips to the end zone for his career, which is nothing to sneeze at. In fact, at the exact moment I am typing this, it is the twenty-second highest total of all time.

So, Leroy Kelly was a very good running back.

Some might even say a great running back.

He just wasn't Jim Brown.

And you can't really criticize a guy for that.

I mean, Napoleon Kaufman wasn't Jim Brown either, and he just got his own entry in this book, too.

(AH)

Knowledge, Lack Of: It Is *Not* Easy To Write A Book About Football

As you now know, I am one of the authors of this book, which happens to be about football.

Whenever I mentioned to friends or family that I was writing (actually, co-writing) a book about football, they invariably and unwittingly adopted precisely the same facial expression. It was the expression you would associate with someone who had just swallowed pickle juice.

Not because they don't like football.

Like most Americans, they love football. Love it like they love God and country.

No, they wore those pickle-juice faces because they don't understand how or why *I* would write a book about football.

How do I know this?

Because often they would expressly state, "Mike, we do not understand how or why *you* would write a book about football."

Their thinking was certainly understandable.

When I wrote—excuse me, co-wrote—a baseball book several years ago (*The Baseball Uncyclopedia*), they understood. I am, you see, a baseball fan.

When I said I was co-writing a football book (*The Football Uncyclopedia*), they did not understand. I am not, you see, much of a football fan. Or at least not in the same way that I am a baseball fan.

With baseball, I will happily spend hours talking about Roberto Clemente, and Albert Pujols, and the Red Sox, and the effects of steroids on home-run totals. I can and will debate virtually any baseball-related subject just for the heck of it. (Best hitter ever? Ted Williams. Most underrated pitcher? Tom Seaver. Worst uniforms? The mid-1970s Chicago White Sox. Most overrated baseball movie? *Field of Dreams*). I have more baseball statistics and anecdotes stored in my brain than I should.

With football, I will happily discuss Roger Staubach, and Reggie Bush, and the Jets, and the effects of rule changes on passing statistics. I can and will debate virtually any football-related subject just for the heck of it. (Best quarterback ever? Johnny Unitas. Most underrated defensive player? Charles Haley. Worst uniforms? The 1980s Tampa Bay Buccaneers. Most overrated football movie? *Brian's Song*). As with baseball, I have more football statistics and anecdotes stored in my brain than I should. (Only quarterback to complete 5,000 passes? Brett Favre. Longest wrong-way return of a fumble? Jim Marshall.)

But, for me, there's a critical difference between the two games.

Now, you probably expect me to argue that baseball is more interesting or more "intellectually challenging" than football, as many baseball fans do. I'm not going to do that. That's a fool's argument.

Baseball has nothing on football when it comes to being challenging. When he steps on the field, the right fielder for the Kansas City Royals needs to remember to do two things: 1) catch the ball if it's hit toward him, and 2) throw the ball back in to someone else wearing a Royals' uniform. At the same time, however, the left tackle for the Eisenhower High School Diplomats football team needs to memorize a playbook the size of the Yellow Pages, each page containing detailed movements that, if carried out improperly, could result in the quarterback being dumped on his noggin by one of the kids from rival FDR High.

And therein lies my problem.

I understand baseball. It is a relatively simple game that can be made to appear complex.

I do not understand football. It is a complex game that only appears simple.

And the truth of the matter is that you probably don't really understand football as much as you like to pretend, either. You're just not willing to admit it. (A note to any and all readers who played high school or college football: no need to write a biting letter to the publisher of this book explaining that I'm a moron because you do in fact understand football. I'm not talking about you. But, while we're on the subject, you may want to take the trophies down in your living room. It's really kind of sad. It's not like I have my chess club plaques hanging up in my office. At least not anymore.)

I'll give you an example.

When I (and perhaps you) watch a football game, we know when a tailback has made a nice run. If he picks up 12 yards, we all say, "Great play!" And we also know he didn't do it on his own. We know that the offensive linemen have contributed to the run in a very meaningful way by opening up a hole or dumping some defensive player on his buttocks.

But what I see (and what you may see) is just a mass of bodies, which the (relatively) little guy with the ball evades before being tackled.

I (and you) see a "running play."

But what kind of running play was it?

Was it a trap?

Was it a draw?

Was it some other kind of running play, the name of which coaches and players recognize, but I (and you) do not?

I have watched hundreds upon hundreds of football games in my lifetime, and I cannot recognize a trap play or a draw play as one or the other is unfolding.

And which linemen were responsible for the play's success? The heck if I know. All I saw was a bunch of enormous men banging into each other like overdressed sumo wrestlers for about ten seconds.

I am a little better recognizing pass routes, and maybe you are, too. I've actually said, "It looks like Marvin Harrison ran a post on that one," and been right about it.

Defenses?

I couldn't even begin to recognize the differences among the many complex defensive packages most pro (and many college) teams now run. You used to be able to tell what position a player

Seriously, is this a trap play or a draw play? Heck, it could be a pass.

played by where he lined up on the field. Now, thank God for the announcer explaining to me that the Giants are playing a 4–3 defense this year, because every time I count, it looks like they've got eight guys on the line.

Kicking?

Okay, I get kicking. They snap the ball and the guy with the ill-fitting helmet kicks it. (And don't tell me that it's a coincidence that kickers' helmets never seem to fit right. The manufacturer does it on purpose.)

Punting?

That's easy. They snap the ball to the other guy with the ill-fitting helmet, and then he punts it.

So, in watching a game, I understand what the kicker is doing. And I understand what the punter is doing. But the other guys running around and beating the living hell out of each other? I'm sorry, but while I *generally* understand what they're doing, I don't *specifically* understand what they're doing. It's too complicated. It's way over my head.

You can certainly see how this might make writing a book about football difficult. Sure, I could fake it like most writers, but I'd feel like a slut. No, I had to learn the intricacies of football—and fast.

A couple years ago, after I had already committed to co-writing *The Football Uncyclopedia*, I had to make a trip from my home in Los Angeles to Atlanta. On the return flight, an enormous man wearing a light blue Lakers throwback jersey sat beside me. Although I usually don't make much conversation on planes as I understand that most people just want to be left alone, particularly on a cross-country flight, I struck up a conversation with him when I saw he had a photo of an infant as the screensaver on his computer. As I had a newborn, too, we spoke at length about our children.

After a brief time, I learned that the man was Jamie Dukes, a studio commentator on the NFL Network. He played center in the NFL for the Falcons, Cardinals, and Packers. He was headed to the NFL Network studios in Los Angeles.

I explained to him that I was writing a football book, and before I could embarrass myself I explained my predicament. I explained that I understand football on one level, but I understand little of it on another level. Among other things, I told him that I can't tell the difference between a trap play and a draw play.

That was when he explained that a trap play can also be a draw play.

Well, that's just lovely.

Over the course of a four-hour flight, he mapped out play after play for me on the blank placemats that the flight attendant gave us. They looked like LeRoy Neiman paintings. A few other passengers leaned over our seats to watch me and my new friend drawing Xs and Os and arrows.

For four hours, I nodded and said, "I get it now."

For four hours, I lied through my teeth.

I didn't get it.

And you wouldn't have either.

(MK)

Landry, Tom: The Dallas Cowboys Are *Not* America's Team

When I was a little kid, my favorite team was the Dallas Cowboys. The reason? My dad's favorite team was the Dallas Cowboys.

That is pretty much the way favorite teams are decided in the years before you get your driver's license. You either root, root, root for the home team, or you pledge your allegiance to your father's favorite club. Eventually people move to new cities, attend colleges, marry wives with alma maters, and pick up new favorites along the way. But there isn't much complication to fandom in those first couple of decades.

Growing up in Portland, Oregon, I had no automatic NFL local rooting interest (since the Seahawks were largely terrible), so the family favorite was the team of my dad's youth, the Dallas Cowboys. He grew up rooting for Roger Staubach, Drew Pearson, Calvin Hill, Walt Garrison, and Bob Lilly. He can still remember watching the Ice Bowl when he was fourteen, and I still remember when he gave me his weathered, flannel Cowboys pennant to hang up in my room.[65] We loved the Cowboys.

I didn't realize at the time that I was rooting for a frontrunner, but at some point, it dawned on me that the favorite team of my youth was also running around claiming to be "America's Team." The revelation was a bit disturbing, to say the least.

Was I rooting for the NFL version of the Yankees? What did "America's Team" imply, exactly?

These were not easy questions. But before I had a chance to decide how I felt about rooting for a football franchise held in possession by a world superpower, the Dallas Cowboys lost me as a fan forever. I'm pretty sure they also lost their claim to the status as America's Team that very same day. It was February 25, 1989, the day they fired head coach Tom Landry.

The word "legend" gets thrown around a bit too much in sports, but the fedora-wearing Cowboys coach was an NFL legend in every sense of the word. Landry was the franchise's first head coach and held the position for twenty-nine years. He tallied a career regular-season record of 250–162–6; he led the Cowboys to two Super Bowl titles; and was inducted into the Pro Football Hall of Fame in 1990. He led the team to thirteen divisional titles and had an incredible streak of twenty consecutive winning seasons from 1966 to 1985. Not only that, but he invented the 4–3 defense (while serving as defensive coordinator of the Giants); introduced pre-snap formation shifts on offense; and used former track star Bob Hayes to revolutionize the downfield passing game. Oh, yeah, he was also a decorated World War II veteran, survived a crash landing in his bomber, and was an outstanding defensive back as a player.

---

[65] As many readers know, the Ice Bowl was the 1967 NFL Championship Game played between the Cowboys and the Green Bay Packers. It was played in minus-thirteen-degree temperatures and was won by the Packers 21–17 when Hall of Fame quarterback Bart Starr ran in a quarterback sneak in the fourth quarter.

On top of all that, Landry was seen as a quiet, humble man, making the Cowboys such an accessible team to so many.

All of which makes it so despicable that shortly after becoming the team's owner, Jerry Jones ran Landry out of town.

Jones scooped up the franchise in 1989 from Bum Bright when the latter's finances took a nosedive along with the Texas economy. Jones then made his next order of business to hop on his private plane and fly to Austin to fire the only coach the Cowboys had ever had, pushing Landry aside in favor of college football darling Jimmy Johnson. While the record clearly shows that Johnson was extremely successful (and well coiffed) as head coach of the Cowboys, the way Jones tossed aside one of the sport's most important and innovative figures was nothing short of an outrage.[66]

Landry was inducted to the Hall of Fame shortly after leaving the game, and while Jones eventually included the coaching legend in the "Ring of Honor," somehow it feels like these accolades did little to rectify the fact that a wrong that had been done in the first place.[67] If anyone deserved to end his involvement with football on his own terms, it was the longtime coach of America's Team. Jones robbed Landry of a proper exit and in doing so, ruined much of the goodwill the franchise had built up over twenty-nine years.

That's why the Dallas Cowboys ceased to be America's Team on February 25, 1989.

The drugs and the prostitutes didn't help either.[68]

(AH)

---

[66] It is worth noting that Jones eventually ran Johnson out of town as well, and replaced him with Barry Switzer after Johnson took credit from Jones for the two Super Bowl victories during Johnson's tenure. Imagine that, the coach taking credit.

[67] The fact that Bobby Hill's school in the TV show *King of the Hill* is known as Tom Landry Middle School didn't rectify the wrong, either, but it is nice to know that even the writers of a TV cartoon know a legend when they see one.

[68] See the entries titled *Apples, Bad* and *Busts, Drug*.

Language, Foul: Herm Edwards Has *Not* Appeared On *The Best Damn Sports Show Period*

At the time of this writing, Herm Edwards is the head coach of the Kansas City Chiefs.

He is an excellent, well-respected coach, and he seems to be beloved by players wherever he goes.

Now, on a number of occasions, he has been asked to appear as a guest on the Fox Sports television show *The Best Damn Sports Show Period*. The show frequently invites players and coaches to join the hosts on their stage to talk sports and crack jokes. From appearances, everyone seems to have a wonderful time of it, laughing at each other's comments and patting each other on the back. It is not a show where the hosts aim to humiliate or degrade their guests. To the contrary, the hosts seem thrilled just to be around someone who has actually worn or touched honest-to-God athletic equipment.

Repeatedly, Herm Edwards has refused invitations to appear on the show.

Not because he is unavailable.

Not because he thinks the show is, at least occasionally, pretty damn silly.

Not because he believes it is beneath him to appear on a TV show.

No, Herm Edwards has refused to appear on the show because he is a Christian.

And, as a Christian, he cannot abide by the word *damn*, which, not incidentally, appears right smack dab in the middle of the show's name.

Now, I happen to be a Christian. Not a particularly good one, mind you, but I'm still banking on using it to get into heaven someday when someone finally kills me. And, as a pretty lousy Christian, the word *damn* doesn't bother me in the least.

In fact, there are lots of words that bother others that don't bother me in the least. Got a funky name for a part of the anatomy? It doesn't bother me at all.

A curse you like to use around the house? That's cool with me.

A word to describe the act of performing sexual intercourse? Trust me, I won't be offended.

In fact, *damn* wouldn't even show up on the list of the top one hundred words that bother me. The word *utilize* bothers me more than the word *damn*. Seriously. Is there any time when someone says *utilize* that he couldn't have just said *use*?

But the word *damn* is offensive to Coach Edwards, and I respect that.

And I respect the fact that he refused to appear on *The Best Damn Sports Show Period* for that very reason.

If the show were called *The Best Utilized Sports Show Period*, I would refuse to appear on the same basis.

But wait a moment, you say, *I saw Herm Edwards on television on that show in the fall of 2006.*

No, you didn't.

I saw him questioned by the hosts of that show.

No, you didn't.

Yes, I did.

No, you didn't. The fact remains that Edwards has never appeared on *The Best Damn Sports Show Period.* Never. Ever.

How is that possible when I saw him on TV? Are you saying it wasn't Herm Edwards? Are you saying it was someone dressed up to look like Herm Edwards? Are you accusing me of being a liar?

Whoa, whoa, whoa. Let's slow down a moment.

Edwards did not appear on *The Best Damn Sports Show Period.*

Instead, on the day he agreed to appear, they changed the name of the show for one day only to *The Best Darn Sports Show Period.*

You gotta give them points for creativity.

But you know that as soon as Edwards left the set, everyone started shouting, "Damn! Damn! Damn!"

(MK)

Leaf, Ryan: A Little Girl Has *Not* Played In The NFL

When Ryan Leaf was wrapping up his undistinguished NFL career by throwing interceptions for the Dallas Cowboys, I overheard someone say, "What a little girl," while pointing to the TV screen where Leaf was pouting.

Please let the record reflect that Leaf was not a little girl, but in fact was, and presumably still is, a full-grown male adult.

In fact, I have researched the NFL records rather extensively, and they reveal that no little girls have ever played in the league. In fact, every NFL player has been an adult male.

Just thought you'd want to know that.

You can thank me later.

(MK)

Leaf, Ryan: Ryan Leaf Was *Not* The Worst Draft Pick Of All Time

It is virtually required that all football fans poke a little fun at Ryan Leaf whenever his name comes up. Or whenever they hear the word *leaf.*

For instance, when your son comes home from school with a maple leaf pressed in wax paper, you are all but required to say, "That reminds me of Ryan Leaf! Boy, did he stink!"

You might even say, "Ryan Leaf was the worst draft pick of all time," a statement I've heard hundreds of times, as you likely have.

The problem is that many people, including diehard San Diego Chargers fans, recall the draft imperfectly. They recall that, in 1998, the two best quarterbacks coming out of college were Peyton Manning and Ryan Leaf. They recall the enthusiastic debate about which one should be chosen first in the draft. And they know that Peyton

Manning has become one of the greatest quarterbacks in NFL history, while Ryan Leaf has become. . . well, no one really knows what he's doing these days. It may involve used clothing.

In remembering the draft, people mistakenly believe that the Chargers had a choice between Manning and Leaf, and that they chose Leaf. This is simply wrong. The Chargers had no such choice. The Colts had the first pick and selected Manning. So the Chargers were left to choose Leaf—a decision every single GM in the NFL would have made, and a decision you would have made, too.

Now, if the *Colts* had chosen Leaf instead of Manning, we'd be having a very different discussion, because that choice would now look insane. But the Colts made the right choice. And the Chargers didn't have a choice to make.

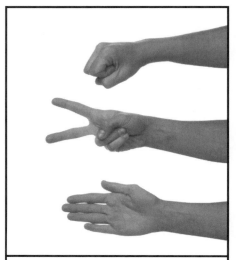

This is an actual photo of the Colts' management choosing between Peyton Manning and Ryan Leaf. Fortunately for Colts fans, rock ended up beating scissors, changing football history.

So, who was the worst draft pick in the history of the NFL draft?

I'd like to nominate the Seattle Seahawks' selection of Brian Bosworth in the 1987 supplemental draft or the Green Bay Packers' choice of Tony Mandarich in 1989. Both had careers as undistinguished as Ryan Leaf. And one of them made some terrible movies, which should certainly count for something in this analysis.

(MK)

Leaf, Ryan: Ryan Leaf's Family Should *Not* Read This Book For Obvious Reasons

If you are related to Mr. Leaf, kindly put this book down and step away.

(MK)

League, No Fun: The NFL Should *Not* Dish Out Fines Or Penalties For Creative Touchdown Celebrations

If you are a football fan, then you have no doubt heard the NFL referred to as the "No Fun League." This reputation comes courtesy of completely ridiculous rules that are often accompanied by stiff fines. Most of the rules have an impact on the game and can be justified as necessary. However, there are plenty of instances in which the NFL seems to be enacting policy with no other rationale than the reduction of good, old-fashioned fun. How else to explain Brian Urlacher being fined a whopping one thousand dollars during the 2007 Super Bowl for wearing a Vitamin Water hat to media day? Crazy rules regarding uniforms are probably the most glaring example of the NFL's overly conservative and restrictive nature, but it isn't the one that irks me the most.

My biggest NFL pet peeve is that players are penalized and fined way too often for touchdown celebrations. Brandon Jacobs of the New York Giants was fined nearly ten thousand dollars during the 2006 season for putting the football under his jersey and rubbing it as a tribute to his pregnant wife. Chad Johnson was fined for carrying a sign onto the field. Terrell Owens got tagged seventy-five hundred dollars in 2007 for pretending the ball was a movie camera. Teams are being flagged for a 15-yard penalty every time a player uses a "prop" during a celebration.

These rules are a creative buzz kill that threaten to drastically reduce the number of creative, humorous, and memorable players who play the game. Football players are anonymous enough with the helmets, and padding, and insane amount of distance between the fans and the action on the field. The last thing the league needs is to encourage robotic behavior while stifling individualism. Would the rich history of the NFL be better without Billy "White Shoes" Johnson's "Funky Chicken" dance (one of the first truly awesome touchdown celebrations) or Ickey Woods' "Ickey Shuffle"? Is football better off without the "Dirty Bird" or the "Mile High Salute" or the "Lambeau Leap"? For that matter, can you imagine the NFL today had the Giants' Homer Jones not performed the first touchdown spike way back in 1965?

Sports are a form of entertainment, and the product needs to be interesting and memorable and visually pleasing. Enacting extreme rules to combat a few cocky wide receivers seems like an example of throwing the baby out with the bathwater. Sure, it might be refreshing to watch LaDainian Tomlinson simply hand the ball to the ref after—yawn—yet another touchdown. However, it would be downright boring if *everybody* did that, wouldn't it?

Even if you are a purist and like your NFL players nice and robotic, I think we can all agree that the strict rules regarding touchdown celebrations are missing the point. The NFL is focusing on the quantity (how long, how many players are involved, what props are used, and so on) rather than quality. Celebrations should not be banned if they are excessive. They should only be banned if they stink.

Celebrations and dances should be judged on their merits. Those that meet the creative standard are allowed. Those that aren't good enough would result in the traditional penalty or fine. . . plus, a healthy dose of ridicule.

The logistics would obviously need to be worked out, but it seems easy enough to round up a panel of three judges to quickly weigh in electronically with a score. Scores over the threshold are allowed; the rest get the gong treatment.

This method seems to work on every level. Players would still be a bit nervous about trying out an elaborate celebration, as failure to achieve success would lead to embarrassment and the anger of one's coach. Announcers could spend time breaking down the celebrations and then analyzing the score from the judges. Fans and players would enjoy the entertainment value. Refs could stop worrying about making difficult judgment calls. There's no downside!

Touchdowns would obviously get the most leeway, considering the fact that the player in question had managed to dodge giants, lunatics, and probably a few steroid users on his way to the end zone. Surely he deserves to celebrate.

That said, there would still be standards.

Originality would count for a lot, which means that mimicking the Ray Lewis dance might not be a good idea for any future Terrell Owens touchdowns.

Obscenity doesn't get all of the First Amendment protections of free speech under constitutional law, so it probably wouldn't get much wiggle room in the end zone either. Which means that Randy Moss' moon job at Lambeau would likely still be fine-worthy (although not the fifth sign of the apocalypse, as Fox announcer Joe Buck would

Within seconds, this very referee will be throwing a penalty flag for excessive celebration.

have had us believe at the time) and that players should think twice before pretending to poop the ball or hump anyone with it.

Other factors would be taken into consideration such as aesthetic appeal, technical execution, nods to history and tradition, and tributes to the armed forces and pregnant women.

I'm telling you, this would work. Chad Johnson's pylon putt, T.O.'s pom-pom dance, Deion Sanders' high step, Kelley Washington's "Squirrel," and Merton Hanks' chicken dance would all have been allowed; while the New York Giants' jump-shot sack celebration, Shaun Alexander's sprinkler (or whatever that is), and any version of the Riverdance would be outlawed. Ray Lewis would be restrained from celebrating assisted tackles, Joe Horn would be exposed as ridiculous, and Steve Smith would make the Hall of Fame purely on the strength of his celebration highlight reel.

Most importantly, the NFL could get back to being fun again. This is football, not nuclear physics.

Although that gives me an idea for a pretty sweet celebration dance. . . .

(AH)

Leagues, Fantasy: Professional Football Players Do *Not* Care If They're On Your Fantasy Team

What I am about to say is not original, by any means. In fact, I wrote pretty much the same thing a couple years ago in *The Baseball Uncyclopedia* in discussing fantasy baseball leagues, and I was sorely tempted to just insert the same text here, changing "baseball" to "football," and "home run" to "touchdown," and so forth. But I won't do that. At least not completely.

In any event, as I said in the baseball book, grown men tend to do stupid things.

It's in our DNA.

We memorize lines from *The Godfather, Caddyshack,* and *Fight Club.*

We quote lines from *The Godfather, Caddyshack,* and *Fight Club*. Old episodes of *Saturday Night Live*, too.

We watch golf on TV.

We suck in our guts when attractive, younger women are near. Especially blondes. Especially ones that sort of look a little like that cheerleader we liked back in high school. Debbie Something. Remember her? Man, she was hot.

We type in our own names on www.google.com once a day just to see what pops up. (For instance, did you know there's another guy with my name who's a dentist? That might not be that impressive if my name were Tim Jones. But two guys with my unusual name is pretty odd.)

We fool around with co-workers at the office Christmas party. Or holiday party. Or whatever the company is calling it this year so as not to offend anyone.[69]

We put lime slices in our beer because we believe that's what they do in Mexico.

We look at pornography on the Internet and assume our girl-friends or wives will never find out because we carefully erase our browser histories.[70]

We write impassioned letters to *Sports Illustrated* about college basketball and horse racing.

We forget our parents' birthdays and anniversaries.

We get upset when someone takes our parking spot, even if there is another spot right next to it.

And we participate in fantasy baseball. Um, I mean fantasy *football*. That's right, I'm writing about football this time.

Actually, it would be more accurate to say, "And we participate in fantasy football with a misguided passion that makes one question our sanity."

---

[69] I'm using the royal "we" here and am not including myself or my co-author Adam. We behave at office parties.

[70] Again, I'm using the royal "we" here. And if you think erasing the browser history is going to keep your girlfriend or wife from figuring out what Web sites you were accessing, you, sir, are a bonehead.

Look, a fantasy football league can be good, harmless fun.

Really, it can.

Draft a bunch of players, compare their stats each week, maybe win a few bucks.

It also provides a healthy and safe outlet for teasing your friends and co-workers.

"Hey, Todd, what were you thinking when you picked Priest Holmes in the first round" won't hurt anyone's feelings, not even Priest Holmes'.

"Hey, Todd, your girlfriend is a whore" might. Unless she is in fact a prostitute, in which case you may be doing Todd a favor.

No, like fantasy baseball, the problem with fantasy football isn't fantasy football itself.

The problem is that some people take fantasy football far too seriously. So seriously that it damages their relationships with other people, like their wives, their children, their friends, and their co-workers.

To put it another way, fantasy football doesn't kill people.

People kill people.

There is no reason for grown men to stay up all night pondering the lineup of their fantasy teams. There is no reason for grown men to read the statistics of players on their *fictional* teams before reading what happened in the *real* games played by the *real* teams in the *real* world.

Above all, there is no reason whatsoever for a grown man to stand among the autograph-seeking kids outside a stadium after a game and shout, "Hey, Amani, you're on my fantasy league team! Amani! Over here! You're on my team, Amani!"

I don't care who "Amani" is or how well he's doing for your team.

I don't care if "Amani" is rushing for 100 yards each week.

I don't care if "Amani" has scored 3 touchdowns a week for the past month.

I don't care if "Amani" just caught 15 passes for 250 yards.

I don't care if "Amani" is going to help you win the one-thousand-dollar league championship.

I don't care if "Amani" is going to get you that championship trophy that you'll keep on your desk at work, pretending to do so ironically when in fact you want everyone to be in awe of your fantasy football skills.

I don't care.

And neither does "Amani."

I am willing to bet that if you ask a bunch of NFL players what kind of fans bother them the most, they'd say that the worst are the ones who hound them for autographs that are only going to be sold on eBay. But a close second are the guys who expect them to be excited to be on their fantasy league teams.

"Hey, Amani," you shout, "we're in second place in our fantasy league! You and me, buddy! We're going to win it all! Woo-hoo!"

Really, what do you expect "Amani" to say in response?

"Gee, mister, thanks so much for selecting me"?

Or, "It's an honor to play for Bob's Sloppy Drunks"?

Or, "Wow, maybe you and I can be friends and spend time at each other's homes"?

That's what you were thinking, weren't you? Admit it.

You were thinking that you and "Amani" would become buddies just because he's on your fantasy team, weren't you?

That there is now a special bond between you and "Amani"?

Well, stop it.

Go take your wife or girlfriend out for dinner and a movie already.

She already likes you.

Unless she's figured out what Web sites you were accessing when she was out shopping.

All women know that there are no legitimate Web sites with the words "teen," "wet," and "hot" in them.

Trust me.

And telling her that it was some crazy site that popped up when you were on www.espn.com didn't work, did it?

Next time, try telling her that one of your buddies must have looked at the Web site while he was using the computer.

Pick the friend she already dislikes.

You know the one.

(MK)

Legislature, Illinois: The 1972 Miami Dolphins Are *Not* The Greatest Team In Pro Football History

In 2005, the Indianapolis Colts were 13–0 and debating whether to rest their starters for the playoffs or go for the perfect season. In 2007, the New England Patriots went 16–0 during the regular season. In each instance, the 1972 Miami Dolphins, owners of the only perfect record in NFL history, were *everywhere*. Champagne on ice, rooting against whatever current team is undefeated, daily segments on *SportsCenter*, the whole nine yards.

It's not just that the 1972 Dolphins are insufferable and annoying, it is that their "perfect season" is maybe the most misleading stat in NFL history.

Did they go 17–0 that year (fourteen regular-season wins and three in the postseason)? Yes.

Should they be commended for doing so? Of course.

However, merely going undefeated does not automatically endow upon a team "greatest ever" status. You might be thinking: *Wait a minute, no one is saying the Dolphins are the greatest team. In fact, all of the attention given to these undefeated seasons focused on just that; the undefeated seasons.* Good point. In fact, I will concede that most magazines, shows, and pundits do a good job of focusing on the record and not slipping into hyperbole about where that team stacks up in the history of great teams.

Nevertheless, one can't help but lump the two things together. No one bothers to say, "Members of the 1972 Dolphins will be gathering this weekend to watch the Colts, wondering whether their perfect season will remain the only of its kind. We should point out, however, that the 1991 Washington Redskins may have actually been much better than those Dolphins." This would *never* happen. Any time a baseball or basketball team rattles off win after win, the conversation inevitably focuses on how "great" that team is and where they might fit in the sport's history. Because it is impossible to go undefeated in those sports, the quest for a perfect record never comes into play. There is nothing to cloud the issue of greatness. Current juggernauts are simply compared with the best teams of all time. Period. Of course, most of those great teams had tremendous records, but one thing isn't necessarily linked to the other. In the NFL, 16–0 or 19–0 is plausible, if not possible, and therefore becomes a distraction. The stories about the Colts and Patriots were all focused on "Can they go undefeated?" when they should have been focused on "How great are they?" "Are they as great as teams X, Y, and Z?"[71] If that was the conversation, I'm not so sure it would have started and ended with the 1972 Dolphins.

First, let me get one thing straight. That Dolphins squad was certainly a great team. I've heard theories that suggest otherwise, and that is simply ridiculous. I don't care about the era, the schedule, the luck, or anything else—winning all your games is impressive and you have to be great to do it. That said, are they the greatest team ever?

As mentioned above, going undefeated is not proof of ultimate greatness, but it helps, so we'll consider the Fins a candidate. For the sake of simplicity, we'll match them up with only one other candidate. There are at least half a dozen teams that could make a claim for the title of "greatest ever," but these are supposed to be short entries and I don't want to give my editor a coronary. Therefore, I am quickly passing on the following teams (get ready for some footnotes!): the 1962 Green Bay Packers,[72] the 1991

---

[71] It is worth noting that neither the 2005 Colts nor the 2007 Patriots wound up winning the Super Bowl during those seasons; so, regardless, the answer wound up being "no, they weren't as great." After all, you have to win the Super Bowl to compete for the title of Greatest Team Ever.

[72] The 1962 Packers won their first ten games (after winning all six exhibition games), and then throttled the Giants in the NFL Championship Game. Their dominance was on full display in one game in which they outgained the Eagles 628 yards to 58.

Redskins,[73] the 1999 St. Louis Rams,[74] the 1989 San Francisco 49ers,[75] the 1979 Pittsburgh Steelers,[76] the 1971 Dallas Cowboys,[77] and the 2004 New England Patriots.[78] Any one of those teams could make a legitimate case for the honor of being the best ever, and I encourage you to waste half of a day coming up with your own list. However, I am going to take my lead from Tom Cross and the Illinois Legislature by forwarding the 1985 Chicago Bears as my candidate for the best NFL team of all time.[79]

The Dolphins were definitely a great team. They had Bob Griese throwing to Paul Warfield; Larry Csonka and Mercury Morris running the ball; Garo Yepremian doing the kicking;[80] and Jake Scott anchoring a fantastic defense. They had nine players make the Pro Bowl and six that were inducted into the Hall of Fame. Legendary coach Don Shula was at the helm. They led the league in both points scored and points allowed. And, yes, they went undefeated. Has anyone ever mentioned that?

---

[73] Washington went 14–2 against a tough schedule, and outscored opponents 485–224 during the regular season and 102–41 in the playoffs. However, they did all this with Mark Rypien at quarterback and it is hard to imagine that Rypien could have been the field general of "the greatest team of all time." Seriously, try saying it out loud a few times.

[74] Kurt Warner was in the midst of the "grocery store clerk turns into Dan Marino" stage of his career; Marshall Faulk was at the height of his powers; and the Rams were the "Greatest Show on Turf." However, despite scoring over 33 points per game, they could be scored upon, and they had to win three tough games (Minnesota, Tampa Bay, and Tennessee) in the playoffs.

[75] San Francisco had Joe Montana completing over 70 percent of his passes; Jerry Rice and John Taylor both topping 1,000 yards receiving; and Roger Craig gaining over 1,000 yards on the ground. They are best remembered for annihilating the Denver Broncos 55–10 in Super Bowl XXIV, as they outscored three opponents 126–26 in the playoffs. The only strike against this team is that the NFC simply wasn't very good in 1989. I personally think this Niners team is right there among the best ever. Again, though, we're simplifying the analysis, so they are reduced to a footnote. Life is tough.

[76] Representative of the great Pittsburgh teams of the 1970s. Strangely, none of the four Super Bowl-winning Steelers squads really stands out as one of the great single-season teams of all time.

[77] The Cowboys scored over 40 points four times during the regular season and allowed only 3 points in both the NFC title game (against the Niners) and the Super Bowl (against the Dolphins). Not a bad offense/defense combo.

[78] The year 2004 featured the third Super Bowl win in four years for the Patriots, as they finished off a 21-game winning streak; went 17–2; throttled the Colts 20–3; and beat a 15–1 Steelers team on the road in the AFC title game.

[79] Illinois state congressman Tom Cross introduced and passed a resolution in the General Assembly that proclaimed the 1985 Chicago Bears as the greatest football team ever.

[80] See more on Yepremian in the entries titled *Ventura, Ace.*

As always, there is another side to the story. The Dolphins played one of the easiest schedules in NFL *history* that year, as the combined record of their opponents added up to a winning percentage of less than .400. In the playoffs they had to scratch and claw their way to victory, edging a mediocre Cleveland Browns team[81] 20–14, beating the rising Steelers 21–17 in the AFC Championship Game, and topping Washington in the Super Bowl by the count of 14–7 in a game in which they were *underdogs*. In fact, doesn't that say it all? The Dolphins were 16–0 heading into the title bout, looking to stake their claim to the first undefeated season in Super Bowl history. . . yet, the Redskins were actually favored to win.

The Bears, on the other hand, left nothing up for debate. In fact, they had been so impressive for so long that by the time Super Bowl XX rolled around, nobody even batted an eye when they shot and recorded "The Super Bowl Shuffle"[82] *before* the actual game. Led by the running of Walter Payton[83] and the play of enigmatic quarterback Jim McMahon,[84] the Bears offense put up 456 points in the regular season (second in the NFL). On the other side of the ball, one of the greatest defenses of all time, led by the likes of Mike Singletary, Richard Dent, Dan Hampton, and William "the Refrigerator" Perry, held opponents to a mere 198 points (best in the NFL). Mike Ditka was the head coach and was so popular in Chicago that he probably could have supplanted Harold Washington as mayor if he wanted to. They had charisma, star power, and a certain charm that led to all of the music videos and songs and nicknames. More

---

[81] The Browns outscored their opponents by a mere 19 points for the season and featured nary a Pro Bowl player on the roster. Their quarterback (Mike Phipps) threw more interceptions than touchdowns, their leading rusher (Leroy Kelly) ran for only 811 yards and 4 touchdowns on 3.6 yards per carry, and they failed to rank in the top ten in the NFL in any statistic except for passing yardage defense. Not to come down too hard on the 1972 Browns, but I didn't want you to think I was throwing the term "mediocre" around loosely.

[82] A music video in which high-caliber athletes took a break from the playing field to embarrass themselves completely. Of course, at the time it was somehow cool and embraced by all. Now though, it is pure comedy of the highest form.

[83] Water Payton, known as "Sweetness," was one of the greatest people and players to ever put on a uniform. He had one of his greatest years in 1985, rushing for 1,551 yards in his eleventh season in the NFL.

[84] See the entry *Utensils, Dangerous*.

than anything though, they just had a swagger and a dominance that made them unforgettable and virtually unbeatable.

Unlike the 1972 Dolphins, the "Monsters of the Midway" encountered no trouble during postseason play. They shut out the entire NFC, beating the Giants 21–0 and the Rams 24–0. In the Super Bowl, they destroyed the Patriots 46–10, as even the Fridge found his way into the end zone for a celebratory touchdown.[85] All told, they outscored their opponents 101–10 in the postseason and finished the year 18–1 while outscoring teams by over 300 points. Miami was great in that magical 1972 season, but the Bears ultimately had more wins[86] and did it in more impressive fashion, winning each game by an average score of 29–11 (versus the Dolphins' average win of 26–12) against far tougher competition.

I hope the next time a team embarks on a quest for a perfect season, columnists and experts everywhere will spend their time comparing that squad to the greatest team of all time. . . and not to the 1972 Dolphins.

(AH)

Lineman, Offensive: Offensive Lineman Do *Not* Get Enough Credit

If there is one thing I know about the National Football League, it is that offensive lineman do not receive the credit they deserve. Nearly every player, coach, scout, and general manager recognizes that games are won and lost at the line of scrimmage. Quarterbacks can't succeed without enough protection to get time to throw. Running backs can't scoot for big gains without holes to run through. Wide receivers can't make plays down the field unless the quarterback has enough protection. . . well, now I'm just repeating myself.

---

[85] See the entry titled *Appliances, Kitchen*.
[86] Granted, thanks to the sixteen-game regular season schedule, the Bears had two more games in which to do it, but that also means that the Dolphins had two fewer games they could have lost. I think the two ways of looking at it cancel each other out and make each teams' record equally impressive.

The bruisers up front are consistently top draft picks.

These giant men often warrant even larger contracts.

Sometimes, they even get to show up on a commercial with the star quarterback.[87]

So why can't they get the proper respect in the form of awards and plaques?

Never in the history of the NFL has an offensive lineman won the MVP award. Nor has an offensive lineman won a Super Bowl MVP award. In fact, while there are eighty-two quarterbacks and running backs in the NFL Hall of Fame, there are only forty-eight offensive linemen enshrined in Canton. Despite the fact that offensive linemen outnumber backs by more than two to one!

It is painfully obvious that offensive lineman simply do not receive the credit they deserve. Not from the Hall of Fame, not from the media members who vote on major awards, and (gulp) not from this book.

You see, this is the only entry in this entire book devoted to offensive linemen. We barely snuck in a Jackie Slater reference back in the entry titled *Bay, Green*.

Hey, what can we say? Quarterbacks sell.

(AH)

Lombardi, Vince: Originally, There Was *Not* An Entry In This Book About Vince Lombardi

I showed an early draft of this book to a friend who happens to be a huge football fan, and the one comment he made was, "How could you guys write a book about football without writing an entry about Vince Lombardi? He was the greatest coach of all time!"

I dutifully explained that I was well aware of the championships Lombardi had won with the Packers, but that the purpose of the

---

[87] The most memorable instances are Dan Marino's Isotoner ads in the early 1990s and Tom Brady's Capital One commercials that ran a few years ago.

book wasn't to write about every great player or coach. The purpose was to give readers a book that might provide them with a few laughs and to point out a few misconceptions about the game, as well as some of the game's unusual feats, interesting achievements, and quirky players.

"But still," my friend said, "it's *Vince Lombardi*. You can't have a football book without having an entry about him."

"You can't?" I asked.

"Well, I'm not saying 'can't' like it would be illegal, but it sure seems like every football book has an entry on him. Isn't there some way you can sneak him into your book?"

"You'd have to tell me something unusual about him that warranted him being mentioned," I said.

"Fine," my friend said. "I'll get back to you."

More than a month passed before my friend called me back and said, "Did you know that Vince Lombardi had his picture on a United States postage stamp?"

I had not known that. "Still," I said, "Lots of people have had their pictures on postage stamps."

"Aha!" my friend said. "But, in the history of the United States, dating back more than two hundred years, Vince Lombardi is the only Italian-American football coach from Brooklyn to ever appear on a postage stamp while smiling."

"While smiling?"

"Yes, he's smiling on the postage stamp. The players are carrying him off the field, and he's smiling."

"Is that an important fact?"

"What do you mean?"

"Well, are there any Italian-American football coaches from Brooklyn who appear on a postage stamp and *aren't* smiling?"

"I don't know. I didn't research that."

And I haven't either.

In any event, to appease my friend and any other readers who may believe that Vince Lombardi must have an entry in each and every football book, I ask that you kindly note Vince Lombardi is the only Italian-American football coach from Brooklyn to ever appear on a United States postage stamp.

While smiling.

(MK)

Man, Mystery: Ricky Williams' Retirement Was *Not* The Strangest In NFL History

Days before the 2004 NFL season kicked off, the Miami Dolphins' star running back, Ricky Williams, stunned the sports world by announcing that he was retiring from professional football at the ripe old age of twenty-seven. While Williams had always been eccentric,[88] the move was shocking given that he was coming off a season in which he accounted for 1,733 yards from scrimmage and scored 10 touchdowns. In addition to torpedoing fantasy football drafts everywhere, he also left his real-life team in a bind and eventually got his head coach, Dave Wannstedt, canned.

Adding to the bizarre scenario were the reports that came after the announcement. "Ricky was about to fail a third drug test and decided to retire so that he wouldn't be suspended," was a common story. "Ricky doesn't want his life regulated," was another. "Ricky simply hates football," was very popular. He was soon the source of massive amounts of ridicule and criticism, and being referred to as Reefer Williams more often than not.

Next, it was discovered that he was hidden away in a remote clinic in Northern California where he was learning to be a "holistic healer." He was traveling the world, enjoying his comforts, taking the road less traveled, and generally staying as far away from the gridiron as humanly possible.

---

[88] Among other things, Williams had dealt with rumors regarding his sexuality; had posed for the cover of *ESPN the Magazine* wearing a wedding dress; was arrested for refusing to sign a traffic ticket; and was profiled in a column titled "A Story of Social Anxiety Disorder."

Meanwhile, back home, the pundits wrung their hands in disgust; Mike Ditka scolded the former apple of his eye;[89] and the Miami Dolphins did what anyone would do when they get the rug pulled out from under them: they hired some terrific lawyers and started looking over the contract that Ricky had no doubt breached twenty times over. It soon became apparent that as much as Williams hated the game that had made him a famous millionaire, he wasn't going to be able to avoid playing it. Well, not if he wanted to keep all that money that Miami had paid him in signing bonuses. The edict was handed down through the typical channels (read: leaked to the media): Ricky, get back here or pay us a whole lot of money.

The next thing you knew, Super Agent Leigh Steinberg[90] was brokering deals left and right, the rumor mill was churning at full speed, and Ricky Williams was back in the NFL. It was all very exciting until he actually returned and proceeded to be completely average for the entire 2005 season. He wasn't spectacular, he didn't flop, and he wasn't bizarre in any way, shape, or form. Therefore, the story died. In addition, he lost his toehold on the desirable title of "Strangest Retirement in Recent Football History."

Ironically, the man who regained the title had perhaps the most famous quote regarding Williams' retirement. "It seems strange, even for me." Those were the words of former Detroit Lions' great, Barry Sanders. They were words that truly gave some perspective to the odd mechanisms of Ricky Williams, because they were coming from a man with a sudden and fascinating and downright strange retirement of his own.

---

[89] As coach of the Saints, Ditka famously traded a boatload of draft picks for the rights to Williams, leading to the *ESPN the Magazine* cover. Get it? Ricky was Mike's bride that he had wooed so relentlessly. Yes, I think even the good people at ESPN would agree it wasn't one of their finer moments. For more on the folly of trading the future of your team for a star running back, see the entry titled *Exception, The Marshall Faulk*.

[90] Leigh Steinberg is one of a handful of NFL Super Agents. After the Williams saga, he was forever upstaged by chief rival, Drew Rosenhaus. In addition to being the man upon whom the Bob Sugar character in *Jerry Maguire* was based, Rosenhaus was also the puppet master pulling all of Terrell Owens' strings during T.O.'s trainwreck 2005 campaign and the heroic rescuer of a young boy from an Orlando area swimming pool. To say that he's been in the news a lot would be a bit of an understatement. Someone could probably write an entire Uncyclopedia about Rosenhaus—or at least about sports agents—so I'll stop there.

This guy is still looking for Barry Sanders.

In 1998 Barry Sanders ran for 1,491 yards in his tenth NFL season. He made his tenth Pro Bowl. He finished in the top five in the NFL in rushing yards for, that's right, the tenth time. He was widely regarded as the most exciting player in football. He scored his 99th rushing touchdown and moved into second place on the all-time rushing yardage list (one of the few lifetime football stats that anyone truly cares about) with 15,269 yards and was poised to cash in for one final contract that would pay him well into his mid-thirties while allowing him to take a shot at pretty much any record he wanted. Instead, to the surprise and chagrin of football fans everywhere, he retired. He cited frustration with management and a host of other reasons that are quite commonplace in sports, took his 5.0 yards-per-carry average, and went home.[91]

The sports world waited for the inevitable comeback. After all, this was only a few years after Michael Jordan made his (first)

---

[91] The second-best career yards-per-carry average in NFL history, trailing only the great Jim Brown's 5.2 mark.

comeback to basketball, so it seemed natural to assume that Sanders would return to the game. Like MJ, he had retired at the height of his powers and at the relatively young age of thirty.[92] Granted, life after thirty is better for a basketball player than for the typical NFL running back, but Sanders seemed to have at least three or four good years left.[93] The optimism regarding a comeback was natural.

Unlike Williams (and Jordan, for that matter), Sanders kept a low profile. The media swell crested quickly after his press conference, started dying down within a few months, and when there was no word regarding Sanders by the time a full season had passed, it dawned on everyone that he was gone for good.

To this day, no one is 100 percent sure why he left the game and stayed away. Looking back, Jordan's retirement from basketball was for personal reasons and is a fun event for conspiracy theorists to discuss in hushed tones. And he certainly didn't stay away. Williams left the NFL because he hated playing football and only came back for money, so that doesn't present much of a puzzle. Sanders, on the other hand, is the ultimate enigma. He always seemed to love playing football when he was on the field. He was set to get one more payday before hanging up his cleats,[94] while picking off a few revered NFL records in the process. Other than a few beefs with management, there wasn't a whole lot to the story. It seems that he simply didn't feel that his organization, the Lions, was committed to winning. Hindsight proves that he was correct in that assessment, and maybe that was indeed reason enough to get out on top.

---

[92] Jordan retired from the NBA in 1993 after winning a third straight NBA title and a seventh straight scoring title, going for 32.6 points per game. He was also one year removed from back-to-back MVP awards. Sanders was a year removed from one of the greatest seasons in NFL history when he ran for 2,053 yards on 6.1 yards per carry and won the MVP award.

[93] Even the greatest running backs suffered a noticeable drop-off after the age of thirty. Emmitt Smith rushed for 878 yards per year in his five seasons after turning thirty. Walter Payton averaged a solid 1,139 yards per season but only managed to play three seasons after turning thirty. Tony Dorsett went for 803 yards per season over four years. Eric Dickerson averaged only 452 in his last three seasons. Marcus Allen kept scoring touchdowns for seven seasons after turning thirty, but only averaged 612 yards per season. Obviously, there is a huge drop off, but, even conservatively, it looked like Sanders could get 800–1,200 yards per season for at least three more years, which would have put him at about 18,000 yards for his career.

[94] Technically, Sanders didn't wear cleats in over half his games, since he played on artificial turf, but I didn't feel like writing "hanging up his cleats/athletic shoes."

One can't help but wonder if things might have been different if only a Super Agent like Leigh Steinberg or Drew Rosenhaus could have come to the rescue and forced a trade. If Ricky Williams can come back to football after absolutely screwing over his team and if Terrell Owens can demand trades whenever he feels like it, why couldn't a good guy and all-time great like Barry Sanders get a few strings pulled to keep him on the field? Like his retirement itself, the answer to that question will remain a mystery.[95]

(AH)

Mexico, Ron: The NFL Should *Not* Have Been Surprised By Michael Vick's Involvement With Underground Dogfighting

In the summer of 2007, the sports world was rocked by one controversy after another.

Under a cloud of controversy due to his suspected steroid use, Barry Bonds broke Hank Aaron's Major League record for career home runs.

The entire legitimacy of the NBA came into question when referee Tim Donaghy was indicted in a point-shaving scandal.

There was also the annual doping scandal in cycling; illegal spying in both the NFL and in Formula One racing; and a horrible domestic tragedy involving a WWE wrestler, who killed his wife, his son, then himself.

Not the best of times.

Perhaps the most controversial and explosive incident in a summer full of them was the scandal involving Michael Vick of the Atlanta Falcons. One of the "Faces of the NFL," Vick was brought up on criminal charges for dogfighting and gambling across state lines and found himself embroiled in a massive controversy. In a league that still

---

[95] Rumor has it that Sanders addresses this in his autobiography. But who has time to read?

sells O.J. Simpson jerseys on its Web site, embraces Ray Lewis as a hero, and lets Leonard Little collect massive paychecks every Sunday, it was odd to see Vick served up as the sacrificial lamb.[96]

But then the details started coming out, and it seemed a little less odd. It was reported that Vick killed dogs that wouldn't fight, and that he performed some of these executions himself, sometimes in horrifying fashion. It is unclear whether that last part is true, as Vick wound up pleading guilty to several charges, but not to killing dogs himself. Either way, it was a sordid affair.

The interesting thing about it was to watch everyone wring their hands and express shock that such a thing could happen. It was interesting precisely because it shouldn't have been all that surprising.

For starters, Michael Vick is the older brother of Marcus Vick, who, to put it kindly, is a troubled man.[97] But having a shady sibling is no reason to assume the worst in people; I think we can all agree with that.

More to the point, Michael Vick had a track record. This is the same guy who flipped off his own fans after a loss to the Saints. Who tried to sneak a water bottle with a hidden compartment through airport security. Who had posse members involved in selling marijuana and theft. And, perhaps most memorably, who settled a civil lawsuit filed by a woman who claimed he knowingly gave her herpes.

In that last incident, it came out that Vick had been visiting various clinics to treat the disease, which proved that he knew about it. Not only that, but it was revealed that he used the alias Ron Mexico when visiting these clinics.

Ron Mexico? Are you kidding me?

This revelation set off a chain reaction that resulted in Ron Mexico paraphernalia being sold on the Internet; the NFL shutting down

---

[96] You can read about O.J. in the entry titled *Simpson, O.J.* You can read about Ray Lewis in the entry titled *Apples, Bad.* Leonard Little's timeline goes like this: a drunk-driving incident that resulted in him killing another person; 90 days in jail; another drunk-driving arrest; and then a giant contract extension.

[97] Among Marcus Vick's many transgressions were his dismissal from the Virginia Tech football team due to his legal transgressions and unsportsmanlike play (like when he stomped on the neck of an opponent), a civil suit for molestation, and being charged with three counts of brandishing a firearm.

those sales; Web sites providing alias engines that would give people their very own Ron Mexico names (like Rocco Aruba); and the real Ron Mexico (an auto-parts supplier in Michigan) getting angry. It was a total fiasco.

And, quite honestly, anyone who treats a venereal disease with an alias like Ron Mexico is pretty much capable of anything.

Which is why no one should have been surprised when Vick was accused of dogfighting and gambling.

(AH)

Miracle, Music City: The Craziest Thing About The "Music City Miracle" Was *Not* The Miracle Play Itself

The "Music City Miracle" refers to an improbable finish to the January 8, 2000, wild-card playoff game between the Buffalo Bills and the Tennessee Titans. The Titans, trailing 16–15 with just 16 seconds remaining, called for a trick kickoff return called "Home Run Throwback." Tennessee fullback Lorenzo Neal hauled in the kickoff, turned and handed it to tight end Frank Wycheck, who then fired a lateral across the field to wide receiver Kevin Dyson.[98] Dyson then raced untouched down the sideline for a game-winning touchdown.

Many people will say that the "Music City Miracle" was one of the craziest plays in NFL history. They might even call it one of the best playoff games ever. These are both fair assessments.

However, want to know what that game *really* was? It was the most insane gambling moment of all time.

Obviously, you are thinking that it was crazy just because the Titans scored on a 75-yard kickoff return (via a lateral) with seconds left, turning certain defeat into miraculous victory. But that's not it.

---

[98] Dyson was only involved in the play because starting wide receiver Derrick Mason was injured and unavailable to play in the game. He was not injured from playing golf, however, which is another Mason story you can read about in the entry titled *Iron, Nine*.

Or maybe you consider the way the play unfolded to be the truly crazy part. Everything from Neal's handoff to the lateral to the bizarre way that Buffalo defended the play adds up to a perfect storm of events.

Or, perhaps, you chose to focus on the controversy surrounding the lateral. The play was reviewed countless times on instant replay to see if Wycheck's lateral was actually an illegal forward pass. The call stood, but the good people of Buffalo, New York, are still angry about it.

You could even fixate on the way Bills' quarterback Rob Johnson played the final series with just one shoe or even express amazement that a Bills kicker (Steve Christie) nailed a clutch 41-yard field goal to set the whole thing up.

All of that stuff is certainly crazy.

But that's not what made it crazy from a gambling perspective.

You see, the most bizarre aspect of this play was one that went unnoticed by nearly everyone. Everyone except for the people gambling on the game.

By kickoff, the gambling line on the game was Buffalo +5, meaning that the Titans were 5-point favorites and would need to win by six or more points to cover the spread.

And when the Titans ran back that kickoff and took a 21–16 lead, we saw gambling implications and sound football strategy collide.

With just a few seconds left, Buffalo's only hope was to counter by running the final kickoff for a touchdown. The odds of this were long, but had the Bills accomplished the feat, they would have scored 6 points for the touchdown and likely tacked on the extra point, good for 23 total points in the game.

So with 21 points on the board and the only possible negative outcome being the Bills reaching 23 points, why on earth would Titans coach Jeff Fisher opt for an extra point rather than a 2-point conversion?

Think about it. An extra point turns a 5-point lead into a 6-point lead, which is pretty much worthless. Whether Tennessee led by 5 or 6, they were going to need to prevent a Bills touchdown on the kickoff. Allowing a score would have meant a sure loss. Meanwhile, successfully going for two could have taken their "as long as we keep them from running this kick back, we are golden" situation and turned it into a "worst case, we are going to overtime" result.

Going for two was the only play there. Seriously, the only one.

Yet the Titans sent out the kick team and tacked on the extra point.

This gave them a 22–16 lead, which, as explained above, was no better than their 21–16 lead.

Except when the spread is 5 points.

I have no idea why Fisher sent out the kicking team in that situation. Perhaps he just got so excited that he didn't think it through. Maybe someone did some terrible math. Perhaps the little 2-point conversion cue cards that coaches use were inaccurate. I have no idea. But it is certainly suspicious, no?

All I know for sure is that every gambler in the world was watching that game in anticipation of the 2-point conversion that would decide whether it was a push (21–16) or a Titans cover (23–16). All those people betting on the Bills were no doubt praying that the Buffalo defense would do something magical to break up the play. And then. . . out came Al Del Greco.

And that is why the "Music City Miracle" was one of the craziest plays in gambling history.

(AH)

Moore, Herman: Life Is *Not* Fair

As I was reviewing an early draft of this book, the image of Herman Moore, the amazingly talented Lions receiver, popped into my head for the first time in years. It made me feel guilty that we had not mentioned him anywhere in this book. Then, little by little, other great players I had not thought of for some time popped into my head as well.

This is by no means a profound thought, but I am struck by how many of these often forgotten players played in small markets or for poor teams, while lesser players in big markets or on good teams remain household names.

Herman Moore was a better receiver than Michael Irvin or Keyshawn Johnson. But who does everyone remember?

So, that being said, I would like to present the following list of undeservedly overlooked players, all of whom would be household names if they'd only had the good fortune to play in New York or Dallas. It makes me smile to see their names in print.

Roger Wehrli[99]	Bruce Matthews
Clay Matthews	Ken Anderson[100]
Earl Campbell	Danny Abramowitz
John Hadl	Chuck Foreman
Art Monk	Charlie Sanders
Len Barney	Mike Quick
Conrad Dobler[101]	John Mackey
Joe DeLamielleure	Marlon Briscoe
Larry Wilson[102]	Sam "Bam" Cunningham[103]
Floyd Little	Ted Kwalik
Tommy Nobis[104]	Tom Matte[105]
Willie Lanier	Roger Craig
Ed Podolak	

---

[99] Not to be confused with Larry Wilson.
[100] Only the most underrated quarterback of all time. It's either him or Lenny Dawson.
[101] Known for biting other players' fingers if they slipped through his face mask.
[102] Not to be confused with Roger Wehrli.
[103] Randall's big brother.
[104] Best player to wear a Falcons uniform. If you are willing to forget that the Falcons had Brett Favre and let him slip away.
[105] Quarterbacked the Colts to victory in a critical game. Even though he was a running back. He filled in when the team's quarterback was injured, taping a list of plays to his wrist.

Please feel free to write in the names of any of your favorite overlooked players.

Seriously, go ahead. It will make you feel good.

(MK)

Moore, Herman: Herman Moore Was *Not* Better Than Michael Irvin

I hate to disagree with my co-author, but while Herman Moore was good, he wasn't as good as Michael Irvin.

Michael Irvin had more catches (750 to 670), more receiving yards (11,904 to 9,174), more touchdowns (65 to 62), more yards per reception (15.9 to 13.7), and more Pro Bowls (5 to 4) than Herman Moore.

That said, I couldn't resist making my own list of players who were criminally overlooked because they got stuck on mediocre teams or played in small markets.

Warrick Dunn	Terry Allen
Curt Warner (see *W, The Letter* for a bit more on Warner)	
Jimmy Smith	Rob Moore
Charlie Hennigan	Bobby Mitchell
Randall Cunningham (see *Cunningham, Randall*)	
John Brodie	Dave Krieg[106]
Ron Mix	Mark Bruener
Antonio Freeman and Donald Driver[107]	
John Henderson	Donnie Edwards
Lenny Moore	Brian Sipe
Roland Harper	Steve Atwater[108]

---

[106] If not for all the fumbles and playing his career in Seattle, Krieg would have been remembered as a great signal caller.

[107] Who do you think caught all those Brett Favre passes? Green Bay wide receivers, that's who.

[108] I'm convinced that Atwater hit harder than any safety who has ever played. Please don't hurt me, Ronnie Lott.

You're right, Mike, that did make me feel good.

But you're still wrong about Herman Moore being better than Michael Irvin.

He was better than Keyshawn Johnson, though. You've got that right.

(AH)

Mouth, Insert Foot In: Tony Romo Is *Not* A Genius

We have already mentioned Dallas Cowboys quarterback Tony Romo far too many times in this book considering the fact that, at the time of publication, he has played all of two full seasons in the NFL. George Blanda played in the NFL for approximately two hundred years and held the record for points scored in a career, and he's mentioned far less often than Romo. And even though he had a longer and more distinguished career than Romo is likely to have, Hall of Famer Anthony Munoz wasn't mentioned at all in this book. Until now. You get my point.

Nevertheless, I have something else to say about Romo, and I'll make it as brief as possible.

Here it is: the man's a moron.

In the short time that he has been in the NFL, Romo has already earned a reputation for dating celebrities. Among others, he has dated country singer Carrie Underwood and singer/actress Jessica Simpson. Of course, that doesn't make him a moron. That makes him awfully darn lucky.

Now, football fans know that there was more than a slight uproar when photos came out in January 2008 showing Romo on a Mexican vacation with Simpson during a bye week before a playoff game. And when the Cowboys promptly lost that next playoff game, commentators swiftly placed the blame on that little trip.

Did going on a trip with Simpson during the bye week make Romo a moron, you ask.

Nope. It was the players' free time, and they could do whatever they wanted with it. Going to Mexico for a few days with his girlfriend was no more stupid than going hunting or fishing or whatever else his Cowboy teammates chose to do that week.

So, you ask, what exactly did Romo do that makes him a moron? I'll tell you.

Apparently, Romo and Simpson were out with friends, and Romo told Simpson that he thought Carrie Underwood, his former girlfriend, was a better singer than Simpson.

What's wrong with that, you ask. Isn't Underwood in fact a better singer than Simpson?

Absolutely. Underwood is a Grammy award winner with a very strong voice. Simpson has never won a Grammy and has a thin, sometimes whiny voice that is masked by producers.

So, how does it make Romo a moron for knowing that Underwood is a better singer than Simpson?

He's not a moron for knowing that Underwood is a better singer than Simpson.

He's a moron FOR SAYING IT OUT LOUD.

TO SIMPSON.

IN FRONT OF HER FRIENDS.

I'm sorry, Mr. Romo, but this is right out of Dating 101.

If your girlfriend asks you, "Do I look fat in this dress?" your answer is always, "Absolutely not, you look fantastic." It doesn't matter how she looks—that's your answer. And it should be stated immediately, without a moment's pause, to convey the impression that the question is so ridiculous that you need not even ponder it before answering.

If your girlfriend asks you, "How many women have you been with before me?" the answer should be, "Three" (unless you can honestly say, "One" or "Two"). It doesn't matter how many women you've actually been with—that's your answer. Telling her that you have been with dozens of women before her cannot lead to anything positive. (And don't let her trick you into telling her the truth by promising that she'll tell you the number of men she's been with because that really won't lead to anything positive.)

If your girlfriend asks you, "Were you just checking out that girl that passed by?" your answer should be, "Of course not." Unless it was pretty obvious that you were looking at the other woman, in which case your answer should be, "I was just thinking how much better her outfit would look on you."

If your girlfriend asks you, "Did you go to a strip club when you were on your business trip?" your answer should be, "Of course not." Unless you paid for something with a credit card, in which case you'd better make sure she doesn't see the credit card statement at the end of the month.

If your girlfriend asks you, "What are you getting me for my birthday?" your answer should be, "I'm not telling you."

If your girlfriend asks you, "Am I prettier than your ex-girlfriend?" you answer is always, "You are much prettier than her." It doesn't matter if your ex-girlfriend was a supermodel—that's your answer.

And, if your girlfriend is a professional singer and asks you if she is a better singer than your ex-girlfriend, who is also a professional singer, your answer is always, "Of course you are." It doesn't matter who you really believe is a better singer—that's your answer.

Heck, my wife is the worst singer I've ever heard, and if she asked me if she is a better singer than Carrie Underwood, I'd say, "Of course you are" without hesitation.

Because that's the way this dating stuff works, Mr. Romo.

The woman you are currently dating is the most attractive, most talented, most wonderful woman you've ever dated.

So, please don't make this mistake again.

And please be prepared for your next girlfriend to ask you if she looks fat in that dress.

Because she will.

And you better not hesitate before saying, "Absolutely not."

(MK)

Namath, Joe: A Third-Grader Should *Not* Do A Book Report On Joe Namath's Autobiography

Like many writers, good or bad, I started out as an avid reader.

How avid?

Well, back in second grade, our teacher had a competition to see which one of us could read the most books. We were to read at home, and every time we finished a book, our parents were to sign a slip of paper stating the name of the book we had read. Then, upon receipt of a duly signed slip, our teacher would put a paper leaf on the wall for every book each of us had read. The leaves started at the very base of the wall and would climb the wall as each of us read more books. If you read three books, your row of leaves would be three leaves high. Five books, your row would be five leaves high. You get the point.

It wasn't much of a competition, I'm afraid.

Very, very quickly my row of paper leaves climbed the wall, then made a turn and began to sneak across the ceiling. Putting aside the excitement of seeing our teacher standing on her desk as she tried to tape a paper leaf to the ceiling, the number of leaves I was accumulating was causing a problem.

First, our teacher called my mother in to school to confirm that I in fact had read each of the books I had claimed to have read. My mother confirmed that I had. You see, she usually sat across from me, reading her own books while I read mine.

Then, several weeks later, our teacher called my mother back to school to ask if she could convince me to stop reading. Apparently, my collection of paper leaves was demoralizing the other students.[109]

So, I slowed down. I stopped reading. I let a few other students get close to catching me, then I pulled away at the end, making sure I beat them by a good three or four leafs.

The leaf incident would only be the beginning of my reading troubles. It would be nothing in comparison to what would happen the next year.

---

[109] Oddly, no one called any students' parents in to school to tell them to stop climbing the ropes so well because their skill was demoralizing *me*. But that's an issue for me and my therapist.

You see, in third grade, we were all given an assignment to do over Christmas vacation. Each of us was to read a book, then give an oral report on it once we returned to school.

And, it was then that, dressed in my beloved New York Jets jersey and helmet, I gave an oral report on Joe Namath's autobiography, *I Can't Wait Until Tomorrow 'Cause I Get Better Looking Every Day*.

Now, *I Can't Wait Until Tomorrow 'Cause I Get Better Looking Every Day* wasn't one of those sports books written for young boys. You know the ones I'm talking about, the ones about squeaky clean athletes who win the big game through hard work and love of God, family and country. No, *I Can't Wait Until Tomorrow 'Cause I Get Better Looking Every Day* was written for adults. Dirty-minded adults.

Although it is pretty tame in comparison to books that are now published, *I Can't Wait Until Tomorrow 'Cause I Get Better Looking Every Day* was pretty darned racy. Oh, sure, there were stories about Namath's success on the playing field. His victories at Alabama. His success with the Jets—particularly his guaranteed victory in Super Bowl III. But it also contained stories of his success in the, ahem, boudoir.[110]

And there I was, standing in front of my third grade class, talking about those victories.

"So there was Joe Namath," I explained, "taking off this woman's stockings!"

I did not get to finish my oral report.

The teacher called both of my parents in to meet with her to share her dismay that I had read such a book. She did not know that my parents had bought the book for me for Christmas. She ended up giving me a D for my oral report.

The kid who read *A Train Goes Zoom* got an A.

I'm sorry, but I got gypped. And I'd give my second-grade teacher a piece of my mind if I weren't pretty sure she's dead. I may just have to say something to her children, though.

As for Joe Namath, in recent years he has been best known for

---

[110] "Boudoir" is French for "bedroom." A "bedroom" is where people have sex.

drunkenly telling ESPN sideline reporter Suzy Kolber, "I want to kiss you" when she questioned him about the current state of the Jets.

I don't know what all the hubbub was about. I mean, have you seen Suzy Kolber?[111]

(MK)

Nightmare, Nigerian: Christian Okoye Was *Not* A Figment Of Your Imagination

His story was meant for the big screen—one of those feel-good stories about family and sports and the American Dream. Christian Okoye had all of the required plot elements.

He came to America via Nigeria and first learned how to play football[112] when he stepped onto the campus of tiny Asuza Pacific University in Southern California. It was there that he thrived as a track star, winning several national titles in field events and drawing the attention of NFL scouts with his incredible combination of size (6'1" and 260 pounds) and speed. In 1987 the Kansas City Chiefs made this hidden gem a second-round selection in the NFL Draft.

His pro career was like a shooting star: brilliant but brief. He played only two full seasons as the starting running back for the Chiefs, earning a Pro Bowl appearance in each of them. Over his six-year career, he ran for 4,987 yards before being forced to retire due to chronic knee problems. At the time, he was the all-time rushing leader in Chiefs history.

Since retiring from the game, Okoye has largely disappeared from the public eye. He is a successful businessman and investor who started his own line of nutritional supplements. He was elected to the

[111] For those of you who did not see Namath play or who are not familiar with his accomplishments, you should know that a great many people consider Namath to have been overrated as a quarterback. As an admitted fan of Namath, I must tell you that those people. . . are absolutely right. If you put aside his image and his history-making guarantee that the Jets would upset the Colts in Super Bowl III—a game in which he did little—Namath was a pretty mediocre quarterback. He routinely threw more interceptions than touchdown passes, and he had a terrible record against good teams. But he would score with the ladies, if you know what I mean. And I think you do.
[112] Not to be confused with fútbol, which he already knew how to play.

Chiefs Hall of Fame in 2000. He remains one of the great video-game athletes of all time, thanks to his dominance in Super Tecmo Bowl.[113] Beyond that, he lives only on highlight films and in the minds of fans, many of whom aren't quite sure if they trust their memory. Did a giant running back with unbelievable power and speed *really* go by the name of "the Nigerian Nightmare" and dominate the league in 1989?[114] Yes, he did. He was not a fictional character brought to life in a sappy sports movie, nor was he a figment of your imagination. Just a devastating runner whose career was cut short by injuries, and a guy who deserves to be remembered in books like this.

(AH)

Oilers, Houston: The Jets Do *Not* Have The Worst Fight Song Ever

As a longtime Jets fan, I can tell you the Jets' fight song without thought.
It is:

J-E-T-S, Jets, Jets, Jets!

Pretty pathetic, don't you think? I mean, it's just spelling the team's name, then shouting it a couple times.

However, it is not the worst fight song.

Without any fanfare at all, I would like to present the somewhat abridged lyrics to the Houston Oilers' fight song:

Look out, football, here we come, Houston Oilers, Number One.

Houston has the Oilers, the greatest football team.
We take the ball from goal to goal like no one's ever seen.
We're in the air, we're on the ground—always in control,
And when you say the Oilers, you're talking Super Bowl.

---

[113] It should be noted that Okoye—and all other players from Super Tecmo Bowl—take a backseat to Bo Jackson where video game greatness is concerned.
[114] When Okoye ran for 1,480 yards and was named the AFC's Offensive Player of the Year.

We've got the offense, we've got the defense,
We give the other team no hope.
'Cause we're the Houston Oilers, Houston Oilers,
You know we're gonna hold the rope.

Yes, we're the Houston Oilers, Houston Oilers,
Houston Oilers, Number One.
Yes, we're the Houston Oilers, Houston Oilers,
Houston Oilers, Number One.

"You know we're gonna hold the rope"?
What on earth does that mean?
"When you say Houston Oilers, you're talking Super Bowl"?
Oh, really?
Let's go back and tally up all those Super Bowls the Oilers won.
Hmm, I come up with zero. How many did you come up with?
(MK)

Paint, Balls Of: Paintball Is *Not* A Good Hobby For A First-Round Draft Pick

The NFL draft has become one of the most over-reported stories on planet Earth. The coverage lavished on this event by ESPN makes the major networks seem lax in their handling of presidential elections and wars. There are mock drafts and player profiles and interviews and myriad other forms of coverage of the two-day event that amounts to guys in suits reading off the names of other guys in suits.

Then. . . nothing. As soon as the draft ends and the "report cards" are in for each team, the coverage just sort of goes away. Sure, there might be the occasional news item that a top pick signed with his team and will report to camp and—on the other end of the spectrum—the occasional rookie training camp holdout will spark a flurry of coverage. But other than that, during the time between the actual draft and the beginning of the season, NFL draft picks are largely ignored.

LaRon Landry—look out!

That is probably why my favorite NFL news item of the 2007 offseason went largely unreported.

The Associated Press report of June 15 read like this: "A paintball shot in the groin left rookie LaRon Landry unable to practice when the Washington Redskins opened their minicamp."

According to the report, Landry was injured during a team-building outing, which saw the defensive players going to play paintball, while others on the roster opted for bowling or lunch.

It seems safe to say that Landry and his fellow defensive mates made the wrong decision.

(AH)

Papale, Vincent: Do *Not* Believe Everything You See In The Movies

I love a good sports movie as much as the next guy.

Really, I do.

North Dallas Forty? Loved it. (Mac Davis. Nick Nolte. Women. Drugs.)

Bull Durham? Loved it. (Kevin Costner. Tim Robbins. Women. Alcohol.)

The Rookie? Loved it. (Dennis Quaid. Babies. Milk.)

Miracle? Loved it. (Kurt Russell. Hockey. Those stinking Soviets.)

Quarterback Princess? Loved it. (What, you don't remember Quarterback Princess? It was a TV movie with Helen Hunt. She was the quarterback of the high school football team—*and the homecoming princess*. She had to play in the big game, then race to get to the school dance. Imagine that!)

Breaking Away? Loved it.

The Longest Yard? Loved it. (I refer to the original, with Burt Reynolds.[115] My dad took me and a bunch of my friends to see it for my twelfth birthday. How cool was that?)

Bang the Drum Slowly? Loved it.

You get the point.

And I purposely omitted *The Replacements* and *Remember the Titans*. Remember, I didn't say I love all sports movies. I said I love *good* sports movies.

In any event, another sports movie on my list of movies I enjoyed is *Invincible*.

Invincible, which was released in 2006, is the story of how a Philadelphia bartender named Vincent Papale overcame the odds and earned a spot on the Philadelphia Eagles roster back in 1976 after attending an open tryout. It's an inspirational and well-told film, and actor Mark Wahlberg did an excellent job of portraying Papale. Not incidentally, Greg Kinnear did an excellent job of portraying coach Dick Vermeil, although he never cried. Dick Vermeil used to cry. A lot.

If you saw the movie, I suspect that you, too, enjoyed it. You probably walked out of the theater with a smile on your face and the

---

[115] For my opinion on the remake, see the entry titled *Jewels, More Family*. The title will make more sense when you get there. Trust me.

thought that you, too, might just get into shape and try out for your local team.

However, if you left the theater thinking that what you had just seen was accurate, well, I'm going to have to burst your bubble. As they are wont to do, the filmmakers took more than a few liberties with the truth. And I don't just mean that they had an actor who is only five feet eight inches tall playing the role of a six-foot-two football player. (They do stuff like that all the time in Hollywood, where very few actors are tall enough to be allowed to ride on rollercoasters. Seriously. I live in Los Angeles, and we bump into movie stars all the time. We are always surprised by how small they are. Owen Wilson actually came to a book signing I did in Hollywood a few years ago. A lovely, charming man. It was a pleasure to meet him. If he weighs 130 pounds, I'd be shocked.)[116]

What liberties did they take in making *Invincible*?

Well, here are a few:

• In the film, Papale had not played organized football since high school. In fact, he had not only played organized football, but he'd played *professional* football as a wide receiver for the Philadelphia Bell of the World Football League for a couple years. And don't think that doesn't mean something. Maybe the WFL wasn't the same level as the NFL, but it was as close as you could get, and more than a few NFL players in their prime jumped to the WFL. (See **WFL, The**). If you think you could have played in the WFL, you are very, very wrong.

• In the film, the Eagles coaching staff had never heard of Papale, and Papale merely showed up among hundreds of other wannabes at an open tryout staged by the Eagles. In fact, Papale and a few other members of the Philadelphia Bell were *invited* to try out for the Eagles. There is a big difference between being picked out of a crowd of eight hundred people of all shapes and sizes, and being invited to an event where people already know who you are and what you do.

---

[116] He's about the same size as Dennis Quaid. See *Quaid, Dennis*.

• In the film, Papale is motivated to try out for the Eagles after his wife suddenly leaves him. In fact, she had left him at least five years earlier, at least according to a number of fairly reputable Internet sources. A minor detail? Not really. A person's motivation to act is a critical part of who he is and what he does.

• In the film, the Philadelphia Eagles fans are portrayed as being clever and fun-loving, albeit a bit obnoxious. In reality, Philadelphia Eagles fans would skin you alive just for saying the word "cowboy," let alone wearing a "Cowboy" sweatshirt.

• In the film, Papale met his second wife while he was trying out for the Eagles, and their romance during this time of struggle is a major part of the movie. In fact, Papale did not meet her until after his career with the Eagles had ended.

• At the very beginning of the film, a hot dog, a box of candy, and a soft drink container dance while singing a song called "Let's All Go to the Movies." In fact, hot dogs, candy, and soft drinks do not have vocal chords or limbs and, as such, do not possess the ability to sing or dance. (Technically, this may not have been part of the movie. It might have been part of the previews. I'm afraid I don't really remember it that well.)

Anyway, I believe I have said enough.

I'm not telling you that you shouldn't enjoy *Invincible*.

I'm just telling you that you should remember that it's just a movie.

And not everything in the movies is true.

For instance, Rocky did not really beat Clubber Lang in *Rocky III*. If it were real, Clubber Lang would have kicked Rocky's rear end ten times a day, seven days a week, for the rest of eternity.

Really. Clubber Lang was tough.

(MK)

Parts, Body: You Do *Not* Need All Of Your Body Parts To Play Professional Football

One of the intriguing things about football is that, unlike other sports, people of nearly every size and shape can play the game at an advanced level.

Are you a bit on the short side? Great. Let's get you a kicking tee.

On the short side but fast as heck? You'll be returning kicks. You might even see some time at halfback.

A little overweight, are you? Congratulations, you're our new nose tackle. Oh, you'd rather play on offense? Fine. You're now a tackle. Or center. Or guard.

Tall and thin? How would you like to play wide receiver?

Ah, yes, there's room for everyone on the gridiron.

So much so that it appears you do not even need all of your body parts to play professional football.

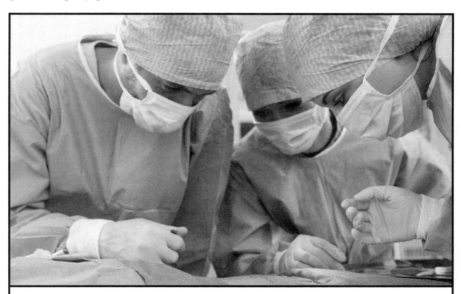

Amputating Ronnie Lott's broken finger so he wouldn't miss a big game was easy. Telling him that he was going to end up having to play for the Jets? Not so easy.

Tom Dempsey, the placekicker best known for kicking the longest field goal in NFL history when he played for the Saints, was missing part of his kicking foot.[117]

Ronnie Lott, the Hall of Fame safety from the 49ers, was missing the tip of his broken, left pinky finger. He had it amputated rather than miss a game. No kidding. He chose to disfigure himself.

Tampa Bay Buccaneers quarterback Chris Simms played after having his gall bladder removed.

A great many players took the field without their appendixes and/or their tonsils.

Jim Otto of the Raiders was missing his teeth.

And Ryan Leaf of the Chargers did not have a heart.

Or a brain.

Now, I'm sure you're saying to yourself, "That's an awfully long way to go just so you can make a joke about Ryan Leaf."

Yes, it is.

But it was worth it.

And I make matters worse in the entries titled *Leaf, Ryan.*

Promise.

(MK)

Philadelphia, Pittsburgh And: The Steagles Were *Not* An Imaginary Team

At some point, maybe at a cocktail party or sitting on your grandfather's lap or driving in your car with talk radio on, you may have heard someone claim that there was once an NFL team named the "Steagles." And that this was a combination of the Eagles and the Steelers.

And you would surely believe that to be a lie, because, honestly, isn't that the most absurd thing you've ever heard?

Ah, but it's true. Amazingly, remarkably, and—get ready to loathe yourself for laughing—nobly true.

---

[117] We have an entire section about him. See *Dempsey, Tom.*

You see, during World War II the United States was forced to send off virtually all of its able-bodied young men to defeat the Nazis and their allies. Seriously, almost all of them. Ted Williams, arguably the greatest hitter in baseball history, put his career on hold while he taught pilots how to fly in the Marines. And NFL players went overseas by the dozens to fight.

In fact, so many players from the Philadelphia Eagles and Pittsburgh Steelers were lost to the war effort, that the only way they could field a team for the 1943 season was to merge their squads and form a single team. Thus, the Steagles were born.

While NFL records officially list the team as the Eagles (or, in some cases, the Eagles-Steelers), that isn't what they were known as to fans. No, that team that went 5–4–1 was known to fans as the beloved Steagles.

True story.

(AH)

Piccolo, Brian: *Brian's Song* Was Not A Great Movie

Football fans, for the most part, have pretty thick skin.

Oh, sure, you and I support different teams, and we can each argue passionately—and loudly—about all the reasons why our respective teams are better.

Then, after your team has defeated my team, I can argue just as passionately—and just as loudly—as to why the outcome of that particular game isn't a true reflection of the quality of our teams.

Yes, your team won. But my team is still somehow *better*.

Debating is an essential part of being a football fan. If you're not willing to defend your team, even when you're wrong, then you just aren't a football fan.

That said, there is little that can be said in the heat of argument that will actually lead reasonable fans to fisticuffs. (I am excluding

Oakland Raiders fans from this analysis. Please note that I qualified my statement by limiting it to "reasonable" fans. Raiders fans scare me. Seriously.)

Tell a Miami Dolphins fan that Dan Marino's statistics were inflated by rule changes, and you will get a retort, not a sock in the jaw.

Tell a New Orleans Saints fan that Reggie Bush is soft, and you will not get into a fistfight.

The same is true if you tell a Chicago Bears fan that the 1985 team was overrated.

Or a Washington Redskins fan that the name of their team is racially insensitive.

There is one and only one statement that will lead a reasonable football fan to fisticuffs: saying that *Brian's Song* is not a great movie.

I'm not kidding.

Say it in front of a group of football fans, then prepare to have the stuffing kicked out of you.

Brian's Song was a television movie that first aired back in 1971. If you're a football fan, you've seen it. You've seen it a hundred times. If you're not a football fan, you've probably only seen it fifty times.

It's the story of the friendship between two young Chicago Bears running backs—Brian Piccolo, portrayed in the movie by James Caan (Sonny from *The Godfather*), and Gale Sayers, played by Billie Dee Williams (Lando in the *Star Wars* movies.)

Piccolo was white.

Sayers was black.

Piccolo was outgoing.

Sayers was shy.

Piccolo was a good running back.

Sayers was one of the greatest backs ever.

Piccolo had a man's first name.

Sayers had a woman's.

You get the point: they were very different.

Not only did these two men compete for the Bears' starting halfback position, but they were paired up as roommates, supposedly the first time the Bears had ever assigned players of different races to room together. If it seems odd to you that there was a time when teams wouldn't pair up players of different races, it should. Of course, there were worse things that were done based on race. If you were paying attention in your high school history class, I don't need to detail them for you here.

Rather than lead to fireworks, the pairing of the boisterous white Piccolo and reserved black Sayers led to a great friendship, with each player pushing the other to change. For instance, Piccolo became more sensitive, while Sayers became more social. They each became better players as well. When Sayers tore up his knee in a game, paving the way for Piccolo to start at halfback, Piccolo did not celebrate as others would have. Instead, he helped Sayers to rehabilitate his knee so that Sayers would eventually return to reclaim his starting position, pushing Piccolo back to the bench.

That is one heck of a story.

Sadly, it is not the end of the story. Early one season, Piccolo was diagnosed with lung cancer. Sayers helped his friend battle the disease. He would not win the battle. This was a time when few people won battles with cancer.

Piccolo's death, like many tragedies, is a great and interesting story, and much can be learned from it. It is a story about the importance of friends and family. It is a story about race relations. It is a story about the importance of hard work and dedication, of earning something rather than having it handed to you. It is the story of the relative meaninglessness of football in the greater scheme of life.

Having said all of that, and after much contemplation, I will repeat what I said earlier with the understanding that I may well face dire physical retribution: although it is a great story, *Brian's Song* is not a great movie.

Not even close.

I'm sorry to offend, but it's true.

Yes, the theme song is moving and can bring a grown man to tears. (*"Da da da da da da, da da da da da DA!"*)

Yes, James Caan and Billy Dee Williams were excellent, each carrying himself with that swagger that is peculiar to athletes and cowboys.

The problem is this: the movie is poorly written and poorly directed. When I watch it now, I either laugh when I am not supposed to, or I get angry about something that was inadequately handled. When I watch it now, I wish it were better.

Now, I understand it's difficult to tell a great story in a short period of time. Here, because it was a TV movie, they had only seventy-three minutes to tell the story of Piccolo and Sayers. And they had a lot to pack into those seventy-three minutes. Whether that was the reason or not, the events in the movie proceed too swiftly and unconvincingly.

One minute Piccolo is concerned he won't make the team. The next, he's on the squad.

One minute, Piccolo and Sayers are strangers. The next, they're best buddies.

I'd appreciate Piccolo's struggle to make the team if I saw him actually, you know, struggling to make the team.

I'd appreciate the friendship Piccolo and Sayers developed if they didn't become such close friends seemingly overnight.

Now, there are two scenes in particular that bother me and will always bother me, until the day I die. (Which may or may not result in a seventy-three-minute movie about my life. We shall see. Or, more accurately, you shall see. I'll be gone.)

The first is a scene in which Gale Sayers is at an awards banquet receiving a trophy honoring him for his comeback from knee surgery.

With Piccolo in the hospital battling cancer, Sayers wipes a tear from his eye and says that his friend is the one who really deserves the trophy.

"Brian Piccolo," he says, "has a hearty vagina."

Okay, he doesn't really say that Brian Piccolo has a hearty vagina, whatever that might mean. What he says is, "Brian Piccolo has the heart of a giant." It just sounds like "hearty vagina" because he's mumbling.[118]

And no matter how many times I see the movie, I laugh, even though I know it's supposed to be a sad and poignant moment.

I understand that they were trying to show that Sayers was uncomfortable speaking in front of an audience. But why did they have him mumble one of the most important lines in the movie? Didn't someone see an early cut of the movie and say, "Brian Piccolo has a hearty *what*?"

The other scene, which occurs earlier in the movie, is even more problematic for me. It has to do with people not acting the way people would act in a particular situation. Oh, sure, I can suspend disbelief and have no trouble, for instance, imagining that Luke Skywalker has the ability to use the Force to make objects move. But if he puts down his light saber in the middle of a battle in order to get a chocolate milk shake, well, I can't deal with that. Why on earth would Luke Skywalker get a chocolate milk shake? It just doesn't seem like something he would do.

In *Brian's Song*, when Sayers' wife brings him home from the hospital after his knee surgery, Sayers is so surly that she chooses to leave him alone in their living room to sulk.

"I'm going out," she says, and she does.

After a few minutes alone in the living room, Sayers suddenly decides to limp down to the basement, where he is surprised to find Piccolo setting up some weight-lifting equipment to help him rehabilitate.

Yes, it's touching that his friend is going to help him rehabilitate.

But didn't Sayers see Piccolo's car out in front of his house?

Wouldn't Sayers' wife have told him that Piccolo was in the basement?

I'm sorry, but if that's me, I notice my friend's car in front of the house.

---

[118] For younger readers, if you are not aware of what a "vagina" is, ask your mother. Preferably in front of her boss or a large crowd at the supermarket.

And I know for certain that my wife would tell me if there was someone lurking around our basement.

Thank God Sayers didn't hear someone sneaking around in his basement, retrieve his gun, and hobble downstairs to blow the intruder's brains out. That would be a very different movie.

Stuff like that makes *Brian's Song* a mediocre movie.

Oh, sure, I'll still watch it whenever it comes on.

And I'll still cry when Piccolo dies.

But, every time Sayers says that Piccolo has the heart of a giant, I'll laugh out loud.

And every time Sayers' wife brings him home from the hospital, I'll still be yelling, "Piccolo's in your basement! He's in the basement setting up the weight-lifting equipment! Don't shoot him! Please don't shoot him!"

(MK)

Pirate, Bruce The: The Dolphins Logo Is *Not* The Least Intimidating Logo Ever Used

Comedian Jerry Seinfeld used to do a great bit in his stand-up routine about sports fans. I don't recall it word for word, and copyright laws would prevent me from retelling it verbatim even if I did. In short, though, Seinfeld's joke was that the players on the teams we root for aren't actually from those cities, and the rosters are constantly turning over. Ultimately, we find that we're just rooting for the uniforms.

You'll have to trust me when I say that it is very funny when Seinfeld tells that joke. Really.

Like many jokes, the humor in Seinfeld's joke is found in the fact that the comment speaks the truth. Look at the Chicago Bears, for instance. If you're a football fan from Chicago, you probably root for the Bears with a passion that you do not have for many things in your life. Yet, few of the Bears were born or raised in Chicago. And, if they have any sense, they pack up and move to warmer climates as soon as the season ends. Which, until recently, was just before the playoffs started. That is not meant to be a knock on Chicago. Chicago is one of my favorite cities, and I always look for a reason to make a trip there. As long as it is not in December, January, February, March, or April.

In any event, the Bears' roster is constantly in flux. This year's guard may have played in Seattle last year. And that linebacker from the Patriots who we hated? Well, now that the Bears have signed him as a free agent, we love him. Why? Because he's wearing the Bears uniform, that's why.

Now, regardless of their prospects, it's easy to root for the Bears. It's easy to root for them precisely because of their uniforms—the simple, understated, timeless black-and-white uniforms with the simple capital *C* on the helmet.[119] They're sleek. They're classic. And, not incidentally, they're intimidating in a sport where intimidation actually means something.

There are a number of teams that are easy to root for, during times of struggle as well as times of prosperity, precisely because of their uniforms.

The Giants, with those navy jerseys and the shiny blue helmets with the lowercase *ny* on the side.

The Steelers, with the black, gold, and white uniforms—and the helmet with the sticker on one side only.[120]

The Rams, with the curving ram's horns on the helmets. (I still prefer the white horns to the yellow or gold ones, but I'll take them either way.)

The Vikings, with their horns on their helmets.

The Packers, Raiders, and Cowboys belong on this list, too. Each has a timeless uniform and a timeless helmet logo.

---

[119] I'm ignoring the bright orange jerseys they've taken to wearing from time to time. You know the ones I'm talking about, the ones that look like practice jerseys. I'm assuming they only wear those when someone forgets to do the laundry.

[120] Why on one side only? Because originally the team wasn't sure it would retain the logo, and it would be easier to remove the logos if there were only one per helmet. It's true. You could look it up in a book. Although, technically, you just did.

There are, of course, teams at the other end of the spectrum, teams whose uniforms make it difficult to root for them. Teams whose uniforms and logos inspire few fans and intimidate few opponents.

The Bengals come to mind immediately. For many years, they wore burnt orange helmets with the word "Bengals" stenciled on the side in the most nondescript manner possible, as if they didn't even care enough to come up with a design. Then, they made a dramatic change, switching to helmets covered with faux tiger stripes that look like a stripper's bikini.[121]

Where the Bengals' uniforms are embarrassing and vaguely creepy, the Browns' uniforms are just dull. Fans are asked to root for a team named after, and dressed in, the dullest color God created. God invented brown when he was very, very bored. Just before he invented charades.

For many years, though, the team with the oddest uniforms was the Miami Dolphins. The problem was—and is—the team's name. If you have a team in Miami and you want to intimidate opponents while still recognizing your seaside locale, you name your team the Miami Sharks. But naming your team the Miami Dolphins, after one of the sweetest, most docile creatures on the planet? You might as well call them the Miami Puppies. At least with puppies you have to be concerned that they might crap on you. No such concerns with dolphins.

Once the team was named the Dolphins, they had no choice but to slap a picture of a dolphin on the side. But why did they make it a smiling dolphin? (Only recently have they tweaked the logo so that the dolphin is snarling just a tiny bit, which might frighten a three-year-old visiting Sea World, but not a middle linebacker visiting your quarterback.) Then they wrapped it all up in aqua, orange, and white uniforms. Sure, they're nice looking, but they just don't look right for *football*.

---

[121] *Note to my wife:* that last comment was based upon information from a friend of a friend of some guy I once met who once accidentally went to a strip club. I swear.

Dick Butkus wouldn't have been Dick Butkus if he had to wear that uniform. Deacon Jones wouldn't have been Deacon Jones if he had a smiling dolphin on his helmet.

Nevertheless, the Dolphins uniforms were light-years ahead of the uniforms worn by the Tampa Bay Buccaneers for the first two decades of their existence. They were bright orange, red, and white uniforms that looked like a frozen drink you'd get at a resort. Worse, the helmet bore the logo of a handsome, smiling pirate. The pirate looked like he was a waiter at that same resort offering you a drink. He looked like he was about to wink at you and became known as "Bruce the Pirate."

Why?

Well, hmm, how do I explain this?

He was referred to as "Bruce the Pirate" because, well, his, um, sexual orientation appeared to be, let's say, unclear.

Oh, hell, he was called "Bruce the Pirate" because people thought he looked like he was gay.

Not that there's anything wrong with that, as Seinfeld would famously say on his television show.

And, of course, there is nothing wrong with being gay.

But there is something very wrong with wearing an ugly uniform with a silly logo. Because, ultimately, that's what we're rooting for and against. The uniforms and the logos.

(MK)

Porcelain, Collecting: Football Fans Do *Not* Collect Little Figurines Of Their Favorite Players

In the section titled *Cardboard, Pieces Of*, we explained how football fans do not collect and save football cards, unlike their baseball counterparts.

Well, there's another thing that baseball fans collect that football fans do not.

Figurines.

You may have noticed that many baseball fans have figurines of their favorite ballplayers that they keep on their desks or their bookshelves. A Mickey Mantle figurine. A Ken Griffey, Jr. figurine. An Alex Rodriguez figurine.

And not just any figurines.

Porcelain figurines.

My mother collects porcelain figurines. My grandmother collected porcelain figurines.

Without fear of contradiction, I tell you that no football fan would ever collect porcelain figurines.

Ever.

This simple fact does not necessarily make football fans smarter than baseball fans.

Just considerably less weird.

(MK)

Posts, Goal: The Goal Posts Should *Not* Be At The Back Of The End Zones

As many older readers will recall, the goal posts in the NFL used to be placed at the front of the end zones. They were offset a little from the goal line so that the uprights themselves ran parallel to the goal lines.

In 1974, the NFL made a number of rule changes. Among them, the goal posts were moved to the back of the end zones.

The result, of course, was that it was now more difficult to kick a field goal. Precisely 10 yards more difficult. Thereby, presumably, leading to a decrease in field goal attempts or, at least, forcing teams to try to move the ball closer to the end zone before attempting a field goal.

This rule change was a mistake. A major mistake.

Not because it affected the way the games were played. Or because it affected scoring.

No, those things were fine.

The reason the change was a mistake was that it deprived fans of one of the most enjoyable moments in sports.

The moment to which I refer?

The moment that occurred once every few games when a player—usually a receiver or a defensive back tracking a pass through the air—ran smack into the goal post.

Bam!

They showed plays like that over and over on shows with names like *The NFL's Greatest Bloopers* and *Zany NFL Bloopers*.

"Look, it's Joe Blow in the end zone and. . . " Bam!

Okay, I'm sure a few players ended up being legitimately injured when they ran into a goal post, and I feel very, very sorry for them. Really, I do. Injuries stink.

But, just the same, you have to admit that it normally was funny as hell when it happened. Bam!

I laugh just thinking about it.

And don't pretend you didn't enjoy it when it happened, because you did.

(MK)

Presents, Holiday: Your Father Does *Not* Want A Tie With The Carolina Panthers Logo On It

My father didn't like to receive gifts.

Especially Christmas gifts.

He is no longer with us, as they say, and that is one of the first things I always think of when he comes to mind: my father didn't like to receive Christmas gifts.

I can recall the pained expressions on his face whenever he would open his Christmas presents, steeling himself for the horrors that awaited him inside the box he held on his lap. He tried to smile, but it was an unnatural, forced smile. It was the smile of a man who'd learned to smile by reviewing a series of photographs of men smiling, each step of the smiling process coming a little too slowly.

"No knickknacks," our father would always say when we asked him what he wanted for Christmas, and we would respond by buying him knickknacks. Not because we were trying to be brats, but because we kept seeing things that we liked, not realizing that they were the very things he didn't like.

What kinds of things did we give him for Christmas?

A "World's Best Golfer" trophy.

A Ziggy coffee mug.

A Ziggy tie.

A baseball cap with moose ears on it.

A monkey with a clock in its stomach.

A New York Yankees beer stein.

A tie with the New York Jets logo on it.

A Joe Namath poster.

Only years later did I realize what he was thinking when he unrolled the Joe Namath poster, the forced smile beginning to form: *what the hell am I supposed to do with this?*

Exactly.

What the hell *was* he supposed to do with that?

Was he supposed to frame it and put it up in the living room? Or the master bedroom? Or his office?

What were we *thinking*?

As we handed over our money to the cashier at Spencer's Gifts, what in the blue hell were we thinking?[122]

The answer, I'm afraid, is this: I don't know.

I honestly have no idea what we thought our father was going to do with a Joe Namath poster. Yes, he liked Namath, but a *poster*?

For a forty-five-year old man?

---

[122] Spencer's Gifts is a store that can be found in virtually every shopping mall in the country. In the 1970s, they sold things only a teenage boy could enjoy. Need a black-light poster of Jim Morrison? Go to Spencer's Gifts. Need some fuzzy dice for the car you're not old enough to drive? Spencer's Gifts. Need a poster of Lynda Carter as Wonder Woman? Spencer's Gifts.

What was he supposed to do with it?

But, like many things, what seems like a good idea, subjectively, to a twelve-year-old is not in fact a good idea, objectively, to the rest of the human race.

An example: Putting a bumper sticker that reads "Hairdressers Do It with Style" on your parents' car seems like a great idea to a twelve-year old.

Putting a bumper sticker that reads "Hairdressers Do It With Style" on your parents' car in fact is not a great idea.[123]

Unless your parents are hairdressers, in which case the subject might arguably be appropriate.

And unless they are also blind, in which case they would not see the bumper sticker.

And, if they were blind, they probably would not be hairdressers or have a car to begin with.

But the tie with the New York Jets logo?

That was different.

Unlike the other presents, I defended that gift for years.

That gift made sense.

First, my dad wore ties to work every day. And many of his ties were old and worn out. So he needed ties. Thus, you had the element of necessity.

Second, my dad was a Jets fan. Namath, Sauer, Snell, Boozer, Maynard—that was my dad's team. No, that was *our* team. We used to watch them together on television. We used to listen to them on the radio. We used to read about them in the paper. Even in the most difficult times, my dad and I always had the Jets. Thus, you had the element of affection.

So, with the elements of necessity and affection both present, a Jets tie was perfect, right?

Wrong. And it took me a while to figure that out.

You see, after years of going out of my way to try to be different from my father, I have come to realize that, in too many ways

---

[123] Sorry, Mom.

to count, I am just like him. I do not contend that this is a profound thought. Just the opposite. Almost every man I know has come to the same conclusion that, often against his wishes, he has turned out to be precisely like his father. (And I understand women often draw the similar conclusion that they have turned into their mothers.)

Among the many similarities I could list is this: I don't enjoy receiving Christmas gifts.

Not that I don't enjoy Christmas. Heck, I love Christmas. And I love giving Christmas gifts. I just don't enjoy receiving them. The sight of a box with a tag that says "To Mike" can practically make me shudder.

I know that when someone gives me a Christmas gift, it's supposed to let me know that they have some level of affection for me.

Which is great.

I'm very fortunate to have many close friends who feel some level of affection for me. I'm not sure that such a miserable human being like me deserves so many friends, but I'll take them all, every single one of them.

But all they have to do to let me know they're thinking of me is give me a Christmas card or a hug, and I'm happy.

Giving me a Kleenex holder in the shape of a football helmet is completely unnecessary. Really, you shouldn't have.

Giving me a pill remover, to remove the pills from the sweaters that I don't have because I live in Southern California, is completely unnecessary. Really, you are too kind. It's too much. You should take it back. Get something nice for yourself instead.

There's no need to give me a coffee cup with a drawing of Homer Simpson saying, "D'oh" on it because, as much as I love *The Simpsons*, you know I don't drink coffee. Oh, I can just display it in my house, you say? I hadn't thought of that.

A one-month pass to Gold's Gym, well, you were kidding, right? Oh, it wasn't a joke? Sorry. Yes, it's a great gift. I really should go to the gym. Thank you for reminding me that I'm not in very good shape these days.

The new Bruce Springsteen CD? Great idea, and I'm so glad you remembered that I'm a huge Springsteen fan. But, knowing that I'm a huge Springsteen fan, aren't the odds pretty good that I ran out to get the CD when it first came out? But, seriously, it's great. Now I'll have one for my home and one for my car. This way, I'll never be too far away from the Boss. It's perfect.

Bowling ball salt-and-pepper shakers? They'd be great if I collected salt-and-pepper shakers. Or bowled. But I don't do either. And I don't even use salt or pepper. Oh, they're supposed to be displayed? In my house? I guess I'll put them right next to the Homer Simpson coffee mug.

The dress shirt with the New Jersey Giants logo on the pocket would be absolutely perfect if I weren't a Jets fan. Oh, you're right. I'm sure I must have mistakenly told you I was a Giants fan. My bad. And, you're right, a lot of lawyers and businessmen wear clothes to work that bear the logos of their favorite sports teams. Yes, I see it all the time. Just like my dad, when he used to wear the New York Jets tie to work.

Now, of course, I don't say any of these things.

Instead, I just smile. Slowly. Just like my dad.

I get it. He had no more use for a Jets tie than I had for a Giants dress shirt.

If there's an afterlife, I hope he knows that I'm sorry about the Jets tie.

And I'm very sorry about the *Welcome Back, Kotter* T-shirt.

Very, very, very sorry.

(MK)

Pyne, Daniel: Joseph Robbie Was *Not* As Good At Naming An NFL Team As Screenwriters

A few entries ago, in *Pirate, Bruce the*, Mike made the extremely valid point that the Miami Dolphins were poorly named, which led to a less-than-sinister mascot, logo, and uniform. He makes the argument that an NFL franchise based in Miami, Florida, should be named the Sharks. A good idea to be sure, and you know who agrees with him? Daniel Pyne, John Logan, and Oliver Stone.

Those three gentlemen were the credited writers on the film *Any Given Sunday*, an over-the-top football drama that featured a memorable pregame speech from Al Pacino (as grizzled coach Tony D'Amato) and a breakthrough dramatic performance by Jamie Foxx (as young quarterback "Steamin'" Willie Beamen). The fictional team that employed these stars of the silver screen? That would be the Miami Sharks.

Indeed, with their black uniforms and menacing name, the fake Miami team seemed more intimidating and imposing than the real version. Which means that Hollywood screenwriters in the late 1990s apparently knew a lot more about naming NFL teams than Dolphins' founder Joseph Robbie did in 1966.

At least, that seems true until you pause your DVD player to get a close look at the Miami Sharks' schedule and see that it includes the Seattle Prospects, Oregon Pioneers, and Wisconsin Icemen. Perhaps we should table this one for now.

(AH)

Quaid, Dennis: Dennis Quaid Does *Not* Play A Football Player In All Of His Movies

Several years ago, when I first moved to Los Angeles, I went to a movie theatre in Santa Monica with a friend. I don't remember the name of the movie we went to see. I believe Sean Connery was in it. He played a reclusive, Salingeresque writer. Oh, yeah, I just thought of the name of the picture—*Finding Forrester*.

In any event, when we first arrived at the theater, we took our seats and, not long afterwards, a couple sat down next to us. The woman was an attractive blonde, and the guy who took the seat directly to my left was short with oddly highlighted hair. I recognized him immediately as someone I knew, but couldn't place him. You know the feeling.

Finally, I turned to my friend and whispered to her, "I think I know the guy next to me. I think we went to college together, or maybe we used to work together."

She leaned forward to look past me at him, then whispered back to me, "That's Dennis Quaid, you idiot."

Dennis Quaid, in case you didn't know, is a fairly popular movie star. He used to be married to an actress named Meg Ryan, who was also fairly popular. He did not go to college with me, nor did he ever work with me.

Now, what I think of whenever I think of Dennis Quaid is that he always seems to be playing a football player or a former football player in his movies.

He was a former high school football star in the cycling movie *Breaking Away*.

He was a college and pro running back in *Everybody's All-American*.

He plays a football coach in *The Express*.

He plays a pro quarterback in *Any Given Sunday*.

Now, before you start thinking that Dennis Quaid plays a football player in every movie, let me stop you.

He plays a *baseball* player in *The Rookie*.

In any event, I'm sure there were movies where Dennis Quaid didn't play an athlete. I know there were movies where he played an astronaut—*The Right Stuff*, *Innerspace* and *Enemy Mine*. (In the last one, he slept with an alien played by Lou Gossett, Jr., and they had a baby together. Seriously. I couldn't make that up.)

That said, I am hard pressed to think of any actor who so consistently plays athletes in movies.

Maybe Wesley Snipes. (Baseball? *Major League* and *The Fan*. Basketball? *White Men Can't Jump*. Football? *Wildcats*. Boxing? *Play*

It to the Bone and *Undisputed*. Cross-dressing? *To Wong Foo, Thanks for Everything! Julie Newmar*. No, cross-dressing isn't a sport. I just wanted to see if you were paying attention.)

But here's the thing that struck me upon seeing Dennis Quaid up close and personal in a Santa Monica movie theater: for a guy who always seems to be playing a football player in the movies, in real life the man is small enough to fit in a lunchbox. While I am sure that he is more than capable of beating me senseless if he wanted to (as he certainly looked to be in good shape), he appears to be all of about five feet six inches tall. If you saw him in person, there is no way you would ever imagine he could play football on any level, other than perhaps playing electronic football.

I don't mean that he's so tiny he'd actually be one of the players buzzing around on the electronic football field. No, he's too big for that. I just mean that that's the only type of football I could see him playing, sitting on his couch with his buddies. I couldn't imagine him ever actually suiting up and actually getting on the field.

But, if they ever make *The Doug Flutie Story*, Dennis Quaid is the man for the part.

Although Dennis Quaid would have to get rid of those odd highlights in his hair.

Doug Flutie didn't have highlights in his hair.

I doubt anyone in the history of the NFL ever has.

I mean, could you imagine Deacon Jones or Jack Youngblood highlighting his hair?

(MK)

Quarterbacks, Raiders Starting: The Raiders Have Never Had A Great Quarterback

The Oakland/Los Angeles/Oakland Raiders are one of the most storied franchises in professional football. They have won Super

Bowls. They have Raider Nation: a collection of rabid fans draped in leather and chains, complete with an enormous seating section of pure chaos known as The Black Hole. The owner, Al Davis, is the individual responsible for putting aggressive owners on the map. He's brash and controversial and highly involved. He dresses in all black. He wears hideous sunglasses complete with one of those little chains more commonly seen in southern Florida retirement communities. The man is like a movie villain. If you don't like out-of-control sports owners such as George Steinbrenner or Jerry Jones or Mark Cuban, blame Al Davis.

Perhaps because of the personality at the top of the organizational flow chart, the Raiders are one of those rare sports teams that seem larger than life. Even when they are bad, they are interesting. When they are good, they seem almost cinematic. They are loved by many and hated by even more. They have a rich history full of colorful characters.[124] They are led by an owner who got control of the team through a hostile takeover that defies all logic.[125] They were part of The Tuck Rule Game.[126] They traded one of their coaches, Jon Gruden, for cash and draft picks. They have had 17 Hall of Famers within the organization, including 12 guys who spent the bulk of their careers with the Raiders—players like Marcus Allen, Art Shell, Jim Otto, and Fred Biletnikoff. In short, the Raiders' archives and trophy cases feature nearly everything you would expect from a legendary franchise. The one thing they don't have? A great NFL quarterback has never gone under center for the Raiders.

---

[124] For example: Lester Hayes, the stingy cornerback who played with so much Stick 'Um [AQ-Stickum ?] on his gloves and uniform that he single-handedly forced the NFL to create an official rule banning the use of the product. Howie Long, the bruising defensive end-turned-network superstar and Radio Shack pitchman. Bo Jackson, the freakish two-sport athlete who routinely ran for 80-yard touchdowns on *Monday Night Football* before suffering a career-ending injury. Todd Marinovich, the comically tragic wunderkind quarterback who was nearly a bigger flop than Ryan Leaf. Even in recent years, characters like Warren Sapp have always seemed to find their way to Oakland.

[125] See the entry titled *Takeover, Hostile*.

[126] The controversial game against the Patriots in the second round of the 2001 playoffs, when what appeared to be a game-clinching Tom Brady fumble was overturned and ruled to be an incomplete pass via the "Tuck Rule." New England rallied past the top-seeded Raiders and went on to win their first of three Super Bowls in a four-year span.

Don't believe me? That would be a perfectly understandable re-action considering the many famous, notorious, and briefly sensa-tional Raiders quarterbacks peppering the history books.

You recognize the name Jim Plunkett and assume that he must have been very good, maybe even great. Not so.[127]

You see all the MVP awards garnered by Oakland quarterbacks and figure that those magical seasons must have been par for the course. Again, not so.

The Raiders have two things at work when it comes to creating recognizable quarterbacks: 1) They have had more than their share of players experience a short stretch of magnificent play, often lead-ing to awards and the perception that these players were terrific over the course of an entire career, and 2) They have had a certain "Raid-ers Mystique," especially in the 1970s, that leads you to believe their players were better than they actually were.

We've dispatched of Plunkett as a possible "great," but there are other field generals that have played for the Raiders and warrant anal-ysis in regard to their greatness. Obviously, this whole breakdown hinges on your definition of the word "great," but for my purposes, I am considering a great quarterback to be a Hall of Fame-quality play-er, someone who belongs in the same conversation as guys like Frank Tarkenton and John Elway and Warren Moon. That said, there are four guys who need to be examined closely: George Blanda, Daryle Lamonica, Ken Stabler, and Rich Gannon. If you are a football fan, you no doubt recognize each of their names, and, in fact, you are probably scratching your head this very moment and thinking, "Wait, a few of those guys were great." Not so fast; the powers of short-term success and Raiders Mystique are hard at work.

First, we have George Blanda. This guy is an actual Hall of Fam-er. He won the AFL MVP award in 1961 while playing for Houston

---

[127] See the entry titled *Game, It's Only One* for some information on Plunkett's very average football career.

and took home the Maxwell Club's version[128] of the honor again in 1970 when he was a bonafide miracle worker at age forty-three, leading the Raiders to one late-season comeback victory after another. However, most of his damage was done as a kicker. He was the backup quarterback during that 1970 season, and while no one can doubt his value coming off the bench, he really didn't play much quarterback. In short, his foot was far more valuable than his arm. By extension, you could also argue that he reached the Hall of Fame on the strength of the same appendage.[129] He was a great player, a great competitor, but not necessarily a great quarterback when he was with the Raiders.

Next on the list is Daryle Lamonica. Terrific spelling of his first name, as well as a flashy last name to go with it. Not only that, but he completes the hat trick with a great nickname: "The Mad Bomber." He's off to a perfect start. He appeared in five Pro Bowls and won two AFL MVP awards, so he has the hardware. His completion percentage was never higher than 53 percent, which admittedly wasn't too bad for the era. On the flip side, he only played six full seasons, and in both of the seasons in which he tossed over 30 touchdown passes, he also lobbed up more than 20 interceptions. He's kind of like the quarterback version of former Chiefs running back Christian Okoye, extremely productive for a short period of time.[130] Lamonica makes a pretty good case, but if we call him a "great" quarterback, then we probably have to bestow the same honor on guys like Steve McNair and Marc Bulger. Are you ready to do that? Not only that, but this entry deals with great *NFL* quarterbacks, and Lamonica played most of his career in the AFL. Semantic issue? Perhaps, but it is my entry, so I make the rules here. Therefore, it is with great sadness that I deny the former host of *Outdoors with the Pros* the badge of NFL greatness.[131]

---

[128] For many years the NFL acknowledged MVP or Player of the Year awards from a variety of sources, including *The Sporting News*, the United Press, the Associated Press, *Pro Football Weekly*, the Pro Football Writers Association, and the Maxwell Club of Philadelphia. Now the MVP is awarded solely by the Associated Press.

[129] Particularly when you note that he threw 277 career interceptions against 236 touchdowns. In addition he is the placekicker on the All-Time AFL team.

[130] See the entry titled *Nightmare, Nigerian*.

[131] A fairly ridiculous national fishing show on Fox Sports Net.

The third player under the microscope might be the most famous Oakland signal caller, Kenny Stabler. He reached four Pro Bowls, won an MVP award, and had five seasons in which he completed over 60 percent of his passes. Unfortunately, there is more to the story. He never threw more than 27 touchdowns in a single season, and for his career he threw 222 interceptions against 194 touchdowns. Even some of the all-time greats like .Elway were known for throwing a lot of interceptions, but the Broncos legend was still 300–226 on the good side of the ledger. It is hard to call a guy a great quarterback when he threw almost 30 more interceptions than touchdowns.

In fact, the reason you remember Kenny Stabler probably isn't for his greatness on the field, but for his legendary performances *off* the gridiron. Notorious for his partying and general carousing, Stabler was known for telling the defense to hold the other team down in the first half so that he would have time to sober up and win the game in the fourth quarter. In today's game, the piranha-like members of the media would rip him to shreds, but in the 1970's, he was an icon of cool.[132] A rock star in shoulder pads. So there you have it: Ken Stabler was very cool and very good. But still not great.

We can zoom over the entire Los Angeles Raiders era until we arrive back in Oakland (for the second time) at Candidate Number Four, Rich Gannon. Statistically, he might make the best case. The journeyman quarterback finally got his chance in Oakland and delivered huge numbers for a brief period of time. He won the MVP award in 2002; he threw 180 touchdowns against 104 interceptions for his career; he made four straight Pro Bowls and won the MVP award in two of them; and was a 60 percent career passer. However, I watched this man's entire career. He wasn't great. He was solid, effective, crafty, and tough. But great? Come on.

---

[132] Another aspect of Stabler's personality that was cool then but wouldn't be so cool now was the fact that he routinely chain-smoked cigarettes under the bleachers before games and in the locker room at halftime. Thanks to scientific research, *60 Minutes*, the "Truth" advertisement campaign, Russell Crowe's performance in *The Insider*, and those awful tracheotomy holes, smoking isn't really all that cool anymore.

To recap, we have a great kicker who is sometimes remembered as being a great quarterback and a series of players who were very, very good for a relatively short period of time. The Raiders had several famous quarterbacks, quite a few excellent ones, and certainly a handful of instantly recognizable names at the position, but by my count, they've never had a truly great passer wear the silver and black.

(AH)

Quarterbacks, Scrambling: Scrambling Quarterbacks Are *Not* The Wave Of The Future

Vince Young is a talented football player. He took the University of Texas to an NCAA national championship, earned himself millions of dollars as a first-round draft pick, and has proven himself to be a winner early in his NFL career.

If you've seen Young play, you will note that he is extremely mobile. He's also big and strong and has a great arm, but, above all, he can run all over the field. Young can cut past, juke around, and run over would-be defenders.

And every time Young leads his Tennessee Titans team to a victory, it gets the talking heads drooling about quarterbacks like him, declaring that scrambling quarterbacks are the "wave of the future."

I hate when people say this because it isn't true.

This requires some explanation.

When I say that scrambling quarterbacks are not the wave of the future, I don't mean that scrambling quarterbacks won't be vital in upcoming seasons. I'm not trotting out an old party line that says only pocket passers can win titles.

No, when I say that scrambling quarterbacks are not the wave of the future, I mean that can't be true, because it implies that they weren't a wave of the past.

In fact, scrambling quarterbacks have been winning football games, making Pro Bowls, and playing in Super Bowls for decades.

Here are three great scrambling signal callers who prove my point:[133]

Fran Tarkenton. Tarkenton is one of the most famous scramblers of all time and one of the all-time great quarterbacks in NFL history. He amassed 47,003 yards passing and threw for 342 touchdowns. He also racked up 3,674 yards and 32 touchdowns on the ground. He played in nine Pro Bowls and played in three Super Bowls, and is a member of the NFL Hall of Fame. Fans today who marvel at Vince Young's ability to move in the pocket and dodge defenders haven't seen anything until they track down some old clips of Tarkenton weaving through defensive linemen.

Steve Young. Young had even more success on the ground that Tarkenton, totaling 4,239 yards and 43 touchdowns rushing during his NFL career. His most famous run, an incredible, game-winning 49-yard touchdown against the Vikings in 1988, was even made a part of Burger King commercial lore (and, yes, there is such a thing) when the Burger King plastic-headed "King" character was superimposed over Young's body in an ad. The southpaw quarterback (Steve Young, not the "King") wasn't a bad passer either, completing 64.3 percent of his passes and throwing for 232 touchdowns against just 107 interceptions. He made seven Pro Bowls, won two Super Bowls, nabbed a pair of MVP awards, and is in the Hall of Fame.

John Elway. The former Broncos great was known for his cannon arm and cool head under pressure, but it was his ability to scramble that truly separated him from other great quarterbacks. He ran for 3,407 yards and 33 touchdowns in his playing career, but, more importantly, used his legs to avoid the pass rush long enough to find receivers downfield. He was a master at buying time, which is why he threw for 51,475 yards and 300

---

[133] And I'm not evening going to mention Randall Cunningham, but it goes without saying that he is included in this group. I don't mention him here simply because you can read all about him in a separate entry titled *Cunningham, Randall.*

touchdowns despite never playing with a Hall of Fame receiver. Elway played in nine Pro Bowls, won two Super Bowls, has an MVP award to his credit, and is, of course, in the Hall of Fame.

These players were all great passers and team leaders, but what undoubtedly set them apart was their athleticism, speed, instincts, and all the other tools that enabled them to beat defenses with their feet. Whether it was racing for critical first downs, breaking off game-winning touchdown runs, or simply buying time to make big throws, guys like Tarkenton, Young, and Elway were so great because they could scramble.

So the next time you hear someone rave about Vince Young or whoever the next Vince Young might be, just remember that a quarterback who can run isn't something new. Mobile quarterbacks who can make plays with their legs aren't a passing fad or a modern trend or even some freakish evolutionary process. These guys have been around through the years, elevating the game and carving out a place in history.

The bottom line is that scrambling quarterbacks are not the wave of anything. They're just a great weapon—past, present, or future.

(AH)

Question, Answer To The Trivia: You Did *Not* Know The Answer To The Trivia Question

In *Answer, Trying to Figure Out the*, we presented a football brainteaser about two men who played for the St. Louis Cardinals at the same time, wearing the same number 21. You were told to turn here to get the answer.

Now, I'll admit that there is a part of me that was tempted to leave this section blank or make it look like there was some error at the printing press just to try to drive you crazy. In fact, there is a very large part of me that wanted to do that.

Then I realized that it would be easy for one of you to track me down and beat me over the head with a lead pipe. So, here's the answer.

Terry Metcalf wore number 21 for the Cardinals from 1973 through 1977, and made the Pro Bowl a couple seasons.

Bake McBride also wore number 21 for the Cardinals from 1973 through 1977, and was selected Rookie of the Year.

But while Terry Metcalf was a running back for the *football* Cardinals, Bake McBride was an outfielder for the *baseball* Cardinals.

That's right—for many years the football and baseball teams in St. Louis were both known as the Cardinals.

And no one remembers why.

I mean, how difficult would it have been to come up with another name for one of the teams?

At the same time, how difficult would it have been for Bake McBride's parents to come up with a better first name for their son?

Bake? Seriously?

That's the best you could do, Mr. and Mrs. McBride?

Bake?

(MK)

Rams, Cleveland: That Is *Not* A Typo

Younger readers of this book may believe that the Rams have always played in St. Louis.

Older readers know that is not so. They know that the Rams previously played in Los Angeles (and for a time played in Anaheim, California, although they were still known as the Los Angeles Rams), and they had a storied history in L.A. Roman Gabriel. Jack Snow. Rosey Grier. Merlin Olsen. Lance Rentzel. Eric Dickerson. Warren Beatty in *Heaven Can Wait*.

Living in Los Angeles as I do now, I am not surprised by the number of football fans who bemoan the loss of the Rams to St. Louis.

It still is remarkable to me that a city as large and as entertainment-driven as Los Angeles does not have a professional football team at this time, but we don't.[134] What does surprise me is how many football fans in Los Angeles believe that the Rams "always" played in Los Angeles prior to the move to St. Louis. It's just not so.

I suspect that anyone from Cleveland who was born before 1940 or so would be happy to tell you that the Rams in fact played in Cleveland until 1945. (And if you happen to meet anyone from Cleveland who was born before 1940, please ask him why they built Municipal Stadium right on the lake. Man, that place was cold.)

The Rams are hardly the only NFL team to change cities.

Not to confuse things, but for those fans who believe the Cardinals "always" played in St. Louis before moving to Arizona, eventually leading to the Rams' move from Los Angeles to St. Louis, the Cardinals in fact played in Chicago until 1959.

The Cleveland Rams and the Chicago Cardinals. Say those names aloud a hundred times each, and they still won't sound right. Seriously, go ahead. I'll wait.

The Indianapolis Colts used to be the Baltimore Colts.

Oh, and the Chicago Bears? Used to be the Decatur Staleys. Really. Decatur is a city. Or a town. Perhaps a county.

And the Baltimore Ravens used to be the Cleveland Browns.

And the Kansas City Chiefs used to be the Dallas Texans.

And the Detroit Lions used to be the Portsmouth Spartans. No kidding.

And the Washington Redskins used to be the Boston Redskins.

I haven't even started on the teams that are no longer around in any form—how the Toledo Maroons became the Kenosha Maroons, or how the Duluth Eskimos became the Orange Tornadoes.

I don't know about you, but I feel fairly certain that I would have rooted for the Duluth Eskimos and the Orange Tornadoes, just for their names.

(MK)

---

[134] You can read all about this in the entry titled *Bay, Green.*

Receiver, Unsung: Marvin Harrison Does *Not* Receive Enough Credit

Most fans know that Marvin Harrison is a good wide receiver. Some even recognize that he is a great wide receiver. But I doubt very much that many football fans realize just how great he is.

One way to illustrate his greatness would be to point out his career stats, which are mighty impressive. However, to do so will probably overwhelm the reader in a sea of numbers. Plus, at the time I am writing this entry he is an active player and therefore constantly accumulating statistics. Any numbers I throw at you are going to be irrelevant by the time you read this book.

That said, there is one number that puts Harrison's greatness in the proper perspective. That number is 143.

As in the number of receptions he hauled in during the 2002 season.

As in, the most receptions in a single season in NFL history.

By 20.

Herman Moore (discussed in the entry titled *Moore, Herman*) once held the NFL single-season record for receptions with 123, which was an impressive total.

Rather, it was impressive to everyone except for Marvin Harrison, who caught 8 or more passes in a whopping 12 of his 16 games that season.

Seriously, 143 receptions?

Harrison didn't just break Herman Moore's record, he shattered it. By accumulating 16 percent more receptions than anyone in history, the Colts wideout likely created an impossible standard for receivers to come. It would be like a running back breaking Eric Dickerson's single-season rushing yards record of 2,105. . . by racking up 2,441 yards. Or a quarterback topping Tom Brady's single-season record of 50 passing touchdowns. . . by throwing for 58 scores.

They say records are made to be broken, but the expression isn't "records are made to be shattered."

Except in Marvin Harrison's case.

See, I told you he was great.

(AH)

Reception, Immaculate: Franco Harris' Famous Catch Was *Not* Immaculate

The sports world provides many things to many people: entertainment, competition, a teaching tool for life lessons, a salve for relationships, a way to make a living. One of the underrated services that sports provides is being a lifeline for puns and egregious attempts at word play.

Open up a major sports Web site right at this moment, and you will see at least one headline is a pun or a lame play on words. Pittsburgh pulls out an improbable victory? You get "Steal City." If Cleveland gets off to a 0–7 start, you will see "Brownout." New England gets caught stealing signals and it is "Patriot Games." (Whoops, that last one actually happened.)

There is also an obsession to name everything.

"The Catch."

"The Shot Heard 'Round the World."

"The Drive."

You get the idea.

So when these two incredible sports traditions join forces, the results can be disastrous. Which is probably why we ended up slapping a nonsensical name on one of football's most memorable plays.

The "Immaculate Reception" refers to one of the craziest plays in NFL history: Pittsburgh Steelers running back Franco Harris hauling in a deflected pass just inches off the turf and racing for a touchdown to defeat the Oakland Raiders in a 1972 AFC Divisional round playoff game.

The name supposedly came about because a random fan called up one of the Steelers announcers, Myron Cope, and urged him to use the phrase to describe the catch. And use it he did. And we've been calling it that ever since.

Now, while I can certainly appreciate how these things come into being, that doesn't mean it's accurate. Because this catch was a lot of things, and miraculous is probably one of them, but the one thing it was not was immaculate.

"Immaculate" does *not* mean "miraculous," or "magical," or "surprising." No, "Immaculate" is defined by *Merriam-Webster's Dictionary* as "having no stain or blemish; pure." Do yourself a favor and find some footage of that play. No stain or blemish? Pure? That catch was Barnum and Bailey on the gridiron. The only thing missing was the Big Top.

Obviously, the phrase is meant as a play on words (surprise, surprise) on the Immaculate Conception of the Virgin Mary. The problem is that the phrase Immaculate Conception isn't meant to convey "miracle birth." It is meant to convey "birth without sin, or stain."

A pass thrown on fourth-and-ten with 22 seconds left in the game. A pass intended for fullback John Fuqua that was broken up by Raiders safety Jack Tatum and sent bouncing into the air.[135] A ball scooped off the turf just inches from the ground.[136] One of the strangest, circus-like plays in NFL history. And we call *this play* "immaculate"?

Let this be a lesson to all of us not to use puns or try to make a play on words without knowing all the facts.

Or without knowing the meaning of the words we use.

(AH)

Rentzel, Lance: Lance Rentzel Was *Not* Lance Alworth

See *Alworth, Lance.*

(MK)

---

[135] There is controversy over which player the ball bounced off of before winding up with Harris. At the time, NFL rules provided that the ball could not touch two offensive players successively. It looked as if it may have touched Fuqua just before Harris caught it, which would have made it illegal. None of the footage or photographs of the play clearly shows what happened.

[136] There is also controversy surrounding whether or not the ball bounced before Harris snagged it. Suffice to say, this remains a controversial play.

Returns, Kick: Clipping Penalties On Kick Returns Are *Not* Harsh Enough

If you want, you can go ahead and file this one under its other name: "Yellow Flags, Too Many." If you watch the NFL[137] then you know that recent seasons have been marred by penalty flags. Specifically, nearly every kick return, whether kickoffs or punts, was negated by a penalty. One *Monday Night Football* game in 2005 featured so many special teams penalties that the normally unflappable Al Michaels actually started whining about it on the air.[138] Touchdowns were called back; 15-yard gains were called back; heck, even returns that lost yardage featured a penalty that moved the return team even farther in reverse.

Before doing any more complaining, allow me to discuss why this is so important. First, kick returns should be some of the most exciting plays in each game. Dante Hall of the Chiefs turned returns into an art form during the 2003 season, even getting some MVP hype midway through the season. Of course, a few of those returns featured a questionable block or two that helped Dante fly down the field, but correct me if I'm wrong in saying that it was some exciting football. Desmond Howard won a Super Bowl MVP by virtue of a fantastic punt return. Devin Hester burst on the scene as a rookie in 2006 to pretty much single-handedly garner the Chicago Bears the top seed in the NFC playoffs. You would be hard-pressed to find a play that rivals a punt return for pure excitement potential, and there are few plays that can swing the momentum of a game like a long kickoff return for a touchdown.

Unfortunately, with all the yellow flags littering the field, returns have largely been reduced to a simple waiting game: waiting to see which referee throws his flag first. Which leads us to the second

---

[137] Actually, I am just going to assume that you do, since you are reading this book.
[138] This was way back when ABC was still doing *Monday Night Football* and Al Michaels still worked for ABC, and thus, Al Michaels was broadcasting a Monday night game. Okay, I know it wasn't "way back," but it sure does feel that way.

reason that the excessive penalties are horrible: they slow the game down to a crawl. It is one thing if a guy calls for a fair catch, takes a knee in the end zone, or gets wrapped up for very little gain; fans can live with the occasional boring return. What becomes excruciating is the stoppage of play after nearly every kick. The referees huddle up, waddle around, and then offer up what feels like a five-minute explanation of the penalty.[139] Nothing kills the flow of a game like too many penalties. In fact, I've taken to recording the games on my TiVo just so I can blow through the returns (and inevitable penalties) on triple fast forward.

Despite my hostility toward the referees, I don't blame them for this problem. They are merely trying to do their jobs by calling the penalties that they see during the course of play. No, the real problem is that players are in fact committing those penalties on nearly every special teams plays. Perhaps it is a risk-versus-reward phenomenon that causes these players to attempt a quick push to the back or to take a guy out with a blatant clip. In many cases it is that exact illegal block that springs the return man for a huge gain. However, in a fairly significant number of cases, the illegal block does *absolutely nothing* for the runner. It winds up being a completely idiotic penalty that leaves coaches, teammates, and fans frustrated beyond belief.

All told, we have a brutal situation on our hands. A plethora of blocking penalties are being committed on special teams. The officials are calling them regardless of severity or impact on the play. Players are committing the penalties on pretty much every kick. In many cases, they are committing the penalty even when it doesn't do the return man any good. Taking all that information into account, there seems to be one way, and one way only, to bring the excitement back to the fans: create a severe enough penalty for "blocks in the back" on kickoff and punt returns that players stop trying to get away with it. If the penalty for a block in the back was automatic

---

[139] I never truly appreciated how long and boring the explanations were until my wife pointed it out to me. Every time the referee starts to explain the call, she deadpans, "Once upon a time ..." It brings the house down. Seriously, take note of this next time you watch a game. It will either double the entertainment value or drive you absolutely insane.

ejection, do you think we would see players committing that penalty on every kick? I'm guessing not.

Obviously, ejecting a guy for blocking a player in the back is probably too extreme. It seems easy to follow the old "if you see the numbers on the back of his jersey, don't hit him" rule, but the fact is, things could get dicey. There are plenty of plays in which gunners get pushed into a defender. Other plays feature guys stumbling into mistakes. One can only imagine the reaction of a coach and his player on a controversial call where it could go either way. Did he hit the guy's shoulder? Did he block him in the side or in the back? Things could get ugly. Mike Shanahan could shatter the record for challenges. Jon Gruden could very well kill a special teams player out of sheer intimidation. However, just because an ejection would cause too many problems doesn't mean that the current 15-yard penalty is getting the job done either. Obviously, the penalty isn't severe enough, or players would stop doing it.

Consider the ways that governments can patrol speeding motorists. On one extreme, you can impose very low fines and allocate a tremendous amount of resources in enforcing the penalty. Would-be speeders are deterred from speeding by the likelihood of getting caught. The other extreme would be to create an enormous fine and then send out the occasional patrol car. The thought of having to pay thousands of dollars would scare people into driving at the speed limit, despite the low chance of being caught. Most government bodies choose a regime somewhere in the middle.

Right now, the NFL needs to recalibrate its method of deterrence for "blocking in the back" penalties.[140] The referees are obviously calling a ton of them, so "enforcement of the fine" isn't the issue here. The problem is that the penalty isn't severe enough. The best possible "fine" in this case would have to be discovered by experimenting with various penalties, but I'm guessing that something in the range of 25-40 yards would do the trick. Can you imagine

---

[140] Why did they have to change the name from "clipping" to "blocking in the back"? "Clipping" is easier to write and it flows better in a sentence. Very frustrating.

the difference if a clipping penalty resulted in a 40-yard penalty?[141] Coaches would go insane if players were stupid enough to block somebody in the back. The officials wouldn't have to throw nearly as many flags, because the occasional enforcement would send the proper message. Players would stop committing needless penalties and the excitement would return.

In this world, kick return specialists would once again be faced with the nearly impossible task of eluding an entire team on their way to the end zone. We will hold our breath in anticipation, knowing that when a guy spins to miss the first gunner, jukes the second guy, cuts back against the overpursuing wave of defenders, spots a crease and darts through with a burst of speed, stiff arms the punter, and wins the race down the sideline for the touchdown, that we won't have to hear the play-by-play guy announce in a glum voice, "Hold everything, we've got a flag down on the play."

The most exciting play in football will be back.

(AH)

Riders, Rough: The Rough Riders Are *Not* The Roughriders

They play football in Canada.

Seriously, I'm not making that up.

The field is a little different, the rules are a little different, they have something called a "rouge," and their offensive players seem to be allowed to run all over the place before the ball is snapped. But, still, it is football.

They even have a professional football league called the Canadian Football League. Or, in French, Ligue Canadienne de Football.

Although it has not always been the case, the league has normally had eight teams.

---

[141] That's right, I said "clipping." Kicking it old school.

And, for a great many years, those eight teams included teams known as the Ottawa Rough Riders and the Saskatchewan Roughriders.

Yes, the Rough Riders and the Roughriders. Playing at the same time. And frequently against each other.

It's not too difficult to imagine the confusion for those listening to games on the radio. "It's Roughriders 24, Rough Riders 23, with two minutes left to go. The Rough Riders have the ball on the Roughriders' 40-yard line. It certainly looks like the Rough Riders have the momentum now, doesn't it, Pierre? Hold on a second! There's a penalty flag down! Is it on the Rough Riders or the Roughriders? Oh my god, it's on the Rough Riders!"

Now, I am sure that there is a long and intriguing story as to how two teams in the same league wound up with essentially the same nickname. But I don't care about that story, and neither do you. All we care about is that, with both the English and French languages at their disposal, offering quite literally hundreds of thousands of possible nicknames, the Canadian Football League was unable to come up with eight *different* names for their teams.

I suppose it could have been worse. Like the boxer George Foreman who named all of his sons George, I guess they could have named all eight of the teams the Roughriders. Would've made it awfully easy to inscribe the championship trophy. They could've inscribed it before the season even began.

(MK)

Romo, Tony: Starting Quarterbacks Should *Not* Be Holders For Field Goals And Extra Points

There is an entry in this book (a very funny one) that discusses the plot from the movie *Ace Ventura: Pet Detective*. The plot of this movie is centered on a cross-dressing kicker who wants to kill Dan Marino, because back in the day, Dan the Man held the ball incorrectly ("laces out!"), causing the kicker Ray Finkle to miss a crucial kick.

Hundred bucks says this guy making a perfect hold is a backup quarterback.

An element of that plot always bothered me. No, not the part about a former kicker trying to kill an NFL legend. It also wasn't the part about a redheaded woman turning out to be a dark-haired man. Rather, it was the fact that Dan Marino was ever the holder on a field goal attempt.

It used to drive me absolutely crazy. I mean, everyone knows that the *backup* quarterback does the holding on field goals and extra points. And everyone knows that Dan Marino was never a backup anything. For years, I felt superior to the writers of *Ace Ventura* because of this oversight.

Then the Tony Romo Game happened.[142]

If you aren't clear on the Tony Romo Game, you didn't read the footnote at the end of the previous sentence.

Well you need to, because I'm not going to repeat what happened. But needless to say, the Tony Romo game proved me wrong

---

[142] The Tony Romo game refers to a wild-card playoff game between the Seattle Seahawks and Dallas Cowboys on January 6, 2007. In that game, Dallas had moved the ball down the field to set up a potential game-winning, 19-yard field goal with just 1:19 remaining in the game. Unfortunately for the Cowboys, Tony Romo fumbled the snap, resulting in a Seattle win and the unforgettable image of Dallas' starting quarterback lying face-first on the field in agony.

in regard to my smug feelings toward Jack Bernstein, Jim Shadyac, and Jim Carrey.[143]

On the other hand, it proved me right about another closely held belief.

And that is. . . oh, just read the title. Do we have to spell everything out for you?

(AH)

Sanders, Deion: Bo Jackson Was *Not* The Best Two-Sport Athlete Of All Time

Bo Jackson and Deion Sanders were memorable, flashy athletes who rose to prominence around the same time and became famous for the same reason—they were gifted football players who also played professional baseball.

You could argue that Bo Jackson and Deion Sanders were the best two-sport athletes of all time. You would be wrong, because the best two-sport athlete of all time was Jim Thorpe.

However, setting aside Thorpe, who played in an entirely different era of professional sports, I am still puzzled by the fact that people think Bo Jackson was the best two-sport athlete of the modern era.

Did these people forget about Neon Deion?

Bo's inadequacies as a baseball player are addressed in *Strikeouts, Bo Knows*. Let's focus on football for a minute.

Each of these athletic marvels was far better on the gridiron than on the diamond, so it is only appropriate to resolve the debate about which was the better two-sport athlete by determining which was the superior football player.[144]

---

[143] The three gentlemen with screenwriting credits on the movie.

[144] For those of you who are sticklers for detail and find it unfair that Bo's baseball career is discussed in detail in his entry in this book, while Deion's is dismissed, I present a quick breakdown of Deion Sanders, Baseball Player. Sanders played parts of nine major league seasons, hitting .263 with a rather poor .319 on base percentage. He stole 186 bases and played an adequate right field. His best year was with the Atlanta Braves in 1992, when he hit .304 and pounded 14 triples in just 97 regular season games, and then went on to hit .533 with five stolen bases against Toronto in the World Series. That about sums it up.

Bo was a freakishly talented running back with a Heisman Trophy to his name and big play ability in his game. He was particularly adept at breaking off big runs on *Monday Night Football* and dominating the Seattle Seahawks (often, he performed these feats in tandem). As a side note, I was a youngster growing up in the state of Washington at the time. But, I promise, I'm being objective about this. I should also mention that Bo racked up an impressive 5.4 yards per carry during his short football career. There is no doubt that he was incredibly talented.

But he was no Deion Sanders. "Prime Time" went to eight consecutive Pro Bowls, ran back 9 of his 53 career interceptions for touchdowns, returned 9 kicks (6 punts and 3 kickoffs) for scores, and even caught 36 passes as a receiver for the Cowboys during the 1996 season. In addition, he was named the 1994 AP Defensive Player of the Year and played on consecutive Super Bowl winners in San Francisco (1994) and Dallas (1995).

Bo Jackson was an amazing athlete with a propensity for highlights, a great series of Nike commercials, and one heck of a football card (the one where he is holding a bat over his shoulder pads). But while he might have done so had he stayed healthy, he never actually rose to the level of a Hall of Fame *football* player. Deion Sanders, on the other hand, is a mortal lock for Canton. He, too, was supremely talented and able to generate excitement with highlight reel plays. Except in his case, he reinvented the game along the way, pretty much defining the term "cover corner."

So while Jim Thorpe is probably the right answer to the question of "who is the greatest two-sport athlete of all time," there is no debate that Bo Jackson is the *wrong* answer.

Because among modern athletes, there was nobody better than Deion Sanders.

Which he would probably tell you himself, were you to ask.

(AH)

Scientist, The Mad: Clinton Portis Is *Not* Always Clinton Portis

Clinton Portis is an interesting fellow. More interesting than the average NFL player, in fact.

This is not because of his ability (awesome) or his injury history (checkered), but rather because of his series of alter egos—characters that he breaks out when dealing with the media.

Like a method actor getting into character or Sacha Baron Cohen doing interviews only as Borat, Portis is fond of totally and completely adopting new personas. He dons a uniform, gives the character a "back story," and then settles in. Don't believe me? Check out some of the costumes that Portis sported during press conferences:

The Mad Scientist. The entry's namesake and a Portis favorite, this costume came complete with a white wig and sci-fi sunglasses. Supposedly, this character electrocuted himself—thus, the white hair and ability to break down any defensive formation.

Southeast Jerome. According to **ClintonPortis.com**, this Lone Ranger character, complete with mask, died on October 30, 2005 (just three days after his first appearance at a press conference).

Dr. I Don't Know. Sporting an orange wig and a fake moustache (plus some rather amazing oversized sunglasses), Dr. I Don't Know was the character who announced Southeast Jerome's demise.

Sheriff Gonna Getcha. Perhaps the best name of the bunch, this character was looking into the disappearance of Southeast Jerome. According to the Web site, Sheriff Gonna Getcha has "leather balls" because he's "tough" and was interested in questioning Rhonde Barber of the Tampa Bay Buccaneers.

Dolla Bill. Like a *Saturday Night Live* sketch gone horribly wrong, this Portis persona sported sunglasses spelling out the word cool and copious amounts of chest hair in addition to a purple wig. This character looks a little like Prince and was created to protest a fine from the NFL.

Reverend Gonna Change. A good luck charm brought in to help a struggling Redskins team. It seems to have worked, as the 5–6 'Skins rattled off five straight wins to make the playoffs.

Kid Bro Sweets. More sunglasses (a giant heart-shaped pair), another wig (yellow), and the addition of some shoulder pads on the outside of his clothes, as well as an eye patch. Supposedly, he loves Payday candy bars and lost an eye when a snake attacked him (thus, the eye patch).

Inspector 2-2. This might be Portis' strangest costume. In addition to a glasses-fake nose-moustache contraption that resembled a Mr. Potato Head doll, Inspector 2-2 also managed to wear a cowboy hat on top of same fake pigtails on top of an old-fashioned leather Redskins helmet. This character was brought in to question the other Barber twin, Tiki, about the disappearance of Southeast Jerome.

Coach Janky Spanky. This character came complete with a giant headset, fake ears, a whistle, a clipboard, and coach's tight shirt and shorts.

Dolomite Jenkins. Portis brought this character out in 2006 to encourage people to vote for teammate Santana Moss for Player of the Week. He wore a "Vote for Santana" T-shirt and moon boots approximating the movie character Napoleon Dynamite.

And occasionally, usually for about three hours on Sundays, Clinton Portis just goes by Clinton Portis.

(AH)

Simpson, O.J.: O.J. Simpson Did *Not* Kill His Wife

How many times have you heard someone say that Hall of Fame running back O.J. Simpson killed his wife?

A thousand times, I'd bet.

Well, I would like to state unequivocally that it simply is not true.

O.J. Simpson did *not* kill his wife.

I state that not as a theory, not as a belief, and not as mere speculation.

I state that as a fact.

These things I know are true: the sky is blue, taxes are due on April 15 (unless it is a weekend), and O.J. Simpson did not kill his wife.

Those things are *facts*.

And please do not try to debate me on this issue, because I will not do so.

It is a simple, unassailable fact that O.J. Simpson did *not* kill his wife.

It simply never happened.

Are you relying upon the fact that a jury acquitted him of murder, you ask. *Are you relying on the fact that he was not found guilty so, therefore, he didn't do it in a legal sense?*

Not at all.

Are you relying upon your own belief about whether he killed his wife?

Not at all.

Are you relying upon some inside information you have about someone else killing Simpson's wife?

No.

Then how on earth can you say, unequivocally, that O.J. Simpson did not kill his wife?

Because he didn't kill his wife.

He killed his ex-wife.

A technicality, yes, but in speaking about O.J. Simpson, it is important to always make sure that we get our facts straight. Why? Because those people who still try to defend him always seem to misstate the facts. Those people tend to come up with crazy theories unsupported by the facts.

It was his son who killed them, they say.

It was his friend, What's-His-Name, the guy who was driving the Bronco when Simpson tried to escape! (A.C. Cowlings, formerly of the Bills, 49ers, etc., etc.)

It was an ex-boyfriend!

It was someone trying to frame O.J. because of a bad business deal!

It was the LAPD that did it!

No, no, no, no, no.

It is a plain and simple fact that O.J. Simpson killed his ex-wife.

And her friend, Ron Goldman.

Killed them in cold blood, as they say. Put a knife to their necks and killed them, then fled.

Am I afraid that O.J. Simpson is going to sue me for saying that he killed his ex-wife and her friend, perhaps accusing me of defamation?

Not for a minute.

Why?

For the very same reason that O.J. Simpson hasn't sued anyone else for defamation for saying he is a murderer—the truth is an absolute defense to a defamation claim. And it is the truth that he is a murderer.

Now, here is my problem. As a lawyer, I repeatedly have to explain to people why it is that a murderer like O.J. Simpson somehow was not convicted of murder, and instead has been allowed to walk the streets for more than a decade now. He's been allowed to dine in the same restaurants as those of us who haven't killed other people (and, more specifically, haven't killed the mother of our children or a young man we've never even met). He's been allowed to live in the same neighborhoods as we do. He's been allowed to go to the movies, and attend sporting events, and play golf.

Why?

The answer, I'm afraid, comes in several parts.

First, our jury system is a terribly flawed one. To pull a dozen laypersons off the street and expect them to pay attention during several months of testimony, then to apply a set of sometimes-complex laws, is asking too much. Most people have difficulty sitting through a two-hour movie. Imagine sitting through four of them a day for several months. And imagine that they are boring and dry, like most trials are. We are lucky that the Simpson jury was still awake at the end of the trial.

Second, as much as the system is flawed, the jury in O.J. Simpson's criminal trial simply did not do their job. They were taken in by the wild theories and ridiculous sideshows that were presented by Simpson's legal team. The evidence against Simpson was not just strong. It was absolutely overwhelming. But the jury ignored it because they were taken in by all of the smoke and mirrors presented by Simpson's lawyers. That's what you do when you don't have a case—you try to confuse the jury. Here, it worked.

Third, the prosecutors, Marcia Clark and Christopher Darden, did a poor job. I suspect that even they are not proud of their efforts. I could detail all of the prosecutors' many errors and deficiencies, but that would be more interesting to lawyers than to football fans, so I won't. And I'm not saying that they were overmatched by Simpson's so-called "Dream Team"—and most lawyers will tell you that Simpson's legal team did not deserve such a nickname—but instead that the prosecutors made a number of basic errors. For example, asking O.J. to try on the glove. To this day, I cannot understand why they made such a request. Was there anyone in the world—and I mean anyone—who was questioning whether the glove that was found at the crime scene fit Simpson? Absolutely not. It hadn't even crossed anyone's mind. Until the prosecutors asked him to try the glove on, that is. And, as everyone knows, Simpson proclaimed that the glove didn't fit. And he made that now-famous statement without ever having to take the stand to testify in his own case.

Fourth, and finally, it's the fault of the entire legal profession. I am not an apologist for the legal profession. I believe the profession deserves all the criticisms and jokes aimed at it. There are too many unethical or incompetent lawyers in the profession, and little is ever done about them. Worse, the legal system rewards parties and their attorneys not for telling the truth, but for hiding it, and shaping it, and changing it. O.J. Simpson's lawyers didn't care about the truth. In fact, the rumor has always been that they specifically asked Simpson not to tell them whether he had killed his ex-wife and her friend. You see, if he had confessed to them, then they would not have been allowed to defend him in the way that they did. For them, it wasn't about the truth. It was about winning. And that may be the biggest problem with the legal system. Gamesmanship, trickery, and showmanship are more important than finding the truth. Winning is all that matters, even if the result is patently unfair, even if justice is not served.

Okay, I'm going to get off my soapbox now. I'm tired of typing O.J. Simpson's name. I'm tired of hearing about him. I wish he would just go away forever.

And I'll bet the NFL and the University of Southern California feel the same way.

(MK)

Singletary, Mike: Mike Singletary Was *Not* The Next Dick Butkus

When the Bears drafted linebacker Mike Singletary in 1981, he was touted as being the next Dick Butkus.

He wasn't.

But you have to admit, he came awfully darned close.

(MK)

Size, Field: Most Football Fans Do *Not* Know The Dimensions Of A Football Field

Imagine that you are on a television game show. It is the final round and all you have to do is answer one question to win a million dollars. The host turns to you and says, "For all the money, can you tell us how long a football field is?"

Without a moment's hesitation, you shout, "One hundred yards!"

And you watch a million dollars slip through your fingers, because you are wrong. Very, very wrong.

But everyone knows a football field is 100 yards long, you say.

Well, everyone is wrong.

A football field is 120 yards long.

Everyone forgets to include the two end zones, which are each 10 yards deep. Add that to the 100 yards from goal line to goal line and what do you get? 120.

Admittedly, that is a bit of a trick question. Which is why they saved it for the final round of our fictional game show.

The next time someone professes to be a football expert, ask him how wide a football field is.

I have never received a correct response when I've asked that question, even when I've asked it of people who played high school or college football.

So, how wide is a football field?

It's 53⅓ yards wide.

How hard is it to remember that fact?

Put this book down, wait a couple hours, then see if you remember what the width of a football field is. If you don't cheat by writing it down, there's a 50 percent chance that you'll forget.

Which is why I write it down.

Seriously, I keep it in my wallet. It's on the same slip of paper where I wrote down my wife's birthdate and our anniversary. [145]

(MK)

---

[145] By the way, a Canadian football field is 65 yards wide and 130 yards long. Only God knows why. And my wife's birthday is March 6. Our anniversary is either November 20 or 21—my handwriting got smudged a bit.

Skating, Figure: Terry Bradshaw Was *Not* Married To Dorothy Hamill

If I had a dollar for every time I've heard someone say that former Pittsburgh Steeler quarterback Terry Bradshaw used to be married to former Olympic figure skating champion Dorothy Hamill, I'd probably have a good twenty dollars.

Meaning that I've heard at least twenty people say that Bradshaw used to be married to Ms. Hamill.

And I say "Ms. Hamill," rather than "Hamill" or "Dorothy," as a sign of respect for one of the great American athletes of the twentieth century, and the only one whom I've had a crush on for thirty years.

(I have a crush on Venus Williams, too, but it hasn't been thirty years. Yet.)

(Oh, hold on a second. I just remembered Chris Evert. Maybe I should just stop.)

In any event, the two were never married to each other and, to my knowledge, never dated.

Bradshaw was married to an Olympic figure skater, it just wasn't Ms. Hamill. He was married to Jo Jo Starbuck.

Which really was her name.

And she really was an excellent figure skater. She was a three-time U.S. pairs figure-skating champion with her partner, Kenneth Shelley.

How do I know these things?

Don't ask.

Please.

(MK)

Soul, Selling Your: Kurt Warner Did *Not* Make A Deal With The Devil

The Kurt Warner story is a truly fascinating tale.[146] From 1999 to 2001, Warner went on a tear that rivals any three-year stretch ever compiled by an NFL quarterback. He won a Super Bowl, two MVP awards, and broke several records. In 1999 he threw for 4,353 yards and 41 touchdowns and then threw for 414 yards in route to a Super Bowl MVP award. In 2000 he tied an NFL record by throwing for at least 300 yards in each of the first six games of the season. And in 2001 he threw for a whopping 4,830 yards, which is the second highest single-season total of all time.[147]

The only thing more remarkable about that three-year run (which was very remarkable) was pretty much everything that happened both before and after.

Prior to briefly becoming the most devastating passer the NFL had ever seen, Warner was a journeyman quarterback who bounced around in various professional leagues and famously bagged groceries for a period of time when things hit rock bottom. He played for the Iowa Barnstormers in the Arena Football League and then the Amsterdam Admirals in what was known as NFL Europa before it was disbanded.[148] From the time he left northern Iowa in 1994 to the moment Rams' starter Trent Green went down with an injury during the 1999 preseason, there was absolutely no indication that Warner would be the quarterback destined to run the "Greatest Show on Turf" offense, rewrite the record books, and lead St. Louis to a Super Bowl victory.

Of course, history is filled with rags-to-riches stories whether it is in business, politics, or sports. Warner's ascension may have been on the extreme end of the spectrum, but, if anything, it just proved that

---

[146] Please do not confuse <u>K</u>urt Warner with <u>C</u>urt Warner, the former Seattle Seahawks running back who is discussed in the entry titled *Alexander, Shaun*. They are not the same person. Seriously.

[147] Dan Marino holds the top mark with 5,084 yards in 1984.

[148] The league made it through three names before shutting down in 2007. It was founded in 1991 as the World League of American Football before changing to NFL Europe in 1997.

the little engine really could make it in the big bad world of professional football. No, it wasn't just Warner's humble beginnings that make his career such an enigma.

You see, no sooner had Warner toppled the football world, when everything started to fall apart. Coming off a loss to the Patriots in Super Bowl XXXVI, the Rams opened the 2002 season 0–3 and Warner looked positively brutal. While everyone assumed he would eventually find the range (much like the big guns of the Civil War would require a few shots to get things lined up), this was not the case. Warner struggled throughout the season, and a guy who had amassed a 103.4 career passing rating entering that season, finished 2002 with a meager 67.4 mark.

By 2003 Warner had fumbled six times in the season opener and lost his job to Marc Bulger. He suffered through a miserable stint in New York where he struggled with sacks and fumbles and was eventually replaced by Eli Manning. He put up good numbers in 2005 but couldn't produce touchdowns for a bad Arizona team and eventually suffered another injury that forced Josh McCown to finish the season under center. In 2006 Warner struggled and was replaced yet again, this time by rookie Matt Leinart. The year 2007 was a bit kinder, as Warner replaced an injured Leinart and threw for 3,417 yards and 27 touchdowns for the 8–8 Cardinals. But that's the best Warner has experienced in the past five years.

Needless to say, it isn't what people expected coming on the heels of that glorious stretch of MVP-level performances. And when folks look at the five years of futility leading up to 1999 and the years of struggles after 2001, it only makes that three-year run of success look more magical and improbable than ever.

However, this is where I need to stop you. Do not let your imagination run wild. Do not conjure up images of Kurt Warner rubbing a genie bottle and making three wishes (for three good seasons, which isn't very bright, because he could have wished for an entire great career and had two remaining wishes). And above all, do not let yourself believe that Kurt Warner sold his soul to the devil.

The concept of selling one's soul to the devil in exchange for success seems to have first surfaced in the 1937 short story *The Devil and Daniel Webster* by Stephen Vincent Benet. In the story, a farmer named Jabez Stone sells his soul in exchange for seven years of prosperity. After the seven years have passed, the devil comes back to collect but the gifted orator Daniel Webster intercedes to talk him out of it. Webster bests the devil that day but is saddled with a variety of cursed predictions, including the deaths of his sons in war and an inability to become president.[149]

Another example of this concept comes in the legend surrounding Robert Johnson's music career. The legendary bluesman was supposedly scolded and embarrassed at a local bar by the great musician Son House and after that, disappeared for a period of time. When he returned, he was a genius on the guitar, which led to the myth that Johnson had gone to the "crossroads" to sell his soul to the devil in exchange for musical talent. Obviously, this overlooks the possibility that Johnson was merely *practicing* during that time period, but let's not ruin the story.[150]

Now, to get back to Warner. Like Jabez Stone and his seven years of prosperity and Robert Johnson and his sudden genius, the former grocery bagger from Iowa went from nothing to something seemingly overnight. Then, he went back to (virtually) nothing again. Because of that, people have wondered aloud whether Warner sold his soul to the devil.

Obviously, this is not the case. First of all, this seems like kind of a tough thing to actually do, from a logistical standpoint. Additionally, Warner is a very religious man. Not only that, but his deal would have expired after three years, which seems like a pretty short run. If he did make such a deal, then he's not a very fierce negotiator.

---

[149] Amazingly, all of these predictions came true. Or perhaps it is not so amazing, since the short story was based on Webster's life.

[150] Perhaps the best thing about the Robert Johnson crossroads myth is that it led to the Ralph Macchio movie of the same name. Somehow, Daniel LaRusso found time between *The Karate Kid* and *The Karate Kid II* to shoot *Crossroads*, an unintentionally hilarious movie about Eugene "Lightning Boy" Martone traveling to the crossroads to find a lost song of Robert Johnson. I assure you, it is as awesome as it sounds—particularly the guitar duel at the end with Stevie Vai.

Kurt Warner never went near this place.

Finally, reaching for explanations like "a deal with Lucifer" seems to ignore the obvious reasons for Warner's rise and fall.

Before his success, he was victimized by the whims of the capricious world of NFL sports. He went to the wrong school, probably had the wrong 40-yard dash times, whatever. Therefore, his success was a product of mere opportunity coupled with the perfect system for his quick release and pinpoint style. Unfortunately, a thumb injury suffered during the 2000 season eventually caught up with him and stripped him of that accuracy. So that is why he stopped being great.

It's all pretty simple, actually. Which, I know, is boring, but what can you do? So there you have it folks: Kurt Warner did not make a deal with the devil. If you were holding out hope otherwise, I'm sorry to be the one to break it to you.

(AH)

Stadium, Giants: The New York Giants Do *Not* Play In New York

There is a team in the NFC known as the New York Giants. You know them. They used to be one of the NFL's powerhouses back in the 1950s and early 1960s, when they had Frank Gifford and Y.A. Tittle. They had a great run under Bill Parcells in the 1980s and 1990s, with Phil Simms as their quarterback. Oh, and they just won the 2007 Super Bowl. See *Tyree, David.*

For many years, the Giants played their home games at Yankee Stadium in the Bronx in New York. But that was a long time ago.

For the past several decades, the team known as the New York Giants has not even played their games in New York.

Instead, they have played their home games at Giants Stadium, located in East Rutherford, New Jersey.

Not New York.

New Jersey.

For those of you who are unfamiliar with geography, New Jersey and New York are not the same place. New Jersey is not in New York. It is not a city in New York. It is not a county in New York. No, it is an entirely separate state that happens to be right next to New York.

For those of you who are familiar with New Jersey or anyone from New Jersey, this may help explain the state's gnawing inferiority complex.

The fact that the Giants continue to deny they're from New Jersey is like going out with an attractive girl who won't tell her friends that she's dating you.

In fact, that's exactly what it's like: The Giants are too embarrassed to tell anyone they're dating New Jersey.

Ouch.

(MK)

Stadium, Giants: The New York Jets Do *Not* Play In New York

See the previous entry.

There is a team in the AFC known as the New York Jets. They used to be in the AFL. Led by Joe Namath, they won Super Bowl III against the Baltimore Colts. They haven't sniffed a Super Bowl since.

The New York Jets used to play their home games at Shea Stadium in Flushing, New York. It was a dump of a stadium and still is, but at least it was actually in New York.

Now, not only have the New York Jets not played in New York for years, but they play their home games in a stadium named for another team—Giants Stadium in East Rutherford, New Jersey.

It would be bad enough if they played at Jets Stadium in New Jersey.

But they play in Giants Stadium in New Jersey.

If someone were to come to the United States from a foreign country, they would have no idea how the heck to find the Jets. No idea at all.

And if the Giants are too embarrassed to tell anyone they're dating New Jersey, what does that say about the Jets?

The Jets are so embarrassed to be dating New Jersey that if you saw them together in the mall, the Jets would lie and say that New Jersey was their cousin.

"Oh, I'm not dating New Jersey," they'd say, rolling their eyes, "the Giants are."

Then you'd both have a laugh at New Jersey's expense.

(MK)

Stars, Former Track: You Really Can *Not* Coach Speed

You can't coach speed.

You've heard the expression a thousand times.

It is always muttered by a grizzled old coach or a savvy analyst, thrown in to a stream of dialogue as a way of saying, "Hey, coaching only goes so far." It is used to sum up the concept that at some point, you simply need talent in order to compete.[151]

The problem with the expression is that it is extremely confusing. What it means, traditionally, is that you can't coach someone how to be fast. You can't take them out on the field and actually instruct them to become quicker and faster.[152] However, the other way to interpret that line is: gee, it is so much harder to coach fast players (as opposed to slow ones). That is obviously not true. In football, in *any* sport, speed can only help a team. In fact, it is such a potent and dangerous weapon that we've got another cliché for it: "Speed kills."

Exhibit A: the Tampa Bay "Cover Two" defense in Super Bowl XXXVII.

Exhibit B: Reggie Bush at USC.

Exhibit C: Steve Smith of the Carolina Panthers destroying the vaunted Bears' defense in the 2006 NFL Playoffs.

You get the idea. Sometimes it comes down to simply being faster than everyone else. Obviously, the expression "you can't coach speed" does not mean that you literally can't coach it. It just means that you can't teach it to someone. Right?

I'm not so sure that is true. Not when you consider the "track" record (pun totally intended, as always) of the various sprinters that coaches have tried to turn into NFL players. These aren't cases where coaches are trying to teach people to be fast. They are literally trying to coach speed—to take a fast athlete and harness that speed into something effective on the football field. It turns out, this is not an easy task.

---

[151] The most popular variation of the phrase is "You can't coach size," which means all the same things and is used exactly the same way, except that the phrase implies that in the end, you need big players to compete, rather than fast players. Same general idea, though.

[152] This isn't entirely true, by the way. NFL teams invest a tremendous amount of resources in strength and speed coaches, all in an effort to coax more speed out of their players. I am guessing that the expression became popular in the age before plyometric training, strength shoes, resistance workouts, and agility drills.

Here is a list of NFL players who started out as track stars, only to become football players after the fact.[153]

Bob Hayes. Perhaps the most famous example of the track-star-turned-football-player experiment, Hayes was certainly the most successful. He first became a household name in 1963 when he ran the 100-yard dash in a world record time of 9.1 seconds and claimed the title of "World's Fastest Man." He followed that up with two gold medals and two world records in the 1964 Olympic Games in Tokyo.[154] Then it was on to football, where the Cowboys signed him as both a publicity stunt and a football experiment,

A legitimate candidate for the Hall of Fame, "Bullet Bob" made a huge splash during his first two years in the NFL, going for over 1,000 yards and 12 touchdowns in each campaign. His blazing speed forced defenses to evolve and nearly single-handedly led to the popularization of zone-coverage schemes. Once defenses started employing zones and bump-and-run coverage, Hayes became far less effective, even as a decoy. Regardless, Hayes was without a doubt the best football player to ever be mined from the world of track and field.

Tommie Smith. With the success of "Bullet Bob" Hayes, it was only a matter of time before another NFL team tried to get its hands on a world-class sprinter. The next candidate was Tommie Smith, who won the gold medal and set a world record in the 200-meter dash during the 1968 Olympics Games in Mexico City.[155] Famous for his "Black Power" salute on the medal stand, Smith isn't quite as memorable for his three-year stint with the Cincinnati Bengals. You probably didn't even know he played for them, which is exactly the point.

---

[153] This is an important distinction. Dozens of NFL players were amazing track and field athletes in high school and even college, as the speed that makes them so good on the gridiron translates well to racing around a PolyResin track. Santana Moss, who became a track star after torching defensive backs on the football field at the University of Miami, is one example of a football player becoming a track star. James Lofton, a member of the Hall of Fame, is another example, as he excelled in both track and football while at Stanford.

[154] He won the 100-meter dash, tying the world record in the process. He was also part of the gold medal-winning and record-breaking 4x100 relay team.

[155] Tommie Smith should not be confused with Redskins running back Timmy Smith. Hopefully the police never confused the two. See *Busts, Drug.*

Jim Hines. Another star at the 1968 Games, Hines won the gold medal in the 100-meter dash with a controversial record time of 9.95 seconds.[156] Like Tommie Smith, Hines was immediately signed by an NFL team. However, he never actually played a game for the Miami Dolphins, as Don Shula apparently decided that he couldn't coach speed in this instance.

Gerald Tinker. In a familiar story line, Tinker grabbed a gold medal (4x100) in the 1972 Munich games and then went on to have a fairly horrible career in the NFL, catching only 12 passes in three seasons.

Willie Gault. Gault is a little different from the other names on this list, only because he achieved All-American status as a wide receiver at Tennessee in 1982, so he was more accomplished than the others as a football player prior to entering the NFL. Nevertheless, it was his pure speed on the track that got him the most attention. He was part of a world-record-setting 4x100 relay team and would have been a 110-meter hurdler for the U.S. Olympic team had the United States not boycotted the 1980 Olympics in Moscow. He played eleven seasons with the Bears and the Raiders, highlighted by his 129 yards receiving in the 1986 Super Bowl. He was a pure, deep threat in the passing game, as evidenced by his career average of 19.9 yards per catch and his failure to ever snag more than 50 passes in a single season.[157]

Ron Brown. When the Los Angeles Rams started looking around for world-class speed, they cast their eyes next door to the 1984 Summer Olympics, being hosted in L.A. It was there that Ron Brown won a gold medal as part of the 4x100 relay team. Next thing you knew, he was playing wide receiver in the NFL. While he was certainly more effective than Smith, Hines,

---

[156] There were two different times for Hines' run: a manual time of 9.9 and the electronic time of 9.95. They opted to go with the electronic time, and his record stood for 15 years before Calvin Smith ran a 9.93 in 1983.

[157] Be sure to check out Gault's page on IMDB.com. As an actor, he has had bit roles in a diverse collection of television shows and films ranging from *The West Wing* to *Deuce Bigalow: European Gigolo.* It is a fascinating way to spend five minutes.

General managers, this is not where you want to look for talent.

and Tinker, Brown never had more than 26 catches, 521 yards, or 4 touchdowns in any one of his eight NFL seasons.

Sam Graddy. Graddy joined Ron Brown (as well as Calvin Smith and little-known track athlete Carl Lewis) on the record-breaking 4x100 team in the LA games. He then went on to have a nearly invisible NFL career, catching only 18 passes in five seasons.

After Brown and Graddy, the trail dries up. There have been wide receivers signed purely for their blinding speed and certainly dozens of NFL players with track-and-field pedigrees. However, over 20 years have passed since an Olympic sprinter has been signed to an NFL contract. Perhaps track and field has become a big enough professional commodity that star sprinters no longer need to change sports in order to cash in on their fame and abilities. Or maybe, just maybe, NFL coaches have learned that you really can't coach speed.

And I mean that in the bad way.

(AH)

Strikeouts, Bo Knows: Bo Jackson Was *Not* A Great Baseball Player

Bo Jackson was an exceptional athlete.

There is no question about that.

Arguably, he is one of the greatest athletes of all time, right up there with Jim Thorpe when it comes to all-around athletic ability. If Michael Jordan could have hit a curveball during his attempt to play baseball, you would have to throw him into the conversation, too, I suppose.

How great an athlete was Bo Jackson?

Well, while most people are lucky to play even one sport well, he played two sports—football and baseball—at the highest level. At the same time.

He played professional football with the Los Angeles Raiders at the same time that he was playing professional baseball with the Kansas City Royals.

And it wasn't as if he was a bench warmer for one team or another. No, he started for both teams. Not only did he start, but he played so well that he was selected for one NFL Pro Bowl and one Major League Baseball All-Star Game, even winning the MVP award for the latter.

Pretty impressive stuff.

But, because of the degeneration of his hip known as "avascular necrosis" that resulted from a perfectly clean tackle during a playoff game against the Bengals in 1990, he was more than a bit of a tragic football figure for what could have been. And more than a bit of an inspirational baseball figure for what was—he returned to play professional baseball after hip replacement surgery. No, he did not return to play a game or two in the minor leagues. He returned to play in the major leagues. Then he homered in his first at-bat after returning.

Now, all of this drama—and the omnipresent "Bo Knows" advertising campaign run by Nike—may have clouded people's memories of Mr. Jackson just a little bit, which is perfectly understandable.

Was he a great football player? Absolutely. His career with the Raiders, though cut short, was mighty impressive, and suggested that he might have gone on to be one of the all-time greats but for his injury, or if he had just played football. His season and career stats for the Raiders are a bit deceptive because he did not play full seasons for them. He only joined the team after baseball season had ended, so he normally missed about a third of the NFL season.

Was he a great baseball player? Well, no. And, unlike football, there is little to suggest that he would have been a great baseball player had he just played that sport.

He had a great arm from the outfield, that's true.

And when he connected at the plate, he could hit the ball a mile, as they say.

But, all in all, you would have to say that he was, at best, a very good baseball player, but not a great one. Which is hardly a criticism. Saying someone is a very good baseball player is a compliment.

For his career, Bo Jackson had a .250 batting average. That would hardly qualify as great, or even very good, to be honest.

He only had one year with more than 30 homers and, not co-incidentally, that was the only one year he had more than 100 runs batted in.

He struck out a lot. And I mean a *lot*. He struck out 172 times one season. It was the only time he ever led the league in anything, and it was one of the categories you never want to be the leader in.

He had 12 errors one season, which is a lot for an outfielder.

In short, he was a superb athlete who just happened to be playing baseball, as distinguished from a superb baseball player.

Which is still a compliment.

Really, it is.

But can we please stop saying he was a great baseball player?

Please.

(MK)

Takeover, Hostile: Gaudy Sunglasses Are *Not* The Strangest Thing About Al Davis

Al Davis is an intriguing fellow. The longtime owner of the Raiders is known for his white pantsuits, ridiculous sunglasses complete with a chain, and inventing a phrase ("Just win, baby!") that is now a registered trademark. He's also the guy who moved the Raiders franchise from Oakland to Los Angeles and back to Oakland again. And probably the biggest proponent of the vertical passing game in the history of the league. Not to mention the NFL owner who promoted a woman to the highest position in league history when he made Amy Trask the team president. So he's a mixed bag, to say the least, and the source of many interesting facts, tales, idiosyncrasies, and legends.

However, the craziest thing about Al Davis has to be the way he got his start.

He was hired to be the general manager and head coach of the Oakland Raiders franchise in 1962, at age thirty-three. In 1966, he left the Raiders to become the commissioner of the AFL, but left after just a few months when the NFL-AFL merger was announced. At this point, he returned to the Raiders as a minority partner, joining an ownership group that included the man who hired him, Wayne Valley, and a third partner, Ed McGah.

In 1972, Davis waited for Valley to leave the country before re-drafting the partnership agreement to give himself total control over all football operations. Somehow he convinced McGah to sign the new agreement, which was ratified by a two-to-one vote. It held up in court, and the rest is history.

It is safe to say that no other owner in the NFL has quite the same history, that is for sure.

And it might also be safe to say that Al Davis is the most interesting person in this book. Okay, not safe, but you could say it. In fact, I just did.

(AH)

Team, Naming Your: The Oakland Raiders Were Almost *Not* The Oakland Raiders

Throughout the pages of this book, I have repeatedly written the words "Oakland Raiders." They are, after all, one of the most storied franchises in the NFL. Loved by a passionate few, hated by many, the Raiders have moved around; impacted fashion and music; won titles; launched careers; and generally made an impact on the cultural landscape in addition to leaving a mark on pro football.

Let me submit this question: would all that be true if this team had been named the Oakland Señors? You see, that was the winning entry in a local newspaper contest that was launched to name the team. Seriously.

However, after about a month of being the butt of one joke after another (and just think, there was no *Pardon The Interruption* at the time), the team changed the name to Raiders, which had been the third place winner in the contest.

Makes you wonder what came in second place and why they passed right over it, doesn't it? I mean, it had to be better than Señors, didn't it?

(AH)

Ten, Eleven To: This Could *Not* Possibly Be True, Could It?

It is very rare that something happens in football that makes you scratch your head and say, "Really?"

But it just happened to me.

Toward the end of a preseason football game where the score was 11–10 (which would soon become the final score) a graphic appeared on the television screen. The graphic stated that no NFL regular-season or postseason game has ever ended with the score of 11–10.

Kindly put aside any questions you may have about why I was watching a preseason football game.

And put aside the fact that the graphic clearly was excluding preseason games for a reason—probably because there have been preseason games with a final score of 11–10, including the game I was watching.

Just think about the graphic: no NFL regular-season or postseason game has ever ended with a score of 11–10. Ever.

I thought I may have misread the statement, but one of the announcers dutifully read the graphic aloud, explaining once again that no NFL regular-season or postseason game has ever ended with the score of 11–10. The announcers did not offer any analysis of this oddity. No theories. No discussion. Just the fact: no NFL regular-season or postseason game had ever ended with the score of 11–10.

Really?

For all of the hundreds upon hundreds of games that have been played over the years, could this possibly be true?

I mean, if they said that no game had ever ended with the score of 76–75, I would certainly understand as it is exceedingly difficult for one team to score 75 or more points in a game, much less both teams.

But 11–10?

Really?

How could this possibly be true?

Well, it appears to be a bit of a statistical anomaly based largely on the way points are scored in the NFL.

As you know very well, the only ways to score points are:

- 6 points for a touchdown

- 3 points for a field goal

- 2 points for a safety

- 2 points for a 2-point conversion after a touchdown

- 1 point for an extra-point kick after a touchdown

There are some point totals that are easy to achieve and quite common. For instance, teams score 21 points—exactly 21 points—practically every weekend. Three touchdowns and three extra points. Simple.

And teams never—ever—finish with just a single point. There's never been a game with the score of 10–1, or 21–1, or anything–1. There is no way to score just a single point in a game.

But 11–10?

Well, the fact that there hasn't been an 11–10 game has little to do with the *10*. Teams score 10 points—exactly 10 points—all of the time. A touchdown, an extra point, and a field goal. Fairly common. I suppose from time to time a team chalks up 10 points with a couple field goals and a couple safeties. Or a touchdown, a missed extra point, and a couple safeties. But it would seem that a touchdown, an extra point, and a field goal would be, by far, the most common way to tally 10 points.

The reason the 11–10 score hasn't appeared seems to have everything to do with the difficulty of scoring 11 points—exactly 11 points. What would you have to do to score exactly 11 points? Three field goals and a safety would get you there. A touchdown, a missed extra point, a field goal, and a safety would do it. A touchdown, a 2-point conversion, and a field goal. Four safeties and a field goal. Sure, there are ways to rack up exactly 11 points, but they are all so unusual. I mean, 4 safeties and a field goal? That probably has never even happened in an electronic football game, let alone an NFL game.

So, not only would you have to be awfully creative to score 11 points in a game in the first place, but then you would have to just happen to do it in a game where the other team has scored precisely 10 points.

Yes, now I see why there has never been a regular-season or post-season game with the final score of 11–10.

Why it's happened in preseason games, but not regular-season or postseason games, is a question for someone with a larger brain than mine.

And if anyone can explain to me why they now call exhibition games "preseason" games, I'd appreciate it. If it's just so they can charge regular-season prices for the tickets to these games, I don't want to know.

(MK)

Texans, Houston: The Texans Did *Not* Lose Any Games On Purpose In 2005

At the end of the 2005 NFL season, the very thing that all sports commissioners fear most seemed to be happening right on national television.[158] With USC's star tailback Reggie Bush set to be the top pick in the upcoming 2006 NFL Draft, the incentives were at an all-time high to finish with the worst record in the league in order to possess that pick.

The Texans, Jets, and a handful of other teams were all in the thick of this race for the bottom and, unlike the NBA with its lottery system, a finish in the cellar would guarantee the top pick.

Heading into week 13 of the NFL season, Houston seemed to be in the driver's seat in the Bush Sweepstakes with a record of 1–11 and consecutive losses of the highly dubious variety. All the Texans had to do was lose four more games, draft Reggie Bush, and turn things around once and for all.

This led to an infamous game against the Tennessee Titans that the Texans appeared to lose on purpose. Throughout the game they made play-calling choices that boggled the mind, committed egregious turnovers, and generally kept a horrific Titans squad on life support. By the time the waning moments of the fourth quarter rolled around, Houston found a way to allow a field goal to fall behind 13–10 with just seconds remaining. You could almost hear

---

[158] Technically, the coverage was of the regional variety, but it was still on a national network and, frankly, it sounded more dramatic to say "national television."

the Texan fans sighing with relief as they clung to their lucky Reggie Bush bobblehead dolls.

Unfortunately, no one gave the "We must lose!" memo to return man Jerome Mathis, because he promptly took the ensuing kickoff and weaved all the way to the Tennessee 29-yard line. Not only that, but his face mask was yanked on the play, putting the ball at the and giving Kris Brown a chip shot to tie the game.

Here is where things got ugly. And I don't just mean ugly in the sense that there was possibly an attempt to lose the game on purpose, which would be a stain on the game forever. No, I mean, this got *ugly* in the aesthetic sense. With 0:00 showing on the clock, Brown launched a kick so hideous that it made viewers wince and turn their heads away and howl at the TV screen in shock. It was to "wide left" what Apollo 13 was to "having a problem." There are no official measurements on record, but it seems safe to say that Brown kicked the ball farther to the left than he did forward. And aside from a few kicks that were thrown around by extreme winds, and maybe a particularly bad shank by the kicker of my junior high football team, this was the worst field goal attempt I've ever seen.

No sooner did the ball hit the turf than the accusations came flooding down. The thinking was that no one could miss that badly, so he must have missed it on purpose as part of an organizational directive. And the kick was so bad and that logic so trusty that people still remember it that way. The only problem with that theory is that it doesn't make any sense.

For starters, it ignores the fact that the Texans won the very next week for their second (and last) victory of the season, as they beat the Arizona Cardinals 30–19. It would be impossible for a team to score 30 points if it was trying to lose the game on purpose, even when playing the 2005 Cardinals.

Of course, some would argue that Houston knew they were busted after the kick heard 'round the world, so they had to win or else face the music. Perhaps. But that ignores the second key fact to come after the Kris Brown Incident: *they didn't draft Reggie Bush.*

The whole point of tanking was to get Bush, yet the Texans famously passed on Bush in favor of defensive end Mario Williams from North Carolina State. They could have had Williams with the number two or three pick, paid less money, and avoided all the scrutiny.

The truly cynical conspiracy theorists among us might continue to push forward and say that Houston was forced to pass on Bush as punishment for throwing a game, or that the league demanded that Bush go to New Orleans because of Hurricane Katrina. Not only does this seem like something from a bad episode of ESPN's short-lived drama *Playmakers*, but it also ignores the way the game itself actually unfolded.

You see, there was more to it than Brown just doing his best impersonation of a bad golf hook. Everyone remembers the kick, but people forget what came before it. Not only did Mathis make an improbable return (topped off by Tennessee kicker Rob Bironis' even more improbable face-mask penalty), which shows that Houston was still trying, but it also turns a blind eye to Brown's own activities.

There were three factors that played a role in Brown setting placekicking back two decades:

1) Earlier in the fourth quarter he had a 37-yard kick blocked. That attempt would have given Houston the lead, and the way it unfolded no doubt played havoc with his psyche.

2) Brown had run for a first down on a fake field goal play coming on fourth-and-four. This is important because it not only proves he and his team were trying, but it also might have resulted in Brown being dinged up in some way.

3) Even though he was no doubt going through the motions on the sidelines right before Mathis' return, there is *no way* that Brown thought he would be attempting a tying field goal. There were only ten seconds left, and the ball was bouncing around on the ground before some massive lineman picked it up and shoveled it back to Mathis. The only conceivable ways that game was going to end were a kick return for a touchdown or a Hail Mary for a touchdown. That is no doubt what Brown was thinking. Except he forgot the only other way: a defensive penalty. The game can't end on one of those, which meant that Houston had a shot even with no time on the clock.

The bottom line is that Kris Brown wasn't mentally ready to kick a game-tying field goal. It didn't matter if it was from 60 yards or 20. Which is why he resembled a fan you would bring out during a halftime spectacle to attempt a field goal for prize money.

When people tell you that Kris Brown missed that field goal on purpose because the Texans were tanking the game, know that there is probably no chance that was the case. Houston really wasn't even good enough to lose games on purpose, if that makes sense. And if they did drop contests for a draft pick, they are even dumber than I thought, because they didn't use the selection to draft the consensus number-one pick anyway. No, I just think that "tanking" gave us all an explanation for the abysmal play of the Texans at that time. That sieve of an offensive line. The clueless coaching. And, yes, that truly horrific kick.

In a weird way, losing on purpose would have been preferable to losing accidentally the way they did.

Kris Brown said as much when asked whether he missed the kick on purpose. His answer: "I wish."

I think he speaks for all of us on that one.

(AH)

Theismann, Joe: Joe Theismann's Last Name Does *Not* Rhyme With Heisman

Back in 1970, Notre Dame had a quarterback they hoped would lead them to a national championship. He was a senior with a relatively strong arm and a great deal of poise. His name was Joe Theismann. His last name was pronounced THEES-man.

How good was he?

Good enough that more than a few pundits thought he might just have a shot at winning the Heisman Trophy, awarded annually to the top college football player in the country.

That's the HIGHS-man Trophy.

Never a school to shirk from any publicity, someone in the marketing department at Notre Dame was struck by the proverbial lightning bolt: *Theismann. Heisman. The names sure look a lot a like. Funny that they should be pronounced differently, don't you think? I'll bet Joe THEES-man would have a better chance of winning the HIGHS-man if we suddenly started pronouncing his last name THIGHS-man.*

The thinking, apparently, would be that the voters would be such dullards that they would vote for college football's most prestigious award based not upon Theismann's accomplishments on the field, but instead based upon the sudden similarity between the pronunciation of his name and the name of the award on which they were voting.

Hmm, voters would think, *I see there's this kid named Joe THIGHS-man. He must be the best player in the country because his name sounds an awful lot like HIGHS-man. He gets my vote!*

It's precisely the same type of logic that landed Debbie Zobel the Nobel Prize in Science.

And that's how Scott Wulitzer won that Pulitzer Prize for Poetry.

And we all know about how Juliette Macademy won her Academy Award.

Although you can bet that someone in the Notre Dame marketing department described the idea as "genius," it wasn't.

It was a stupid, stupid, *stupid* idea.

Even putting aside the fact that it was a stupid idea, there was no way the marketing department could convince Joe to suddenly change the pronunciation of his last name, right? I mean, Joe had too much respect for his father and his ancestors to suddenly change the pronunciation of his last name—*their* last name—just to try to win an award, right? *Right?*

Wrong.

Joe went along with it. In the time it takes to snap your fingers, Joe THEES-man became Joe THIGHS-man.

Did he win the Heisman Trophy as a result?

Nope. He ended up finishing second to Jim Plunkett, whose last name didn't rhyme with anything (although, incredibly, Theismann did finish just ahead of Archie Manning, which suggests that maybe some voters, in fact, were taken in by the whole name-change scam.)

But now there was a problem. Now that he was Joe THIGHS-man, he couldn't resort to calling himself Joe THEES-man, could he?

Nope.

We all knew him as Joe THIGHS-man, and Joe THIGHS-man he has remained.

But there's more. If you think that there were no repercussions from Joe's decision to change the pronunciation of his family name, you're very, very wrong.

Karma, you see, is a funny thing. It's not always swift, but it never forgets.

Karma waited. And waited. And waited.

For more than a decade, it looked like Joe would escape any consequences for changing the pronunciation of the name that his ancestors had presumably used so proudly.

Then, in a *Monday Night Football* game on November 18, 1985, Theismann's Washington Redskins faced the New York Giants, led by their legendary linebacker Lawrence Taylor. Everyone of a certain age remembers where they were when the play I am about to describe occurred, just as they remember where they were when they heard that the Japanese had bombed Pearl Harbor, or that President Kennedy had been shot, or that Britney Spears had gotten married.[159] On a flea-flicker, Theismann handed the ball to John Riggins. When Rig-

---

[159] I was watching the game in John Daugherty's dorm room with John, Pete Johnson, Bert Brandenburg, Ty Childress, and Mike Andresino.

gins reached the line of scrimmage, he pitched the ball back to Theismann. Taylor hadn't been fooled. Within a second, he was all over
Theismann. It was more than just a tackle, though. It was one of the
ugliest events ever to occur in a televised sporting event. Theismann's
right leg twisted and snapped so hideously that grown men screamed
in their living rooms. Then they screamed again because the American
Broadcasting Company showed the footage of the injury over and
over again as the *Monday Night Football* commentators analyzed the
injury like it was the Zapruder film: *See, right there, that's the moment
when the tibia starts to poke through Joe Theismann's sock.*

Theismann never played pro football again.

Football record books state that it was Lawrence Taylor who
ended Theismann's career that night.

They are wrong.

It was karma.

That's what you get for insulting your ancestors.

That's what you get for changing the pronunciation of your family name.

And that's what you get for stealing Heisman votes from Archie
Manning.

(MK)

Tights, Spandex: A Super Bowl Champion Should *Not* Embarrass His Family

Let's play a game. I'm going to list several players, and you tell me
what they have in common. It's that simple.

Ready?

Here goes.

What do the following players have in common?

Pete Gogolak	Chris Bahr
George Blanda	Morten Anderson

Al Del Greco   Garo Yepremian

Chip Lohmiller

The answer, which you no doubt got right, was that they were all placekickers in the NFL.

Okay, let's make it a little bit more difficult. What does this next group have in common?

Earl Morrall   Norm Evans

Jim Kiick   Larry Little

Marlin Brisoe   Jim Dunaway

Marv Fleming   Manny Fernandez

You knew that one, didn't you? You immediately recognized them as being part of the Miami Dolphins undefeated 1972 team, discussed in the section titled *Legislature, Illinois*. Congratulations!

Let's try another.

Emmitt Smith   Ricky Watters

Barry Sanders   Errict Rhett

Curtis Martin   Rodney Hampton

Chris Warren   Terrell Davis

Terry Allen   Harvey Williams

Yes, they were all running backs, but I'm looking for something more.

Think for a second.

Think, think.

That's right! You knew that they all rushed for more than 1,000 yards in 1995. That's very impressive!

How about a tougher one?

What do the following players have in common?

Ernie Ladd	Steve McMichael
Bronco Nagurski	Leo Nominelli
Bill Goldberg	Ron Simmons
Brian Pillman	Harvey Martin
Wahoo McDaniels	Bill Fralic
Lawrence Taylor	Russ Francis
Reggie White	William Perry

Tough, isn't it?

And even those of you who know the answer may not be willing to blurt it out because you might have to explain to someone *how* you knew the answer. It's sort of like being in a trivia contest at your local bar and the only thing standing between you and the one-hundred-dollar grand prize is answering a question about the name of the character in *Grease* who goes to beauty school. Oh, sure, you know the character's name is Frenchy, but do you really want your friends to know that you know her name is Frenchy?

For those of you who do not know the answer, how about if I give you a hint about what those players have in common?

Here's the hint: boots.

No, they're not all cowboys.

How about another hint: tights.

No, they didn't all dance in the ballet.

One more hint: it rhymes with "professional mestling."

That's right, all of the football players listed above wrestled professionally.

Some of them wrestled for very long times and were considered to be excellent by pro wrestling standards. Bronco Nagurski, the Bears fullback, held the National Wrestling Alliance championship back before people began to suspect that professional wrestling might be, ahem, fixed. Ron Simmons and Bill Goldberg held the World Championship Wrestling title in the 1990s, long after people began to suspect that professional wrestling might be, ahem, fixed.

Ernie "the Big Cat" Ladd wrestled many of the greats, including Andre the Giant and Bruno Sammartino. And "Chief" Wahoo Mc-Daniel was a longtime fan favorite, known for bleeding profusely from the forehead in his matches. He won a few tag team championships, too, and frequently wrestled "Raging Bull" Manny Fernandez, who was not the same Manny Fernandez who played defensive end on the undefeated 1972 Miami Dolphins. However, the wrestling Manny Fernandez did play pro football for about three years with the Kansas City Chiefs. Got it?

Some of the pro football players listed above wrestled very briefly. Lawrence Taylor only wrestled a few matches, but they included wrestling Bam Bam Bigelow during Wrestlemania, the World Wrestling Federation's biggest annual wrestling event, watched by tens of millions of fans around the globe.[160] Bill Fralic, William Perry, and Harvey Martin appear to have only wrestled in one match each, a "battle royale" with many men in the ring at once, with the last man left declared the winner.

And one of the pro football players listed above was so terrible as a wrestler that it deserves a special mention. That would be Steve McMichael, who is widely recognized as one of the worst professional wrestlers ever by everyone not named Steve McMichael. He wrestled in World Championship Wrestling, and, for some reason, was allowed to be part of one of the greatest wrestling stables ever: a group of wrestlers who went by the name the Four Horsemen, led by the incomparable 16-time world champion Ric Flair.

What exactly made McMichael a bad wrestler?

How can someone be a bad wrestler if everything is predetermined?

Well, plays and movies are predetermined, everything is scripted, and yet we have no problem recognizing a bad actor or actress.[161]

---

[160] Here's some trivia. The World Wrestling Federation had to change its name to World Wrestling Entertainment (or the WWE). Why? Because the World Wrestling Federation's acronym—WWF—caused confusion with the World Wildlife Federation, also known as the WWF. If there was anyone in the world who confused these two groups, I'd love to know who he is. I have some property he might be interested in buying.

[161] I'm thinking of you, Steven Seagal. Yes, you.

In the ring, McMichael moved so awkwardly he reminded you of your grandfather trying to make it to the couch after Thanksgiving dinner. He just, well, lurched around the ring.

Now, a lot of pro wrestlers can make up for their lack of agility in the ring by presenting themselves well in televised interviews, pointing at the camera and threatening their opponents and their opponents' families or developing catchphrases that the fans enjoy. Listening to Steve McMichael being interviewed was like listening to the morning news being read on a high-school radio station. What came out of his mouth sounded vaguely like words. Was English a second language for him? Had he just moved to the United States? Had he been drugged with some powerful sedative that paralyzed his tongue? Whatever it was, whenever he gave one of his wrestling interviews, you laughed at Steve McMichael, not with him, until you completely forgot that he was a part of the freakin' 1985 Super Bowl champion Chicago Bears.

When I think of Steve McMichael now, do I think of that terrific season he and the Bears had?

Nope.

Do I think of how they dominated the Patriots in the Super Bowl?

Nope.

Instead, I think of him struggling to say the word "stupendous" while wearing wrestling tights and a ponytail.

I forgot to mention the ponytail, didn't I?

Well, it's true.

Super Bowl champion Steve McMichael had a ponytail at times during his pro wrestling career. And not one of those somewhat masculine ponytails that some athletes can pull off. No, it was a completely girlie ponytail that reminded me of one of my younger sisters getting ready to go out and sell Girl Scout cookies. Except my sisters could pronounce the word "stupendous."

Now, you're probably asking yourself, *how on earth do you know all of this about pro wrestling? Aren't you supposed to be a serious-minded writer? How do you know so much about pro wrestling?*

I decline to answer on the grounds that my answer would embarrass my family.

Perhaps not as much as Steve McMichael embarrassed his family.

But if I grew a completely girlie ponytail, it would be awfully close.[162]

(MK)

Tittle, Y.A.: You Do *Not* Know The First Name Of One Of The Greatest Quarterbacks Of All Time

Fans of a certain age will remember watching one of the greatest quarterbacks of all time, Y.A. Tittle, leading the San Francisco 49ers or the New York Giants downfield with sharp, accurate passes.

Though he would never lead his teams to a championship, Tittle was a star in the 1950s and early 1960s, passing for more than 28,000 yards on the way to the Hall of Fame.

Even if you never saw him play, you surely have heard of Tittle.

And not just because of his unique name.

He won two MVP awards.

He played in six Pro Bowls.

He held the record for most touchdown passes thrown in a season.

He once threw 7 touchdown passes in a single game against the Washington Redskins.

He is still in the top fifty all time for pass attempts, completions, passing yards, and passing touchdowns, which is remarkable when

---

[162] The truth? You want the truth? The truth is that while I profess to be a fan of foreign movies, the fiction of John O'Hara and Truman Capote, and the poetry of Charles Simic and Anne Sexton, I am also a fan of 1980s new wave music, 7-Eleven hot dogs, and, yes, professional wrestling. When I was a child, my family moved quite frequently, and I ended up spending quite a bit of time alone. Pro wrestling proved to be a perfect hobby for a boy with a rich fantasy life. Later, when I learned the outcomes were pre-determined, I came to enjoy the characters, the spectacle, and the silly humor of it all. The idea that two grown men would agree to wrestle in a Chainsaw Match, whereby whoever reached the chainsaw in the middle of the ring first was allowed to use it on his opponent? Priceless. That the wrestler who first reached the chainsaw would choose to smack his opponent over the head with it instead of revving it up and hacking away? Even more priceless. John O'Hara couldn't have thought of that on his best, drunken day.

you consider how much the rules have been changed over the years to open up the passing game. When Tittle played, a defensive back was allowed to hit a wide receiver over the head with a frying pan before he could even get off the line. Now, a defensive back gets penalized if he even breathes too hard in the direction of a receiver. Okay, I'm exaggerating a bit, but don't think for a second that the rule changes over the years haven't greatly affected statistics. They have.

In any event, no matter what the age of the fan, no matter whether he was a 49ers or Giants fan, no matter if he lived right next door to Tittle, I have never met a fan who could tell me what Tittle's first name was.

Normally, people guess that he had no first name at all, that his parents instead gave him the initials "Y.A."

Wrong.

Occasionally, people guess Yertle.

Which is a fine name for a turtle, but not for a person.

Sometimes, people will guess Yancy.

Nope.

Or Yardley.

Nope.

Or Yulysses.

Nope. And, by the way, Ulysses begins with a U. Trust me. It's right on the cover of a book James Joyce wrote. And James Joyce knew how to spell. It was part of his job.

Young?

No.

Yvonne?

No.

Yelstin?

Do you really believe his first name was the same as the last name of the former Soviet prime minister? Really? That's your guess? Well, you're wrong.

Eventually, people stop guessing, and I just tell them the answer.

Y.A. Tittle's first name was. . . Yelberton.

That may explain how Tittle got a reputation for being so tough. With a name like Yelberton, he had no choice.

(MK)

Todd, Richard: Richard Todd Was *Not* The Next Joe Namath

Richard Todd had the misfortune of playing the same position as Joe Namath—quarterback.

And of going to the same college as Namath—Alabama.

And of being drafted in 1976 by the same team for which Namath had been an icon—the New York Jets.

Naturally, sports writers put together these "facts" and determined that if Todd played the same position as Namath, at the same college as Namath, and would be playing for the same pro team as Namath, well, it was a virtual mathematical certainty that he was going to be the next Namath!

He wasn't.

Which doesn't make him a bad person.

Todd still had a noteworthy NFL career. He threw for more than 20,000 yards for the Jets and, later, the Saints. He tossed 124 touchdown passes. He led the Jets to playoff victories against the Bengals and Raiders in 1982, before they were stopped cold by the Dolphins in the conference championship game.

Although he did throw 5 interceptions in that game against the Dolphins, which I'm sure he'd rather I hadn't mentioned.

Five.

That's an awful lot of interceptions, isn't it?

Namath never threw 5 interceptions in a playoff game![163]

(MK)

---

[163] Namath's name pops up way too much in this book, doesn't it? Almost as much as Adam Sandler's!

Toilet, On The: This Book Is *Not* Waterproof

The moment you finish reading this sentence, I would like you to look down.

Your pants are around your ankles, and the seat you are perched on has a hole in it, doesn't it?

Or, in other words, you're reading this book on the toilet, aren't you?

Well, on the one hand I suppose we should be glad that you're reading the book in the first place.

On the other hand, I don't think many people read Tolstoy during bowel movements.

And please don't pretend that you're offended that I just used the expression "bowel movements." You're the one on the toilet, not me.

In any event, at least do yourself a favor and be careful not to drop the book in the toilet. That image alone might kill us.

(MK)

Touchdowns, Longest: *Not* All Records Are Unbreakable

How many times have you heard a sportscaster say, "Records are made to be broken"?

A hundred times?

A thousand times?

More?

It's a great sentiment in many contexts. However, there are some records that simply cannot be broken. Not many, but some.

And one of them is in professional football.

On January 3, 1983, in a game against the Minnesota Vikings, the Dallas Cowboys were backed up to their own 1-yard line. The ball was handed to their star halfback Tony Dorsett, who broke through the line and just kept going. You could actually hear a whooshing noise as he sped down the field. The fact that he picked up any yardage at all is remarkable when you consider that the Cowboys only had ten men on the field, instead of eleven, because of a miscommunication on the sidelines. When all was said and done, Dorsett had run for a 99-yard touchdown, leaving the entire Vikings defense huffing and puffing behind him. It was the longest touchdown run from scrimmage in the history of the NFL.

And it will *always* be the longest touchdown run from scrimmage in the history of the NFL.

Sure, it's possible that someone might *tie* the record

But it will never be *broken*.

Why is that?

Because you can't have a 100-yard touchdown from scrimmage.

Why?

Because that would mean that the play would have to start from the goal line, and a play can't start from there. And even if the ball is spotted an inch from the goal line, it is always considered to be on the one-yard line as the NFL doesn't recognize any smaller increments than a yard. So, place the ball wherever you want, and run as fast as you can, but the longest run from scrimmage that is possible is 99 yards.

So, Tony Dorsett owns a record that is truly unbreakable.

Having said that, don't be tricked if someone ever asks you what the longest touchdown in NFL history was—because it wasn't Dorsett's. Dorsett's was the longest touchdown run. There have been more than a few touchdown passes that have totaled 99 yards, too. However, Dorsett's run and those 99-yard passes have all been *from the line of scrimmage*. There have been plenty of touchdowns that have been 99 yards or longer. Think of all of the times you've seen a player run a kickoff, punt, or interception out of the end zone and take it all of the way down the field for a score. There have been plenty of touchdowns that have gone for more that 100 yards.

The longest touchdown of all time was a 109-yard return by the Chargers Antonio Cromartie in a game against the Vikings on November 4, 2007. Coincidentally, it was the same game where Vikings running back Adrian Peterson set the all-time record for rushing yards in a game with 296.

Did Cromartie return an interception?

No.

A kickoff?

No.

A punt?

No.

A fumble?

No.

Then how the heck did he get the ball in the first place?

Well, if you guessed that Cromartie returned *a missed field goal*, you'd be right. And you get an awful lot of credit for even remembering that the defensive team can run a missed field goal out of its own end zone as that happens very rarely since most missed field goals still end up in the stands. No, you need a missed field goal that comes up short and stays on the playing field, which is what happened in the Chargers-Vikings game. Cromartie caught a short field goal attempt at the very back of his own end zone, then streaked all the way down the field, only slowing down a bit to showboat as he neared the Vikings end zone.

Like Dorsett's record, Cromartie's 109-yard touchdown return is also an unbreakable record. Sure, someone could tie it some day, but no one could ever break it. Why? Because it's impossible to have a touchdown longer than 109 yards.

Unless you're playing in Canada.

(MK)

Tradition, Break From: Teams Should *Not* Be Afraid To Change Their Uniforms

When a team can't figure out how to get to the next level—when all the tactics have been exhausted—there is one thing they can do to change their luck: Get new uniforms.

It sounds odd, but nothing gets a team out of a rut like a change of gear. It's a proven fix. Of course, I have no idea why it works, but that hardly matters. All that matters is that it does work and that a team in need of a boost should seriously consider shaking things up. Change the colors, change the helmet design, change the logo, whatever it takes. If need be, change your name to the Flamingos and start wearing pink. Sports purists would argue with this suggestion, but I say go crazy. Again, *whatever it takes*.

The uniform change has become the most effective turnaround method in the NFL in recent years. Forget drafting a stud quarterback or hiring a new coach or implementing complex blitz packages. All you need to do is swap fabric and trade paint. Dress for success. Look good to play good. Pick your cliché.

The best part about the power of the uniform switch is that it doesn't matter what your motivations are in making the changes. Whether a team's interests are legal, cosmetic, superstitious, financial, or practical, the results are all positive. Here are some of the different types of uniform changes we've seen in recent NFL history.

The "marketing" approach. When NFL teams want to boost jersey sales and attendance at home games, or basically achieve any sort of jump in revenues, this is often at least accompanied—if not completely accomplished—by a marketing blitz (again, pun intended). One major marketing tool for pro sports teams is to tinker with the uniform. It gives the team a new look and spawns a whole new generation of jerseys that need to be purchased (in addition to rendering the old uniforms "throwbacks," which gives them instant rap video potential). Also, it often distracts from deficiencies on the field. It is all about ushering in a new era.

The marketing approach is usually characterized by major changes in color and appearance. In 2002, the Seattle Seahawks joined the Oregon Ducks from the college ranks to break out some of those metallic bodysuit uniforms. The 'Hawks new blue eyesores took the place of the white, blue, and grey uniforms of the Steve Largent era and helped turn the franchise around. Within four seasons of the new look, Seattle was playing in its first Super Bowl.

The Atlanta Falcons were looking for another color to add to their black (home) and white (road) uniforms, so they introduced some flashy red tops in 2004. No doubt this was done to simply get another pre-Bad News Kennels Michael Vick jersey on the market, but it had the effect of taking a franchise that had gone 30–49–1 over the previous five years and immediately turning them into a squad that won eleven regular season games and reached the NFC championship. Not bad.

The NFL isn't the only place where "uniforms" are changed with marketing in mind. Jay-Z brought the button-down shirt look to hip-hop music and rode the trend to enormous fame, fortune, and his own clothing line. The stars of *The O.C.* were walking billboards for teen and young adult fashion. No, uniform changes are not unique to the NLF, not even those done purely for marketing reasons. The NFL is just the one place where such changes somehow result in instant and dramatic improvement in performance (you didn't see all those trendy outfits improving Mischa Barton's acting, did you?). Of course, this unstoppable power isn't unique to uniform changes made for marketing purposes.

> **Simple cosmetic changes.** Not every uniform swap needs to be dramatic. In fact, some of the most successful changes were subtle in nature. Coming off an abysmal three year run of 8–40 in the mid-1980s, the Buffalo Bills made a minor tweak, switching from an all-white helmet to the all-blue variety. They proceeded to post double-figure win totals in nine of the next thirteen seasons, while reaching four Super Bowls. Likewise, the Cincinnati Bengals snagged a new coach in Marvin Lewis and a franchise quarterback in Carson Palmer, but it took a minor uniform switch (adding more tiger stripes) prior to the 2005 season to finally win the AFC North. It's like when Jennifer Aniston got that nose job and became a huge movie star; when Steven Soderbergh used color filters for various scenes of *Traffic* and won an Oscar; or when New York City made Times Square seem cool again by kicking all the pornographers into the gutters. Sometimes a simple cosmetic solution

goes a long way.

Superstition. Perhaps no uniform swap did more for a franchise than it did for the Tampa Bay Buccaneers when they made a drastic move in 1998. After posting only three winning seasons in their twenty-two years of existence, the Bucs switched from the ghastly orange-and-white threads of yesteryear to their current red, white, and pewter look. They immediately rattled off four winning seasons in a row, culminating in the 2002–2003 squad winning the Super Bowl. Now, I have no proof that they made these changes for purely superstitious reasons, but given the dire situation of the franchise at that time, it seems safe to assume they were in full-scale "we need to try anything!" mode. Kind of like when Enron went business casual in the summer of 2001.

Practical reasons. One very practical need for a new uniform would be the birth of a franchise. The Carolina Panthers and Jacksonville Jaguars introduced new uniforms onto the scene in the NFL and, sure enough, both teams went to their respective conference title games in their second year of existence. What, you think it was skill that got them there?

Another practical reason to alter one's uniforms would be in the event of a lawsuit demanding such a change. In 1996, the team formerly known as the Cleveland Browns switched everything. They changed the colors, the nickname, and even the city by becoming the Baltimore Ravens. However, the real magic didn't occur until they were forced to reinvent their logo in 2000 because they were being sued for copyright infringement. Out went the coat of arms look; in came the purple raven. Amazingly, that was also the year they won the Super Bowl. The case of *Bouchat v. Baltimore Ravens, Inc.*, might have been the best thing to ever happen to that franchise.[164] And you thought intellectual-property law didn't play a role in deciding NFL titles? Shame on you.

---

[164] From 1996 to 1998, the Ravens used a logo featuring the letter *B* inside a shield, which was flanked by raven wings. The United States Fourth Circuit ruled that the Ravens stole this design from Maryland artist Frederick Bouchat, and the team was forced to change its logo.

There is one final reason for a "practical" uniform change, and that is when a franchise moves to a new city and adopts a new nickname. Like the aforementioned Ravens, the Tennessee Titans were a franchise that tried moving to a new city, but ultimately needed only to change its clothes. The Houston Oilers moved to Nashville in 1997, but that wasn't drastic enough as they stumbled along at 8–8 for the next two years. Then they changed their name to the Titans and performed a huge makeover on their uniforms in 1999. What do you know, they went 13–3 in the regular season, enjoyed the Music City Miracle, and went straight to the Super Bowl. See, this is really very easy.

The "modernizing" approach. Last but not least, teams often have the incentive to modernize. Sometimes uniforms are changed simply because the old ones look like they are late for a date with the NFL Hall of Fame in Canton, Ohio. Call it swapping ugly for trendy, trading old school for new school.

The Philadelphia Eagles made a bold move from kelly green to dark green in 1996, and shortly thereafter went to the NFC title game four straight times. In the ten years after the jersey change they won a total of eight playoff games (after winning all of one postseason contest during the previous fifteen years).

Then you've got the Patriots. Prior to the 1996 season, New England finally switched from the old white helmet with the hiking patriot logo (possibly the sweetest logo in pro sports history) to the new sleek, silver version. The change worked right away, as a team that had a losing record in six of the previous seven seasons went 11–5 with their new lids. After the switch, New England had a winning record in 8 out of 10 seasons, won three Super Bowls, and boasted a combined regular season record of 101–59 and a playoff record of 13–4. Not bad.

The final example of the power of modern thinking is perhaps the most uplifting blueprint for teams in desperate need of a lift. The Denver Broncos and John Elway kept getting close to the ultimate prize, only to be turned away time and time again. After the 1996 season, the Broncos switched from those old gaudy blue-and-orange clown suits to their current sleek navy-and-orange uniforms. They promptly won back-to-back Super Bowls.

No matter what reason a team has for revamping their wardrobe, the effect always seems to be the same. Therefore, one could argue that many NFL teams need to get to work right away on some new threads. Add a stripe (cosmetic); go for something flashy (modernizing); add a special black jersey to be used for every eighth road game played on *Monday Night Football* in November (marketing); or even find a practical excuse to wear a new uniform. Whatever the rationalization, just get the players into a new version of that old uniform. Because instead of focusing on cap space or a new quarterback or even draft picks, teams simply need to throw caution to the wind and start switching up their uniforms. It works every time.

(AH)

Tundra, Frozen: The Expression "Frozen Tundra" Does *Not* Make Sense

If you are a football fan, you have no doubt heard Lambeau Field referred to as "the frozen tundra." As in, "The Cowboys travel to the frozen tundra of Green Bay this weekend for a matchup with

When it gets cold in Green Bay, Wisconsin, this grass turns into frozen frozen soil.

the Packers." Usually it is said in a gravelly voice, maybe even while a beer can is being smashed or a piece of steak is grilled over an open flame. It implies brutal conditions and manly men doing manly things. It sounds tough and is actually pretty fun to say.

The problem? It doesn't make any sense. We might need an official ruling on this, perhaps from a reputable scientist, but I believe the expression "frozen tundra" is redundant. "Tundra" refers to terrain where the subsoil is "permafrost," meaning that it is always frozen. It basically means "frozen soil." So, saying "frozen tundra" is like saying "frozen frozen soil," isn't it?

I hate to get all grammatical here, but I'm getting paid to point out things like this.

(AH)

Tyree, David: David Tyree's Catch Was *Not* The Greatest Catch Ever

You know the play.

And you know you will be telling your children and your grandchildren about it.

It's Super Bowl XLII.

The undefeated Patriots against the surprising, wild-card Giants.

Tom Brady, the world's perfect quarterback, versus Eli Manning, the much-maligned brother of Peyton Manning, the world's other perfect quarterback.

Fourth quarter.

It took longer than anyone had imagined, but the Patriots have finally and inevitably taken the lead, 14–10.

The Giants have less than three minutes to drive down the field.

The fans are ecstatic.

Eli Manning is moving the Giants.

The clock is ticking, ticking, ticking.

It's third down.

Manning drops back, and he's swarmed by so many white Patriots jerseys that it's impossible to tell the Patriots defenders apart. There's just a mass of white surrounding Manning.

Manning scrambles, and is consumed by the mass of white jerseys.

Patriots fans erupt.

The Patriots are going to complete a perfect season!

Tom Brady's perfect life is going to continue!

Only. . . what's this?

Manning is still on his feet!

He broke free?

He wasn't sacked?

How?

And now he heaves the ball downfield.

The ball seems to be floating.

It's tossed up too high.

The ball is knocked down.

And Patriots fans erupt again.

Only. . . what's this?

It wasn't knocked down?

Someone in a Giants jersey leapt in the air and caught the ball?

By pressing it against his helmet?

And somehow he kept control of the ball as he fell to the ground?

A 32-yard completion!

A first down!

The game isn't over yet!

Who the heck made that catch?

David Tyree?

Never heard of the guy before he caught a TD pass in the fourth quarter.

Now this?

This?

Making one of the most memorable, most dramatic catches in NFL history?

Pressing the ball against his helmet to keep the Giants last-minute drive going?

And, of course, that would be the crucial play before Manning found Plaxico Burress in the end zone for a touchdown.

Giants win!

Patriots lose!

Wow!

I mean, Wow!

I leapt out of my seat when Tyree made that catch, and I'll bet you did, too. Unless you were too bloated from eating nachos to leave the couch, in which case you probably threw your hands in the air. Or unless you're a Patriots fan, in which case you probably just sunk into your seat. But, even if you're a Patriots fan, you knew you had just seen something special. Admit it.

Special, yes, but now we must ask, Was it the greatest catch ever?

Nope.

And how do I know that?

I know that because I personally made a nearly identical catch in a pickup game in high school, catching a pass from Ken Greene over Greg Bello, who was covering me. Only my catch was better than Tyree's.

First, my catch was for a touchdown, not a measly first down.

Second, my catch ended the game.

Third, unlike Tyree, I was not wearing a helmet. So I didn't catch the ball against my helmet. No, I caught it against my face.

Which may explain why our publisher isn't running an author photo on the back of this book.

(MK)

Uniforms, Powder Blue: San Diego Should *Not* Play Home Games In Anything But Their Special Occasion Uniforms

We live in an interesting time for football uniforms. It seems every team has dozens of variations on their home and away jerseys (in many cases, for good reason—just flip back a few pages to *Tradition, Break From*) and has started breaking out hideous throwback unis to celebrate the third Sunday of every month. It has gotten so chaotic that high schools have had to ban alternative uniforms and institute a home and away policy.

The amazing thing about this exploding trend, is that it would all be worth it if it just meant that the powder-blue San Diego Chargers jerseys of yesteryear were making an appearance eight times a year.

Instead, while other teams break out the throwbacks and flirt with strange colors, the Chargers keep wearing white on the road and navy at home. Sure, they mixed in some white helmets for the 2007 season, but what good is that?

Give us the powder blue more than twice a year.

Give us the best jerseys in NFL history.

Is that too much to ask?

(AH)

Unitas, Johnny: Joe Montana Was *Not* The Greatest Quarterback Of All Time

Joe Montana was a phenomenal quarterback. So were Dan Marino, John Elway, Brett Favre, Bart Starr, Roger Staubach, Peyton Manning, Troy Aikman, Len Dawson, etc., etc., etc.

But Johnny Unitas was the greatest quarterback of all time.

Don't compare statistics. The game has changed too much for raw statistical comparisons to have any relevance.

Don't look at those "quarterback ratings." Those are nonsense. Just trust those people who saw Unitas—and the others—play. Unitas was the greatest of all time. And Starr is a close second. Case closed.

But what about Montana's Super Bowl victories, you ask.

I already said "Case closed."

But. . .

"Case closed!"

(MK)

USFL, The: You Do *Not* Remember The United States Football League

Do me a favor. Skip ahead to the section titled **WFL, *The*.**

Change "WFL" to "USFL."

Then change "mid-1970s" to "mid-1980s."

Then insert references to Jim Kelly, Reggie White, Steve Young, Herschel Walker, Doug Flutie, and Brian Sipe.

Then insert a few references to the Houston Gamblers, the New Jersey Generals, and the Oakland Invaders.

Then pretend I wrote an entire section about the United States Football League.

Pretend it was informative and amusing.

Pretend you nodded your head a lot and laughed.

Thanks.

(MK)

Utensils, Dangerous: Jim McMahon Did *Not* Wear Sunglasses Purely For Fashion Reasons

Jim McMahon was one of the most colorful characters in the NFL during the 1980s. He broke or tied 56 NCAA records while at BYU

Perhaps every Patriot defender should have wielded one of these during the 1985 Super Bowl.

and briefly served as a successful pro quarterback for the Chicago Bears before his career was ravaged by injuries.

While in the NFL, he was known for his notorious temper, partying lifestyle, exotic haircuts, and unusual fashion statements.

Particularly the fashion statements. He often wore ridiculous headbands as well as a pair of trademark sunglasses.

People saw McMahon as a bit of a diva because of those sunglasses.

But the truth is, while McMahon might have been a diva, it wasn't because he chose to wear shades everywhere he went.

You see, at the age of six, young Jim stuck a fork in his eye, forever damaging his retina and forcing him to wear fashionable eyewear.

Or so he claimed.

Don't forget he was eccentric. And a bit of a diva.

(AH)

Vagina, Hearty: Brian Piccolo Did *Not* Have A Hearty Vagina

See *Piccolo, Brian*, for a discussion of this subject. We only mention it here because it makes us laugh when we think about it.

(MK)

Ventura, Ace: Not All Place Kickers Deserve To Be Made Fun Of

Rian Lindell found his way into the NFL as a place kicker for the Buffalo Bills. This role requires trotting out on to the field a couple of times a game to kick extra points and field goals. Raising a hand before jogging up to boot the opening kickoff. Wearing small shoulder pads, a skimpy facemask, and funny shoes. A kicker spends half the game toeing a ball into a net.

For all of this, he gets a free pass to Ridicule City.

It's the nature of the beast. The common perception of kickers, in a nutshell, is that they are lame. At best, a necessary evil. At worst, an element of the game that needs to be corrected as quickly as possible. Pundits have suggested forcing kickers to perform more functions (requiring them to be better all-around athletes), going back to the dropkick so that punters can handle all kicking-related chores, and even eliminating field goals and extra points altogether. Drastic measures, to be sure.

It doesn't seem to matter to anyone that a guy like Rian Lindell was actually a terrific athlete. In high school he dominated pretty much anything he tried. All-State baseball player, All-State football player at tight end, linebacker, and, yes, kicker. He just happened to be better at booting a ball with great distance and precision than he was at any of those other things. If you watch a Bills game closely during the Rian Lindell era and an opponent broke off a big return, you are treated to the rare sight of a kicker laying somebody out like the middle linebacker he was in a past life.

Lindell isn't the only one. You can just tell by watching NFL games that more than a handful of these guys are legitimate athletes. Watch the way the New York Jets' Mike Nugent jogs onto the field—like an athlete, not a "kicker." Check out Miami Dolphins kicker Jay Feely's calves; the man is a monster. Pittsburgh's Jeff Reed looks like he could hit a baseball 450 feet. Yet despite what these players bring to the table, they can't escape membership in an exclusive and undesirable club. Kickers are football's outcasts. They have a handful of individuals to thank for this.

Garo Yepremian. Here is a man who came to America with virtually nothing, wasn't allowed to play college football because of his professional soccer experience, and still found a way into the NFL as a member of the Miami Dolphins. He was named "Kicker of the Decade" for the 1970s, is now a motivational speaker, and, by all accounts, is a terrific guy. Yet all anyone thinks about when they hear the name Garo Yepremian (if they think of anything at all) is "The Pass." As in, the ridiculous, backward, feeble, bobbling attempt that went all of about two feet and landed right in the arms of the Washington Redskins' Mike Bass, who returned the fumble 49 yards for a touchdown in Super Bowl VII.[165] It didn't matter that the Dolphins went on to win the game 14–7 and finish the season 17–0. No, the hilarious image of the ball slipping out of Yepremian's hand like a water balloon is forever part of blooper history. More importantly, it sent a message to football players and fans everywhere: kickers can't do anything but kick; and if they try to do anything but kick, the results are likely to be catastrophic and comical.

---

[165] The phrase "returned the fumble 49 yards for a touchdown" is loaded with tremendous information. First of all, it reveals that the pass attempt was so pathetic that it was ruled a fumble. Second, for a player to snatch a ball in the air and return it for a touchdown and only go 49 yards means that little Garo had done some serious backtracking before getting rid of the pigskin. The former haberdasher from Cyprus was lining up for a 42-yard field goal, which means that the ball was snapped from the 25, the holder was at the 32, and that Garo scooped up the botched snap somewhere around the 35-yard line of the Redskins. It is most impressive that he found a way to move the ball backward 14 yards before transferring it to Mr. Bass. Amazing play, all around.

Scott Norwood. Norwood is the poor sap who missed what would have been the winning field goal in Super Bowl XXV, breaking the hearts of Buffalo Bills fans everywhere. Wide right! It doesn't matter that the Bills' offense failed to put away an over-matched New York Giants team or that the defense couldn't hold the lead against backup quarterback Jeff Hostetler. No one remembers that the field goal was from a healthy distance of 47 yards or that Norwood was a Pro Bowl kicker for the Bills that year. All they remember is "Wide right!" While kickers such as New England's Adam Vinatieri certainly receive accolades for *making* important kicks, they never get all the credit. Guys like Tom Brady will always share in the spoils of victory. However, when the kicker misses a potential game-winner, he shoulders the blame alone, and for what appears to be eternity.

Ray Finkle. Moving chronologically, we come to perhaps the greatest offender: Ray Finkle of a fictional Miami Dolphins team. You might remember Ray as Jim Carrey's cross-dressing foil in the movie *Ace Ventura: Pet Detective*. Finkle was a not-so-subtle homage to Norwood himself, although I have it on pretty good authority that the former Buffalo Bill never blamed his miss on the placement of the ball. I'm also pretty sure that Norwood never decorated his childhood bedroom with the kind of collage that would make a stalker proud, never kidnapped any of his former teammates, and never engaged in cross-dressing. For some reason, the fictional Finkle did more damage to the kicking profession than any actual player could have ever managed. The mere fact that Hollywood—no doubt desperate for new villains to cast in ridiculous movies—created a choke-artist kicker as the bad guy in a film seemed to serve as some sort of message to the general public. And the message went something like this: open season on kickers.

The Brothers Gramatica. As if the Norwood/Finkle "choker" angle wasn't bad enough, a pair of Argentinean brothers made sure to bring bizarre and annoying behavior to the forefront. Martin and Bill Gramatica engaged in comical celebration routines after even the most mundane kicks, eliciting both catcalls and guffaws alike. It started out as a funny idiosyncrasy, but fans and players quickly grew tired of the over-exuberant little men. Things reached a breaking point when Bill actually tore the anterior cruciate ligament in his knee while celebrating a field goal. They could play football for two thousand years, and this incident will still hang over the head of every kicker that ever takes the field.

As you can see, it is not easy being a kicker. Adam Sandler summed up all of these stereotypes in his song "The Lonesome Kicker," when he described them as outcasts, scapegoats, and under-equipped defenders thrust into occasional (and terrifying) action on kickoffs. And he would definitely know, since his football experience includes playing both a mentally challenged linebacker and a felonious quarterback on the big screen.[166] All I am saying is give kickers a chance. Look beyond the funny songs and movies and attempted passes and look for the guys like Rian Lindell—guys who can actually play and just happen to kick the ball.

(AH)

W, The Letter: Your Last Name Does *Not* Have To Start With A W To Be A Pro Bowl Running Back For The Seattle Seahawks

Most of you readers probably didn't realize that there was a magnetic pull between Seattle Seahawks running backs and the twenty-third letter of the alphabet. Well, it's true. Sort of.

Since the inception of the franchise in 1976, the Seahawks have had four running backs reach the Pro Bowl. Until Shaun Alexander, all of their last names started with a W[167] Before Alexander took over as the starting running back in 2001, Seattle was led in rushing by a W in 16 of 25 seasons, including 16 of 18 from 1983 to 2000. It seems

---

[166] *The Waterboy* and *The Longest Yard* remake, respectively.
[167] In 2005, fullback Mack Strong was named to his first Pro Bowl, joining Alexander as a Seahawk running back as a non-W Pro Bowl running back.

almost impossible for something like
this to happen, but happen it did.

It started with Curt Warner, an
All-American at Penn State before becoming the first star running back in
Seattle Seahawks franchise history.[168]
In his first season, Warner ran for
1,449 yards and 13 touchdowns and
led the Seahawks to the AFC Championship game. He reached the Pro
Bowl that year, as well as in the 1986
and 1987 campaigns. All told, he led
the Seahawks in rushing yardage six
of seven seasons from 1983 to 1989.
And the reign of the Ws had begun.

We can't be certain, but we
are pretty sure this was
painted on the Kingdome
walls at one point.

In 1990, second-year back Derrick Fenner took over for Warner
and ran for a league-leading 14 touchdowns while leading the team
with 859 yards on the ground. Fantasy football was just taking off
at the time, so many stat geeks remember Fenner's touchdown bo-
nanza with a touch of nostalgia. Unfortunately for the former Tar
Heel, this was the last season in which he cleared even the 500-yard
mark. There are a lot of reasons for this, but I blame it primarily on
the fact that his last name started with an F.

In 1991, the legend really picked up steam as the Seahawks were
led in rushing by their fullback, John L. Williams. Williams was a two-
time Pro Bowl selection for Seattle, and in 1992, actually led the team
in receptions—so he was a very good player. However, the fact that
he led the way on the ground with 741 yards was proof that something weird was about to happen in Seattle.

Sure enough, when the brass realized that they needed a legitimate
tailback to carry the ball in Seattle, they called the number of seldom-
used third-year running back Chris Warren. The big back from tiny

---

[168] The Seahawks' leading rusher in five of their first seven NFL seasons was Sherman Smith,
whose career high in rushing yards was 805 in 1978. Needless to say, he doesn't meet the definition of a "star."

Ferrum College ran for over 1,000 yards in his first four seasons as a starter, reached the Pro Bowl in three consecutive seasons from 1993 to 1995, and led Seattle in rushing for six straight years.

Despite Warren's solid work on the ground, Seattle did not have a winning season in any of those six seasons, and, by 1996, Warren had begun to slow down. Way down, actually. In 1998, the Seahawks decided to upgrade by prying Ricky Watters away from the Philadelphia Eagles. Waters had been a Pro Bowl selection in each of his first five seasons in the NFL, and since his last name started with a W, Seattle was sure they had found the offensive weapon that would put them over the top in the AFC West.[169]

Despite the fact that Watters never reached another Pro Bowl while playing in Seattle, the former Notre Dame star did a solid job for the Seahawks, rushing for over 1,200 yards in each of his three seasons as a starter. However, the Seahawks remained a mediocre team. Even a coaching change from Dennis Erickson to Mike Holmgren did little to change things.

In 2001, Seattle decided to rebuild. They turned the offense over to Brett Favre's former backup Matt Hasselbeck, who is even known in his own house as "Brett Favre's former backup." They drafted Darrell Jackson to start at wide receiver. Most importantly, they decided to replace Watters with a young running back.

One can only imagine the process by which the Seahawks' management arrived at their decision as to which running back they should build around. No doubt they considered the prospect of acquiring Tyrone Wheatley, who had run for more than 1,000 yards in 2000 for the Raiders.[170] They surely salivated over Ricky Williams from afar. They probably flirted with the idea of trying to turn fullback Moe Wil-

---

[169] Some of the younger readers or recent converts to NFL football might believe that the reference to the AFC is an error, but that is not the case. Seattle was a member of the AFC from its inaugural year in 1976 through 2001. It still seems bizarre to me to see them playing in the NFC.

[170] It was the second consecutive quality season for the former Michigan star. It was also his last quality season. In fact, one would imagine that Wheatley still makes University of Washington fans cry out "Why?" when they think of the 1993 Rose Bowl, for that was the magical day when everything came together for Wheatley, who somehow amassed 235 rushing yards in a 38–31 Michigan victory. Wheatley also broke off a Rose Bowl-record 88-yard touchdown run in that game. Taken in light of his highly mediocre career, you can see why this might upset UW alumni.

liams into an every-down back. There was probably talk of Warrick Dunn, while wondering if first names counted. Perhaps they even tried to tempt Brian Westbrook to leave school early.

Fortunately for Seahawks fans everywhere, the front office escaped the shackles of their most unusual tradition and decided to put the ball in the hands of Shaun Alexander, their first-round pick in the 2000 draft out of Alabama. It turned out to be a pretty solid decision. Alexander became the franchise's all-time leading rusher after a mere five seasons as the starter (and six seasons total), posting 7,817 yards by the end of the 2005 season. He became the first player in NFL history to score 15 touchdowns in a season for five straight campaigns. He won the 2005 NFL MVP award while breaking the record for touchdowns in a season with 28. He led the Seahawks to a 48–32 record during his first five years as a starter and took them to the 2006 Super Bowl.

Most importantly, he showed Seattle that when it comes to running backs, there is life after W.

(AH)

Walkers, Street: Thurman Thomas Misplacing His Helmet Was *Not* The Stupidest Thing Any Super Bowl Participant Has Ever Done

Imagine for a moment that you are a player on one of the Super Bowl teams. Imagine it's the Saturday before the game, the biggest game of your life.

Imagine you have just been presented an award for your sportsmanship.

Imagine your wife and children are waiting for you back at the hotel.

With your sportsmanship award tucked under your arm, you head back toward the hotel.

But, on your way back, you decide to make a brief detour.

Where do you stop?

To sign autographs for some fans?
No.
To visit some ill children??
No.
To go to church to pray for a good, well-fought game?
No.
To stop at the stadium to pick up your playbook?
No.
To pick up some flowers for your wife?
No.
To pick up some video games for your kids?
No.
To pick up a burger and some fries?
No.
To give blood at the local hospital?
No.
How about to solicit a prostitute for oral sex?
Unthinkable, isn't it?
But it happened.
In 1998, against all odds, the Atlanta Falcons somehow fought their way into the Super Bowl, to be played in Miami, Florida. The Falcons were an overachieving, fun-loving team. They celebrated their touchdowns by flapping their arms and doing a dance they called "The Dirty Bird." They were led on offense by their star running back Jamal Anderson. They were led on defense by safety Eugene Robinson. Robinson was their spiritual leader—at least if you believed what his teammates said in the newspapers.

On the Saturday before the Super Bowl, Robinson was presented with the Bart Starr Award for being such a great, inspirational guy. Then, on his way back to the hotel, where his family was waiting for him, Robinson solicited a prostitute for oral sex.[171]

Actually, he did something worse: *he solicited an undercover policewoman for oral sex.*

---

[171] For young readers of this book, you should ask your parents what a "prostitute" is. Preferably in front of some of their friends. Or at church.

And he ended up spending the night before the biggest game of his life in a Miami jail.

If that weren't bad enough, many of his Falcons teammates stayed up all night worrying about their leader and wondering how they were going to play without him if he were not released from jail before kickoff. It was a legitimate question.

If you watched that game, you know that the Falcons played with little energy. From the opening kickoff, they seemed to be a step behind the Denver Broncos, ultimately losing by a score of 34–19. It's amazing it was that close—the Falcons were barely awake. They looked like the entire coach class crawled off a Los Angeles-to-New York red-eye flight.

Now, I lived in Atlanta at the time this event transpired. The entire city was dumbfounded. Everyone—and I do mean *everyone*—was asking the same question: what on earth could Robinson have been thinking?

Years later, we are still waiting for an answer.

And I suspect his wife, his kids, and his teammates are still waiting, too.

Whenever fans speak of Super Bowl blunders, they are bound to mention how Thurman Thomas of the Bills misplaced his helmet at the start of Super Bowl XXVI, causing him to miss the first few snaps of the game.

Big deal.

Misplacing your helmet is nothing.

Betraying your family, your teammates, and your friends by getting thrown into jail for soliciting an undercover policewoman posing as a prostitute the night before the game?

That has to be measured on a completely different scale than misplacing your helmet.

I'll bet Eugene Robinson wishes he had only forgotten his helmet.

And I'll bet his wife has won every argument they've had since that day. Seriously. She doesn't even have to pull out the prostitute trump card to win an argument. He knows she has it and can use it whenever she wants. He knows.

(MK)

Washington, Gene: Gene Washington Is *Not* Gene Washington

In the late 1960s and early 1970s, the Minnesota Vikings had an excellent wide receiver named Gene Washington.

In the late 1960s and early 1970s, the San Francisco 49ers also had an excellent wide receiver named Gene Washington.

No, Gene Washington wasn't traded from the Vikings to the 49ers, or vice versa. These were two difference wide receivers with the same name.

It was, frankly, difficult to remember which Gene Washington was which, particularly for those of us who were in grade school at the time. In fact, for a while, a few of us actually thought there was only *one* Gene Washington who was somehow allowed to play for both teams, even when their games were being played at the same times in different cities. And when the 49ers played the Vikings? Well, it just drove us crazy trying to figure out why he was allowed to play for both teams' offenses. Fortunately, we eventually came to understand that they were two separate and distinct human beings who happened to share the same name. Unfortunately, they seemed to share a lot more.

It would have been easy for us if one Gene Washington were short and the other were tall. We could have identified them as "the short Gene Washington" and "the tall Gene Washington," and everyone would have known which one we were talking about.

But one Gene Washington was about six-two.

The other Gene Washington was about six-three.

It would have been easy if one were thin and the other were stout. We could have referred to them as "the thin Gene Washington" and "the not-so-thin Gene Washington" (or, more likely, "Fat Gene Washington").

But they were both relatively slender, weighing about 205 pounds in their prime.

It would have been easy if one were more talented than the other. We would have had "good Gene Washington" and "crappy Gene Washington."

But they were both good. In fact, one Gene Washington was selected in the first round of the NFL draft and played in several Pro Bowls.

The same is true for the other Gene Washington.

Admittedly, it also would have been easier if one Gene Washington had been white and the other had been African-American because, at that time at least, we would not have had a problem referring to them as "the white Gene Washington" and "the black Gene Washington."

But both Gene Washingtons were African-American.

It would have been easier if one of the Gene Washingtons were a well-known jerk so we could have called them "nice Gene Washington" and "mean Gene Washington"—the latter of which you have to admit has a nice ring to it—but both of them had reputations for being decent, honest men.

Now, one of the Gene Washingtons eventually became the Director of Football Operations for the NFL. And I have to admit that, until I decided to do some quick research for this book, I always thought it was the one who played for the Vikings. I don't know why I thought that, but I did. It turns out it was the one who played for the 49ers who went on to hold that position.

I'll bet you I wasn't the only one to make that mistake.

In fact, I'll bet some of the other Gene Washington's friends and family think he's the NFL's Director of Football Operations.

Which is cool with me.

(MK)

WFL, The: You Do *Not* Remember The World Football League

If you were a football fan in the mid-1970s, you had one of two reactions upon learning of the creation of the World Football League, a new competitor to the NFL following the NFL-AFL merger:

1) "Hooray, now I get to watch even more football than I already watch"; or

2) "There are barely enough decent players to fill the rosters of the existing NFL teams. How on earth is the WFL going to get enough decent players that I would have any interest in watching?"

As a boy, I had the first reaction.

Any reasonable adult would have had the second. Seriously, how on earth did the WFL plan to fill their rosters?

The WFL decided that the best way to populate their teams was to sign away some of the NFL's stars for their marquee value, then fill in the rosters with a bunch of guys who were a heck of a lot more talented than you or I, but not nearly as talented as the last man on any NFL roster. It was not a particularly ingenious strategy in the sense that it was an obvious strategy and also one that failed miserably. Despite the presence of more than a few NFL stars, the WFL was a flop. A phenomenal flop. The league's owners miscalculated how much people wanted to watch mediocre football being played in small markets, a miscalculation that would be repeated years later with the USFL and the XFL. Seriously, did anyone really think that the good people of Birmingham, Alabama, were going to fill the stands to watch some so-so professional football when they could watch some excellent college football whenever they wished? And are there even enough football fans in Shreveport, Louisiana, to fill a stadium in the first place?

The league started in 1974 and went out of business in 1975, but not before it wreaked some havoc on the NFL.

The Dolphins at that time were led, at least offensively, by quarterback Bob Griese, running backs Larry Csonka and Jim Kiick, and wide receiver Paul Warfield. You can imagine the uproar when the last three of those star players announced that they were defecting to the WFL. To play for the same team, no less. The three signed to play with the WFL's new team in Memphis, known as the Memphis Southmen.

The Dolphins were not the only team affected by the upstart league. Suddenly, the Cowboys' Calvin Hill was no longer "the Cowboys' Calvin Hill." Instead, he was "the Hawaiians' Calvin Hill." That's right, the WFL had a team in Hawaii. Called, imaginatively, "the Hawaiians."

And suddenly Ken Stabler was the quarterback of the Birmingham Americans of the WFL, rather than the Oakland Raiders.

There were others who defected. And there were many more who understood that the threat of defection was a great bargaining chip in their negotiations with their NFL teams. How many times do you think someone said, "I'd like a raise or else I'm going to play for the Southmen. Or the Hawaiians. Or the Americans." And how hard did they have to try to keep from laughing whenever they mentioned those team names? Seriously, could the WFL have come up with any worse names for their teams if they'd just opened the dictionary blindly and pointed?

The Birmingham Crops? Sounds good to me.

The Hawaii Igloos? Okey-doke.

The San Antonio Shoelaces? What the heck.

Having said all of this, I have found that even people who claim they remember the WFL do not really remember the WFL. In particular, they do not even remember the names of the teams.

Here is a quiz. Below is a list of team names from the WFL. Your job is to indicate whether it is the real name of a WFL team, or a fictitious one. Write your answer in the margin, unless you are taking this book out of a library, in which case writing in the book is verboten.

1. Birmingham Vulcans
2. Chicago Winds
3. Cleveland Lakes
4. Toronto Northmen
5. Montreal Quebecers
6. San Jose Lightning
7. Southern California Sun
8. Virginia Ambassadors
9. Denver Omlettes
10. Charlotte Hornets
11. Philadelphia Bell
12. Baltimore Keys

13. Houston Texans   **14.** Shreveport Gamblers

(MK)

The correct answers: 1, 2, 4, 7, 8, 10, 11, and 13 were all real WFL franchises. The rest are fictitious, although some of them might have had some pretty cool uniforms.

White, Danny: Danny White Was *Not* The Next Roger Staubach

Danny White was the successor to Roger Staubach as quarterback of the Dallas Cowboys.

He was touted as being "the next Roger Staubach," which set a pretty high standard because Roger "the Dodger" Staubach not only led the Cowboys to a Super Bowl victory, but his clean-cuttedness was the very image of the Cowboys before Michael Irvin came along and changed things forever.

Danny White in fact was not the next Roger Staubach.

Which doesn't make him a bad person.

In fact, he was an excellent quarterback (and, not incidentally, a heck of a punter). He passed for nearly 22,000 yards in his career, and threw 155 touchdown passes, which ain't too shabby for a guy who essentially played ten seasons. He led the Cowboys to a few NFC championship games, and he made a Pro Bowl team, but he never led them to a Super Bowl victory. (And don't write to our publisher to correct me by saying that Danny White led the Cowboys to their 1977 Super Bowl victory. He was the punter on that team. Staubach was the quarterback.)

If Danny White were playing today, he'd be a multimillionaire and he'd probably be dating the winner of *American Idol*.

But people would probably still complain that he wasn't the next Troy Aikman.

Such is life.

(MK)

Wilma, Husband of: Fred Flintstone Did *Not* Play Football For Shale University

One of the great football debates has always been over the identity of the greatest running back ever.

Jim Brown? Yes, you could make a heck of an argument for him.

Walter Payton? Hmm, I can see your point of view.

O.J. Simpson? I'm sorry, but my opinion of him as a football player is clouded by a little thing called a double homicide. See the entry titled *Simpson, O.J.*

Gale Sayers? I see what you're saying. It's a shame about the knee injuries. See the entry titled *Piccolo, Brian.*

Barry Sanders? An excellent nominee for the title of best running back ever.

Earl Campbell? Worth considering.

Marcus Allen? Hmm. It's a shame Al Davis tied him to the bench for a few seasons, isn't it?

Tony Dorsett?

Franco Harris?

Eric Dickerson?

Floyd Little? Maybe not, but since he was one of my favorites, I'm going to include him here anyway.

John Riggins?

Emmett Smith?

I'm sure there are others who deserve consideration, and you should certainly feel free to pencil them in here. Really, go right ahead. It's your book, you can write their names in ink if you'd like.

This is the actual helmet worn by star running back Fred Flintstone. Or it's just a photo of an old helmet we found somewhere. Whichever makes you happy.

But, no matter whom you mention, I will never be convinced that there was a better running back than Fred Flintstone during his years at Bedrock High.

Yes, Fred "Twinkletoes" Flintstone, as he was better known.

If you have had the opportunity to watch any of the archival footage of Flintstone's accomplishments on the gridiron, I have every confidence that you would agree with me that he was the most powerful, graceful player ever to take the field. At least during his high school years. He could bulldoze right over defensive linemen. He could twist and twirl to escape the grasp of linebackers. And when he stood up on his tiptoes—his trademark maneuver, made possible only by the absence of shoes—well, let's just say it was magic. Pure magic.

Sadly, Flintstone's college career was not as successful as his high school career. He would never make it to the pros.

While Flintstone's football exploits are occasionally replayed on cable television, it seems that many football fans are mistaken about his ill-fated college career. I wish I had a dollar for every time I heard someone say that Flintstone played ball at Shale University. It's simply not true. Flintstone played for Shale's rival, Prinstone University.

You can trust me on this.

Flintstone, you see, played football for Prinstone University (better known as "P.U.") while attempting to get an accounting degree in their night school. Unfortunately, the rigors of night school, when coupled with his full-time job working at the quarry for Mr. Slate—who himself was a graduate of Prinstone—left Flintstone too tired and confused to focus on the football field.

It's episode thirty-five from season two of *The Flintstones*.

Why do I know this?

Because we taped it for my daughter, and I've had to watch it five hundred times this past month alone, that's why.[172]

(MK)

---

[172] So who really was the greatest running back of all time, excluding cartoon characters? Jim Brown, end of argument.

WLAF, The: You Do *Not* Remember The World League Of American Football

See the entry titled *USFL, The*.
  Rinse.
  Repeat.
  (MK)

XFL, The: You Do *Not* Remember The XFL

See the entry titled *USFL, The*.
  Change "USFL" to "XFL"
  Change "mid-1980s" to "early 2000s."
  Mention how one player had the words "He Hate Me" stitched on the back of his jersey where his last name should have been, which would have made him famous if anyone could remember is name—which they couldn't do because his last name wasn't on his jersey.
  Throw in a sentence about how the XFL was the brainchild of pro wrestling promoter Vince McMahon, then make a few wrestling jokes.
  (MK)

York, King Of Upstate New: Frank Reich Was *Not* The Guy The Notorious B.I.G. Was Referring To In All Of His Songs

In the 1993 NFL playoffs, Buffalo Bills backup quarterback Frank Reich led his team to one of the greatest comebacks in the history of professional sports, turning a 35–3 halftime deficit into a 41–38 victory over the Houston Oilers. Reich threw 3 touchdown passes in the second half of that AFC wild-card game as his Bills overcame the loss of both their starting quarterback *and* running back to come from 32 points down, the largest lead ever erased in the history of the NFL.[173] It is fitting that the greatest comeback of all time is known to this day simply as "The Comeback."

It is also fitting that Frank Reich was the man behind the wheel of such a dramatic turnaround. You see, Reich was also the mastermind of the greatest comeback in the history of *college* football. More amazing is the fact that he was the backup quarterback in that game too.

In 1984, Reich's University of Maryland Terrapins faced the University of Miami Hurricanes in a clash that featured Heisman Trophy candidate quarterbacks on both sides. The Hurricanes started Bernie Kosar, while Boomer Esiason took the snaps for the Terrapins. Esiason was injured, and Miami jumped out to an enormous 31–0 halftime lead. In came Frank Reich to lead the Terps on one scoring drive after another, as Maryland outscored Miami 42–3 in the second half and won the game by the score of 42–34.

Reich threw for a mere 2,097 yards in his career at Maryland, yet the Bills—who already had an All-Pro quarterback in Jim Kelly— took Reich in the third round of the 1985 NFL Draft. It turned out to be one of the greatest draft picks in franchise history, as eight years later Reich basically replicated his great backup performance from college and helped the Bills reach the Super Bowl.

Despite these amazing efforts by Frank Reich, it turns out that he was not featured on any of the songs written and performed by Christopher Wallace (aka The Notorious B.I.G., aka Biggie Smalls). If you are like me, this might come as a surprise to you. After all, Wallace's *Life after Death* album was released posthumously in the spring of 1997, meaning that the songs had been recorded in the years leading up to, and right after, Reich's amazing performance. I can remember hearing bits and pieces of songs at the time and wondering about the origins of what appeared to be a deep rever-

---

[173] Most people remember that Reich replaced Hall of Fame quarterback Jim Kelly, but it is rarely noted that star running back Thurman Thomas also left the game in the first half and was replaced by backup Kenneth Davis.

ence and admiration for the longtime backup quarterback. The song lyrics I *thought* I was hearing included gems such as:

- *"Frank Reich push the sticks on the Lexus, LS, four and a half, bulletproof glass tints if I want some ass."*[174] (This one obviously hinted at certain lifestyle upgrades that Reich no doubt enjoyed after his fifteen minutes of fame.)

- *"Frank Reich the menacin'."*[175] (Here, Biggie seems to remember Frank Reich as being an intimidating figure, which he no doubt was—at least to the Oilers' defense on that dramatic January afternoon.)

- *"It's unreal, out [of] the blue Frank Reich got sex appeal."*[176] (Pretty obvious that the rapper knew a lot about Reich's personal life.)

- *"You've got to call me Francis M.H. Reich."*[177] (He goes on to refer to himself as the "King of NY" later in the verse.)

Why would a highly successful and gritty rapper interject so many references to a backup quarterback? It seemed puzzling, to say the least. Sure, Buffalo is located in upstate New York, a state that was home to Biggie and many other famous rappers. However, the Bills are hardly the local rooting interest for "Brooklyn's Finest."[178] Why would The Notorious B.I.G. identify so closely with Frank Reich? Furthermore, why would he refer to Frank Reich as the "King of New York"?

The answer turned out to be pretty obvious. That is, once I checked the lyrics and learned that he was actually saying Frank *White*, not Frank *Reich*. As it turned out, there was a movie released in 1990 titled *King of New York* that featured Christopher Walken in the role of Frank White, a Robin Hoodesque mob boss who wanted

---

[174] From the hit single "Hypnotize." To all the kids reading this book, I apologize for the use of the word *ass*. Unfortunately, once you decide to start quoting rap albums, it kind of comes with the territory.

[175] From the song "Long Kiss Goodnight."

[176] From "I Love the Dough," featuring Jay-Z.

[177] From the track "Kick in the Door."

[178] A Jay-Z song featuring Biggie, which served as a reminder that not only were they each from Brooklyn, but that they were also the "finest" rappers from that particular area.

to fund a hospital in the Brooklyn area and engaged in a violent and bloody gang war to raise the money. It seems that Biggie identified strongly with the White character, so much so that he added the moniker to his growing list of aliases.[179]

In the end, it made far more sense that Biggie would name himself after a Christopher Walken character from a gangster movie, but I can't deny that it was disappointing. A comeback master like Frank Reich deserves to be immortalized on one of the great rap albums of all time.

In fact, someone get Kanye West on the phone. I've got a great idea for him.

(AH)

Zorn, Jim: Jim Zorn's Cousin Did *Not* Follow Football

Jim Zorn, who was named the new head coach for the Washington Redskins shortly before this book went to press, was, for a period of about seven years, the star quarterback for the Seattle Seahawks. He was one of my favorite players.

A lefthander, he and Steve Largent formed one of the best quarterback-receiver combinations of the late 1970s and early 1980s.[180]

I used to work with Jim Zorn's cousin Rebecca when I lived in Atlanta.

She didn't follow football very closely and only had a vague notion that her cousin Jim had a very successful NFL career, which always amazed me.

If Jim Zorn had been my cousin, my office would have been decorated with Seattle Seahawks paraphernalia. I would have found ways to work his name into every conversation.

---

[179] Among Christopher Wallace's many handles were "The Notorious B.I.G.," "Biggie," "Biggie Smalls" (the name of a gangster from the 1975 movie *Let's Do it Again*), "Frank White," "The King of New York," and "Big Poppa." All of which would have been great nicknames.

[180] They were an exciting duo, a poor man's Steve Young and Jerry Rice. Largent was Adam's favorite player growing up. Zorn was one of my favorites. What are the odds of that?

Maybe that's why Rebecca Zorn was cooler than I was.

She would've been a lot cooler if she'd have gotten her cousin's autograph for me.

A *lot* cooler.

(MK)

A Guide For Book Clubs

As book clubs become more and more popular, so, too, are guides that help book clubs determine what issues they should focus on or discuss. For instance, if *Moby-Dick* were published today, it might include a guide that suggests that book clubs discuss the symbolism of the white whale and the comment that author, Herman Melville, is making about the human experience.

With that in mind, we would like to suggest that book clubs that read *The Football Uncyclopedia* discuss the following critical issues:

Cheerleaders—blondes or brunettes? How about red-heads?

Cheerleading uniforms—Tank tops? Belly shirts? Both?

Would you cheat on your wife with a Dallas Cowboy cheerleader? How about if you were guaranteed your wife would never find out? How about if God personally gave you the okay?

Same as number 3, but change it to a Miami Dolphins cheerleader. And have her bring you a case of your favorite beer. Now what's your decision?

What do cheerleaders symbolize?

What do cheerleaders tell us about the human experience?

Were there any cheerleaders in *Moby-Dick*? Seriously. It's been years since I read it.

When did you stop finding Dick Butkus' name funny? High school? In your thirties? Or is it still funny?

If there were a giant who was 100 yards tall, couldn't he just fall into the end zone and score a touchdown? How cool would that be?

What would a 100-foot tall giant symbolize?

What would a 100-foot tall giant say about the human experience?

Should a couple of writers try to complete a book when they're polishing off their second bottle of vodka?

Do you have any idea how hard it is to type at this point?

Man, I wish we had some more nachos.

Nachos rock!

Nachos with chili really, really rock!

Don't worry, Adam, our editor will edit this whole section out. Right?

Did you ever date a cheerleader?

How about a gymnast? Gymnasts are cool.

Will you please type "The End" because I'm about to fall asleep.

(MK)

THE END

Index

About The Authors

Michael Kun is the co-author of *The Baseball Uncyclopedia.* He is also the author of the novels *You Poor Monster, My Wife And My Dead Wife,* and *A Thousand Benjamins,* and the short story collection *Corrections To My Memoirs.* He is a trial lawyer and lives in Los Angeles, California, with his wife Amy and their daughter Paige.

This is Adam Hoff's first book. He lives in Los Angeles, California, with his wife Jen.

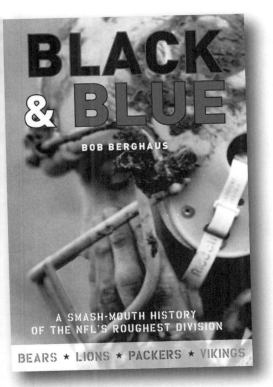

BLACK & BLUE
A Smash-Mouth
History of the NFL's
Roughest Division

by Bob Berghaus

Black and Blue revels in the fierce and long-standing rivalries between the Chicago Bears, Green Bay Packers, Minnesota Vikings and the Detroit Lions, better known as the "Black and Blue Division." Football fans around the country revere these four teams for their memorable games and hard-nosed superstar players.

Through the years, many of toughest men in pro football have played in the Black and Blue—from Butkus to Nitschke, Eller to Spielman, Favre to Singletary to Karras to the Purple People Eaters. Now called the NFC North, these teams still do battle twice a year. Black and Blue celebrates along with them, recalling the great plays and players, the big games and big seasons. From first-hand interviews with players and coaches past and present, to first-rate photography, **Black and Blue** presents the history of this one-of-a-kind football phenomenon like never before. This book has huge appeal to every fan who longs for the "good old days" of gritty, selfless players.

$16.95 • ISBN: 978-1-57860-320-6

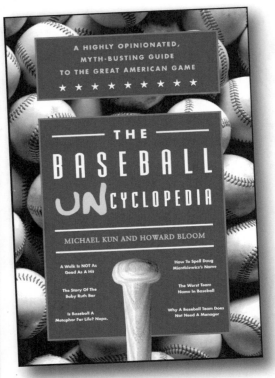

THE BASEBALL UNCYCLOPEDIA
A Highly Opinionated, Myth-Busting Guide to the Great American Game

by Michael Kun and Howard Bloom

"Incredibly funny and easy to relate to. A baseball book that reminds us it's just a game in the much bigger game of life."
—Karl Ravech, Host, ESPN's Baseball Tonight

The Baseball Uncyclopedia reveals the truth about the tall tales, ill-formed oinions, and widely held misunderstandings that baseball fans have clung to for generations.

Packed with surprising baseball facts as well as the musings of two baseball fanatics, crammed almost to bursting with argument starters, bet settlers, and absurd pop-culture references, *The Baseball Uncyclopedia* offers a sound rebuke to anyone who thinks a baseball book can't be smart, funny, and informative all at the same time.

As Michael Kun and Howard Bloom explain, American League teams are not required to use a designated hitter. Nor is it always wrong to root against the home team. They heap scorn upon those who believe Joe DiMaggio was ever "The Greatest Living Baseball Player." They also offer tips on appropriate ballpark heckling and issue a condemnation of the writer responsible for Reggie Jackson's Love Boat appearance. Wild. And crazy. You're gonna love this book!

$14.95 • ISBN: 978-1-57860-233-5